IMAGES
of America

St. Lawrence County

IMAGES
of America

St. Lawrence County

Susan Wood and Christopher Angus

ARCADIA
PUBLISHING

ISBN 978-0-7385-0934-1

Published by Arcadia Publishing
Charleston, South Carolina

Printed in the United States of America

Library of Congress Catalog Card Number: 2001091708

For all general information contact Arcadia Publishing at:
Telephone 843-853-2070
Fax 843-853-0044
E-mail sales@arcadiapublishing.com
For customer service and orders:
Toll-Free 1-888-313-2665

Visit us on the Internet at www.arcadiapublishing.com

This book is dedicated to Otto Hamele, the first historian for St. Lawrence County, whose inspiration it was to organize the St. Lawrence County Historical Association.

Contents

Acknowledgments		6
Introduction		7
1.	Living in the Towns	9
2.	Living on the Land	41
3.	Living in the Mountains	59
4.	Living on the Water	79
5.	Partners on the Land	101

ACKNOWLEDGMENTS

For all their help in the creation of this book, we extend our appreciation to the historians of St. Lawrence County's towns and villages who submitted material from their respective archives.

Carl Goodrich, Town of Brasher
Kathy Colton, Town of Clare
Jeanne Reynolds, Town of Clifton
Dennis Eickhoff, Town of Colton
Virginia Fischer, Town of DeKalb
Nelson Winters, Village of Gouverneur
Joe Laurenza, Gouverneur Museum
Valera Bickelhaupt, Town and Village of Hammond
Terry Fisher, Town of Lisbon
Theresa Sharp, Town and Village of Massena
Leon Burnap, Town of Norfolk
Susan Lyman, Village of Norwood
Emma Remington, Town of Parishville
Betsy Travis, Village of Potsdam
Marie Rocca, Town of Russell
Carl Stickney, deputy, Town of Stockholm
E. Jane Layo, Town and Village of Waddington

We also extend thanks to:

Laura Foster, curator, Frederic Remington Art Museum
Rebecca Hopfinger, curator, The Antique Boat Museum
Jane Subramanian, librarian, Crumb Library, State University of New York (SUNY), Potsdam
Phoebe Tritton, librarian, The Antique Boat Museum
Trent Trulock, executive director, St. Lawrence County Historical Association (SLCHA)

Special thanks to:

Mary Ellen Jones, archives manager, St. Lawrence County Historical Association

INTRODUCTION

St. Lawrence County is sometimes called the largest county east of the Mississippi River. This refers, of course, to its geographical size. In population, it ranks decidedly farther down the list, a characteristic that many residents relish, for the county has not lost its small town and rural nature. It is a wonderful place to live, with clean air and water, beautiful landscapes, and an old-fashioned openness and relaxed pace that are rapidly vanishing from the American landscape.

St. Lawrence County encompasses an unusually wide range of topography and as a result, has become a tourist and recreation mecca for visitors from all over New York State and the Northeast. Much of the southern part of the county lies within the Adirondack Park, a six-million-acre preserve comprising a mixture of state and privately owned lands. The Adirondacks receive some nine million visitors every year who participate in a range of activities including mountain climbing, wilderness paddling, skiing, and boating and who enjoy the world-class facilities of Lake Placid, home to the 1932 and 1980 winter Olympic games. Cranberry Lake, one of the park's most beautiful and popular bodies of water, lies entirely within St. Lawrence County.

The St. Lawrence River and the Thousand Islands, one of the preeminent resort areas in New York State, border the northern fringe of the county. Boating along the St. Lawrence ranges from elegant private yachts to one of the world's busiest shipping lanes through the St. Lawrence Seaway, connecting the region with the Great Lakes. Boaters can also connect via the extensive inland waterway system with the lakes, rivers, and canals of Canada, permitting travel into the heart of downtown Ottawa, where they can tie up their crafts and enjoy fine cuisine and a raft of cultural offerings. Consequently, many Canadians have an interest in and have made real contributions to the history of the region.

Between the mountains and the river lie the prime farmlands, lush forests, and flowing streams of the St. Lawrence River Valley. This area first attracted settlers in the late 1700s, drawn by the rich soils, abundant timber, and an excellent water transportation system. The region also grew into an educational and cultural hub centered around St. Lawrence University, Clarkson University, the State University colleges at Potsdam and Canton, and the world-famous Crane School of Music.

It is our intention to focus on the rich history of St. Lawrence County, showing the movement of various population groups into the area, beginning in pioneer times. Logging, mining, farming, tourism, recreation, and education have all brought differing groups to the region, with each leaving its imprint. A number of famous individuals left their mark as well, including artist

Frederic Remington, boatbuilder Henry Rushton, former U.S. senator and New York governor Silas Wright, and writer Irving Bacheller, to name only a handful. There is a range of interesting architecture from the elegant homes of early industrialists to the beautiful old barns and mills constructed by landowners to an especially rich heritage of sandstone homes built out of native Potsdam sandstone, which was also used to construct the Parliament buildings in Ottawa.

Adding to the rich cultural mix are communities of Mennonites, Amish, Mohawk, Jewish, Armenian, French, Greek, and many other nationalities. For this is a region that has attracted a variety of peoples, many of whom fell in love with the beauty and diversity of life in the North Country.

Above all, the photographs assembled here represent the interaction of people with the landscape, thus our chapter headings, which emphasize living on the land, water, in the mountains, and in the towns that inevitably arose in places that the landscape dictated—along waterways, near waterfalls for power supply, and near rich soils and prime stands of timber. Carving this civilization out of the wilderness demanded a close and all-important partnership between men and women. Each supplied crucial talents, emotional support, and the basics of community that enabled them to serve as partners on the land. This partnership was, and remains, the basis for the success of a county that managed to at once conquer and yet preserve large portions of the wilderness.

As the reader peruses these images of times gone by, it would be altogether appropriate to reflect upon the hard work and wise stewardship of our ancestors. It is through their efforts that we have inherited this most beautiful and inhabitable of counties.

One

Living in the Towns

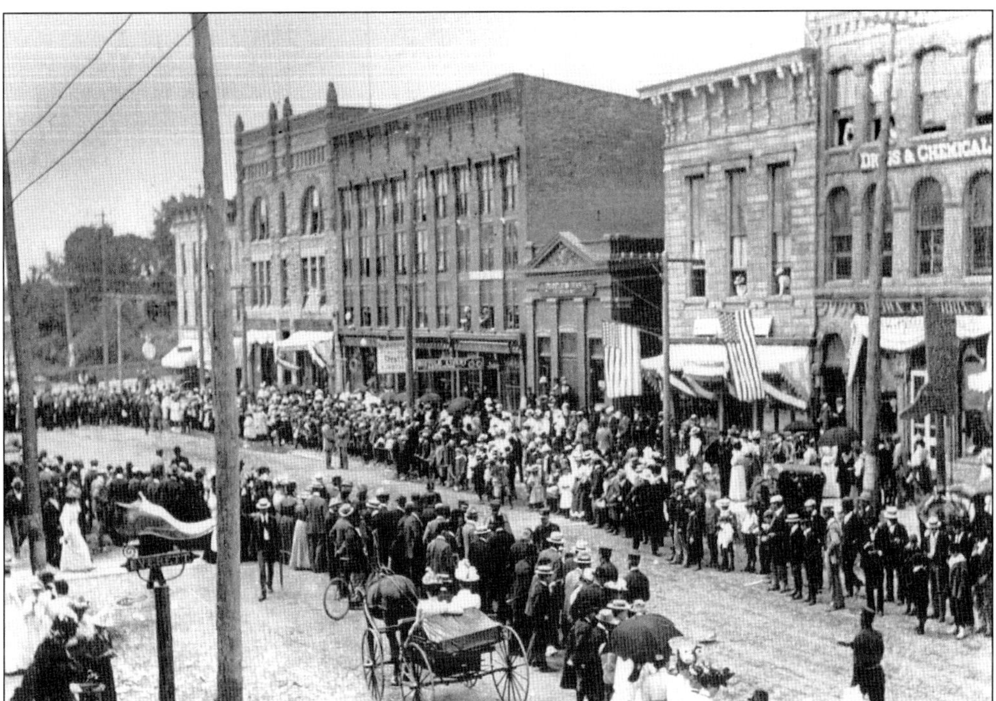

Waiting for a Parade, Market Street, Potsdam. On Market Street in downtown Potsdam, the crowd awaits the Fourth of July parade in 1901. (Courtesy Potsdam historian.)

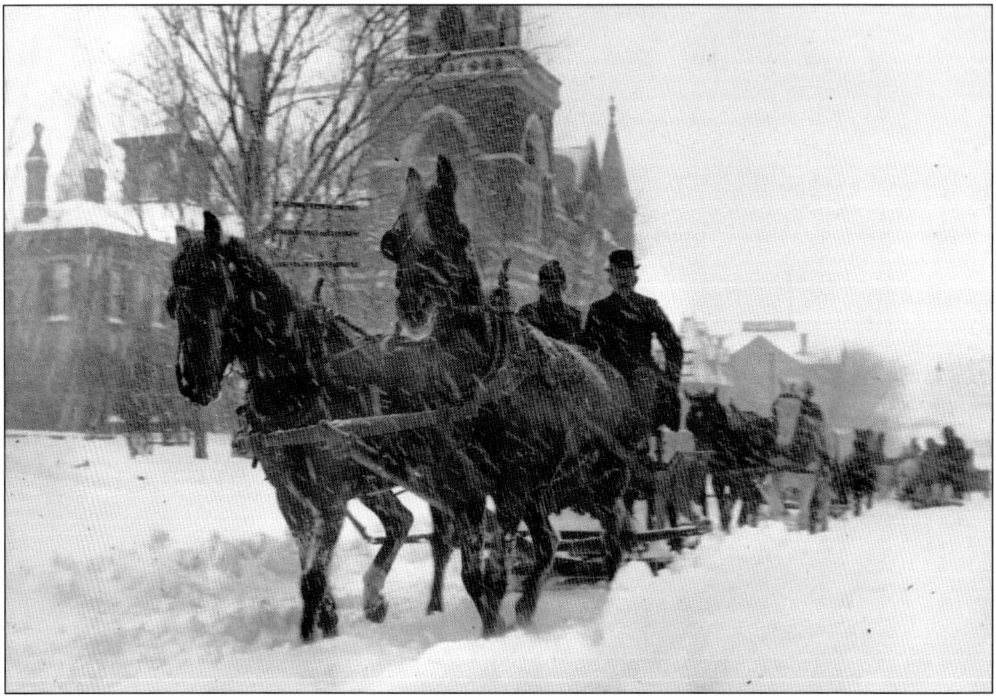

Horse Teams Plowing Main Street, Canton. Farmers brought their teams of horses into town "come a heavy fall of snow" expressly to "break out the road" for automobiles. Here, the horses are seen in front of the old town hall. (SLCHA.)

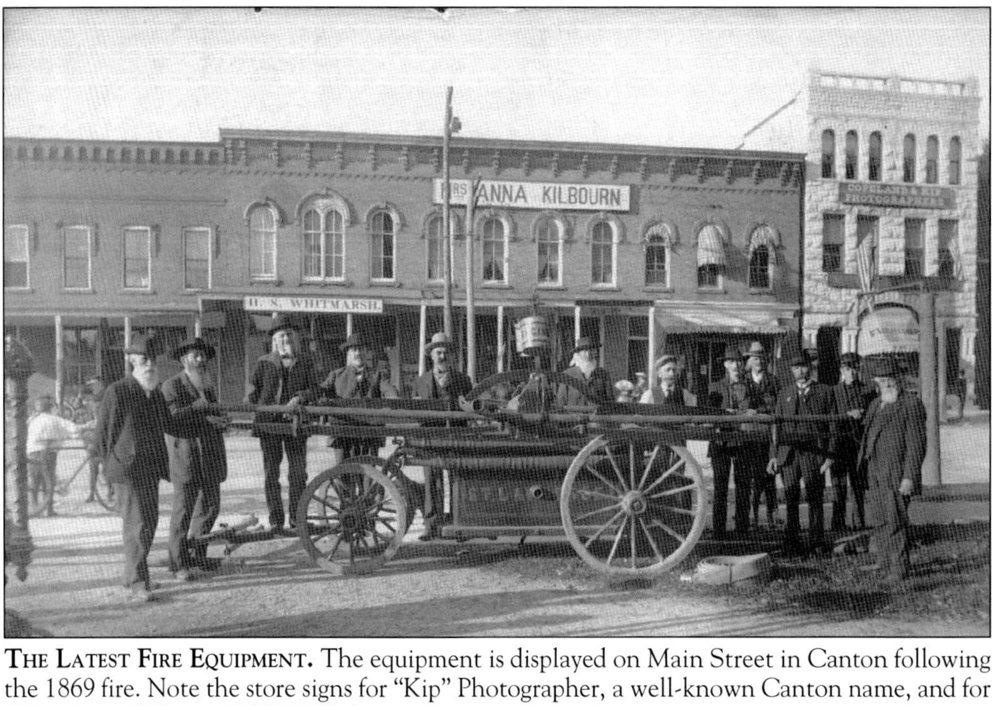

The Latest Fire Equipment. The equipment is displayed on Main Street in Canton following the 1869 fire. Note the store signs for "Kip" Photographer, a well-known Canton name, and for "Mrs. Anna Kilbourn." (SLCHA.)

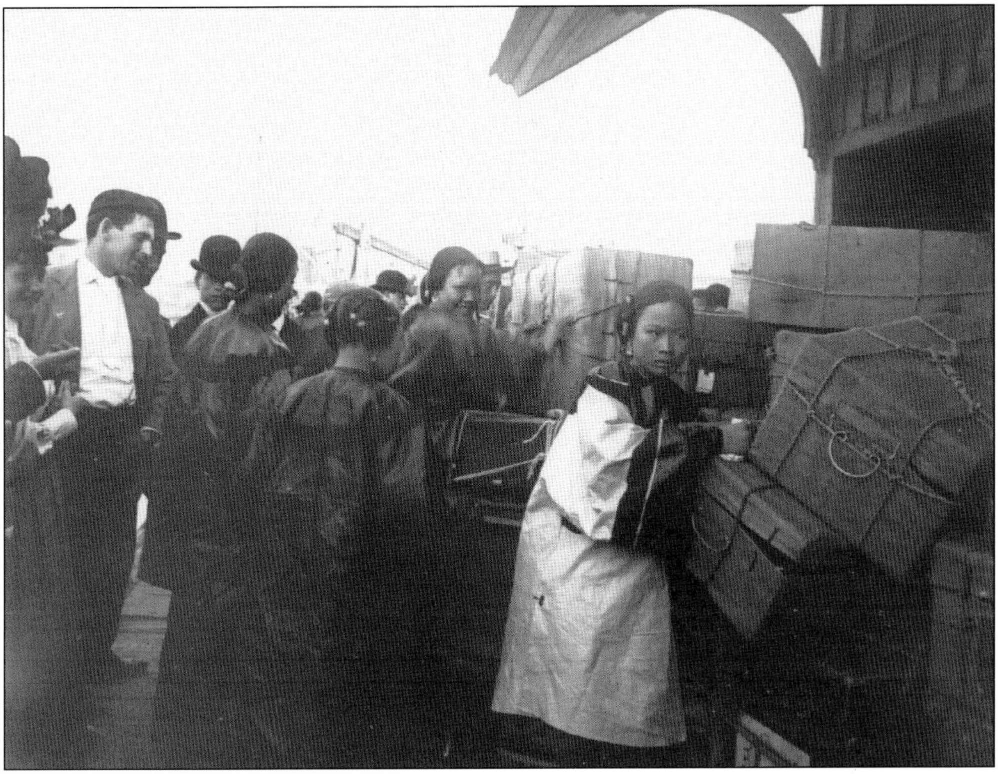

The Ogdensburg Docks. Chinese immigrants are among those pictured at the Ogdensburg docks. (SLCHA.)

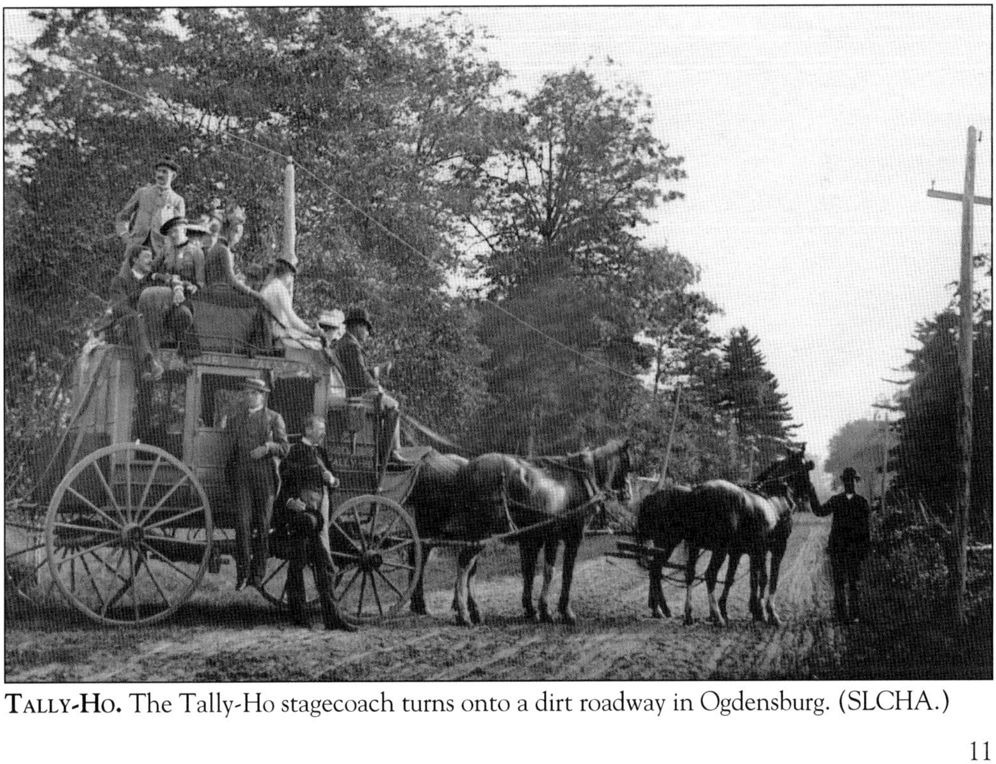

Tally-Ho. The Tally-Ho stagecoach turns onto a dirt roadway in Ogdensburg. (SLCHA.)

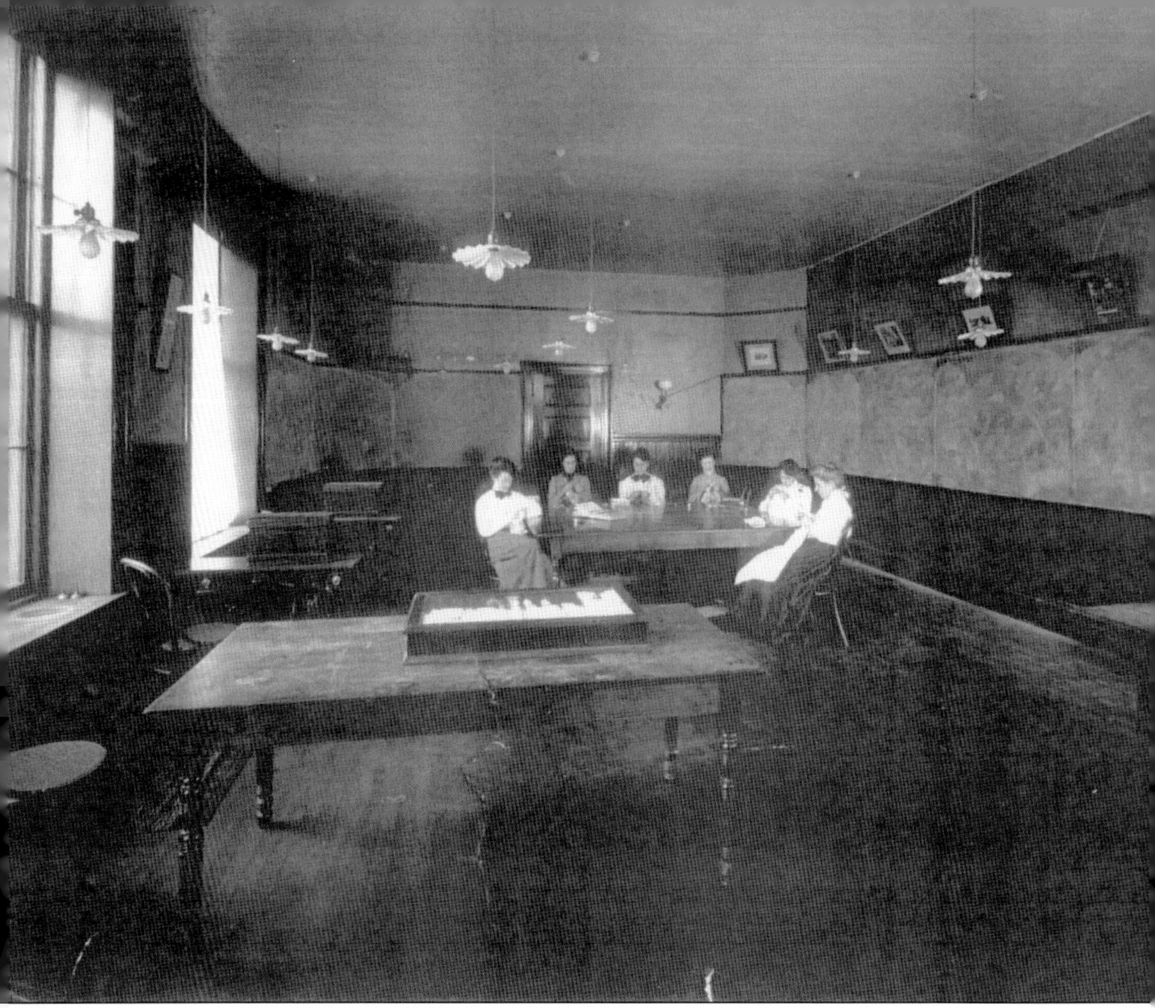

DOMESTIC ENGINEERING, CLARKSON COLLEGE, POTSDAM, 1899. "This four year course leading to the baccalaureate degree offers women a full college training in the applied and economic sciences. Its aim is to thoroughly prepare them for teaching the technical branches of Home Science as well as for the most efficient management and supervision of the home . . . This course for women is arranged to parallel the regular engineering courses given in this School to men. In engineering and technology it comprises instruction in the vocations with woman's sphere as the other engineering course comprises instruction in the respective professions of men."—from the Thomas S. Clarkson Memorial School of Technology Catalogue, 1901–1902. (Courtesy Potsdam historian.)

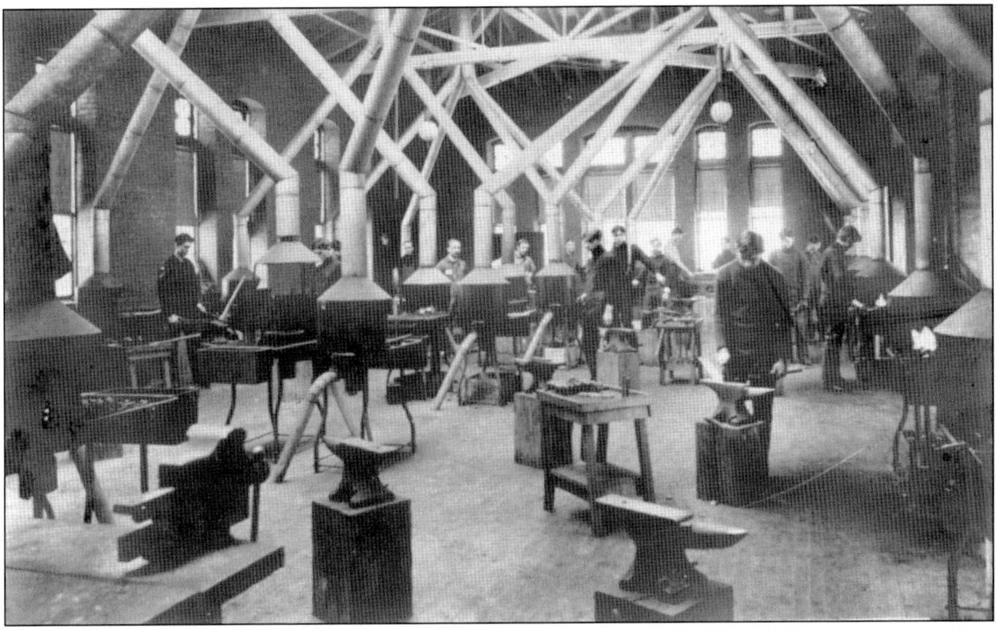

FORGE SHOP, CLARKSON COLLEGE OF TECHNOLOGY, POTSDAM. "The Forge Shop has twenty-four forges and anvils, and necessary small tools, shears, blacksmith's drill, bolt header, vises, swage-block, etc. A few forges are equipped with hand-blowers in addition to motor-driven power blast."—from the Thomas S. Clarkson Memorial School of Technology Catalogue, 1901–1902. (SLCHA.)

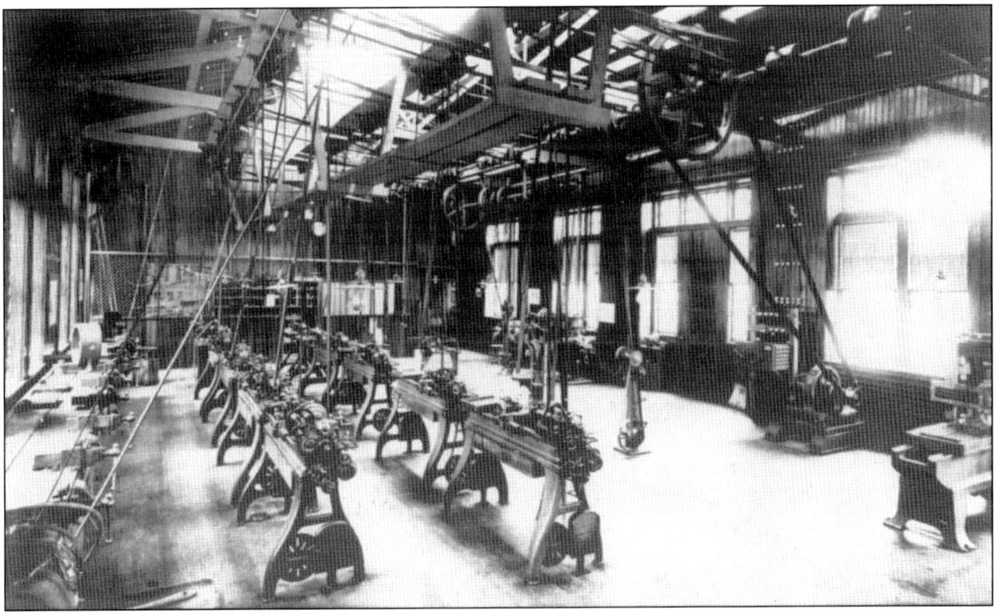

MACHINE SHOP, CLARKSON COLLEGE OF TECHNOLOGY, POTSDAM. The estimated expenses for the school year 1901–1902 at Clarkson were as follows: tuition $80; deposit fee $5; books, stationery, and instruments $15–$30; room and board $99–$126; and washing and laundry $10–$15. (SLCHA.)

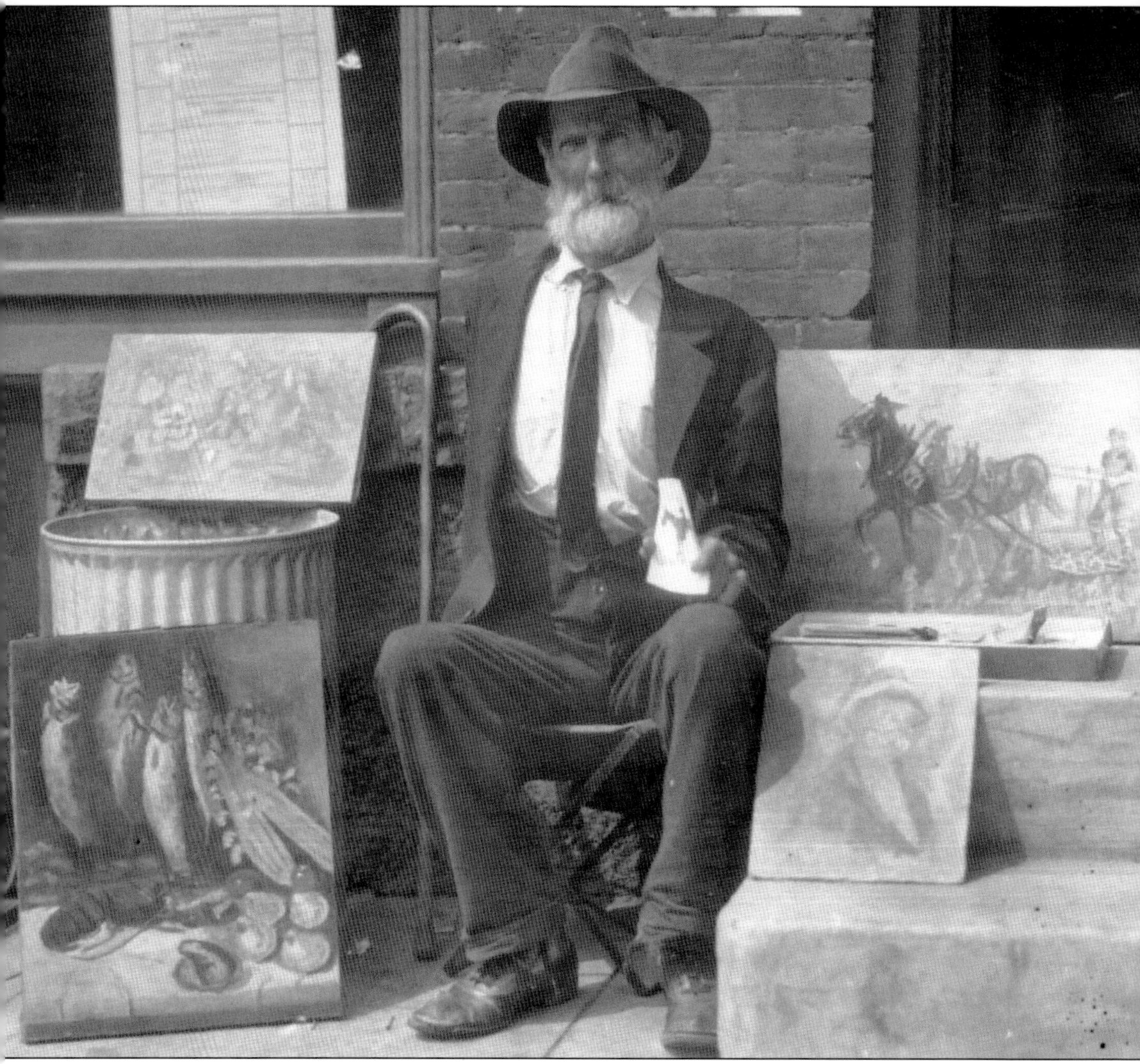

Eddie Perry, Canton Artist, c. 1930. Eddie Perry painted and sold postcards on Main Street. He was a victim of chorea, or St. Vitus' dance, a nervous disorder causing uncontrollable and irregular movements of thc arm, leg, and face muscles. He taught himself to paint, steadying his right, painting hand with his left hand. He was a boyhood friend of and idolized artist Frederic Remington, who offered him help with his painting technique. (Dwight Church photograph, SLCHA)

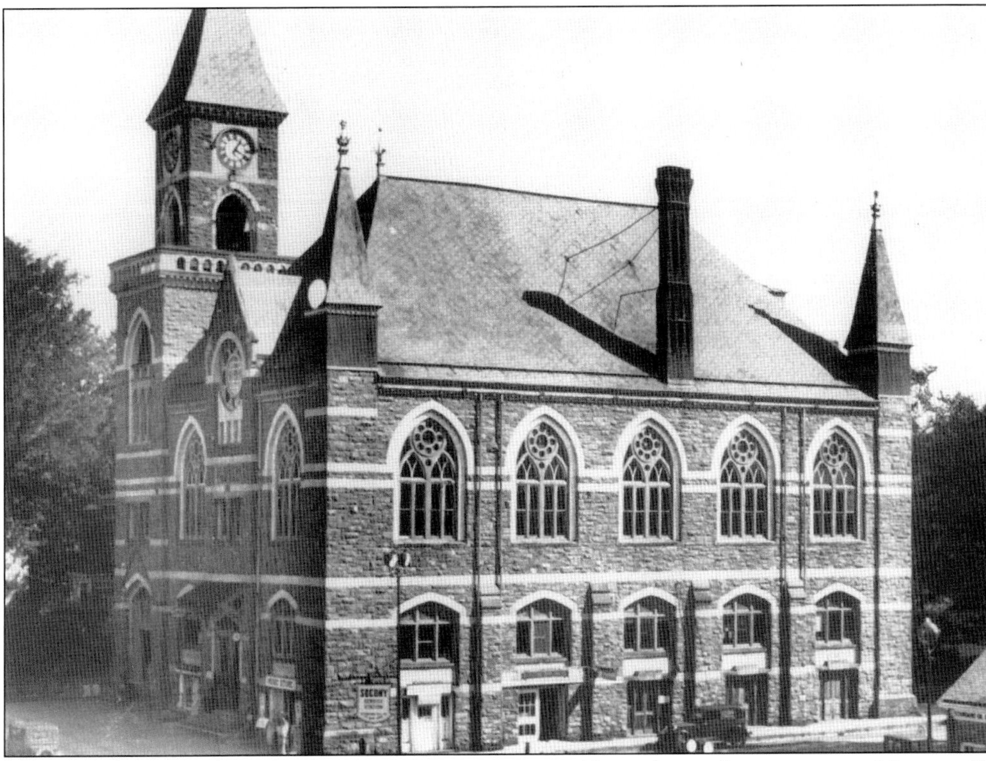

Canton Town Hall and Opera House, c. 1930. Note the early gas pumps. Many well-known performers appeared on stage here. (SLCHA.)

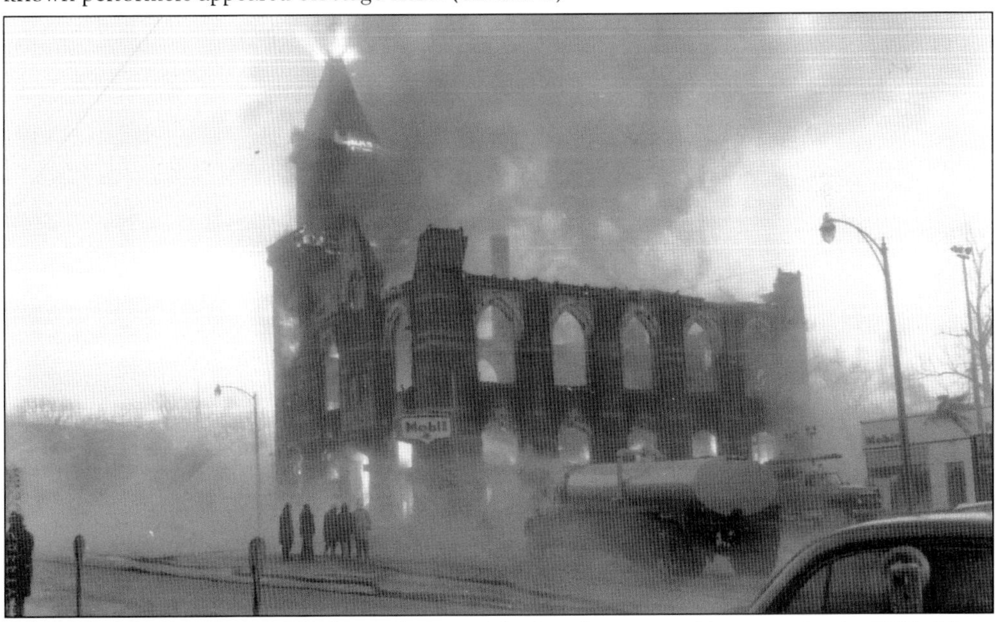

Canton Town Hall. The hall was destroyed by fire during a cold winter day in 1961. Many windows on Main Street buildings shattered from the combination of intense heat and cold. The huge bell in the steeple sounded one last time as it fell to the ground, where it was later retrieved. (SLCHA.)

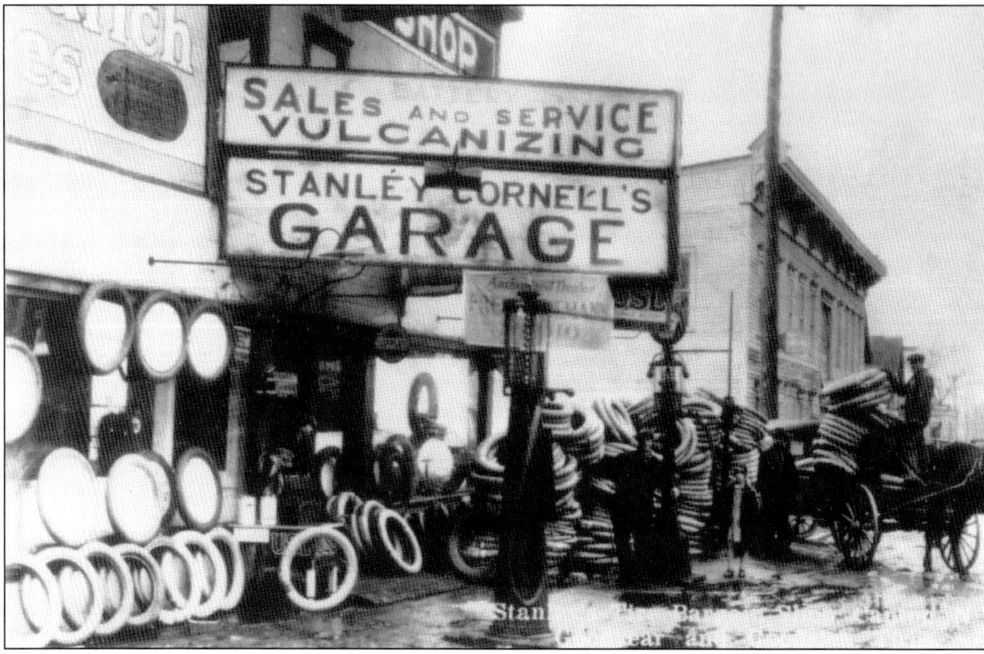

STANLEY CORNELL'S BARGAIN TIRE SHOP, RIVERSIDE DRIVE, CANTON. Note the tires being delivered by a horse. (SLCHA.)

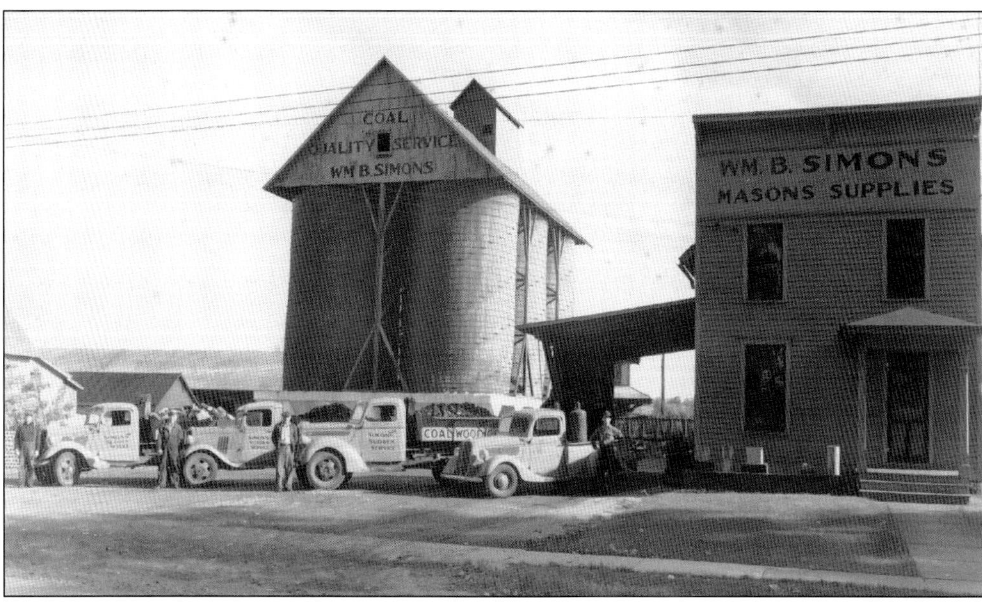

SIMON'S FUEL AND SUPPLIES, 280 EAST MAIN STREET, GOUVERNEUR, 1939. The drivers seen here, from left to right, are Harrison Hull, Frank Chateau, Robert L. Smith, and John Backus. (Courtesy Gouverneur Museum.)

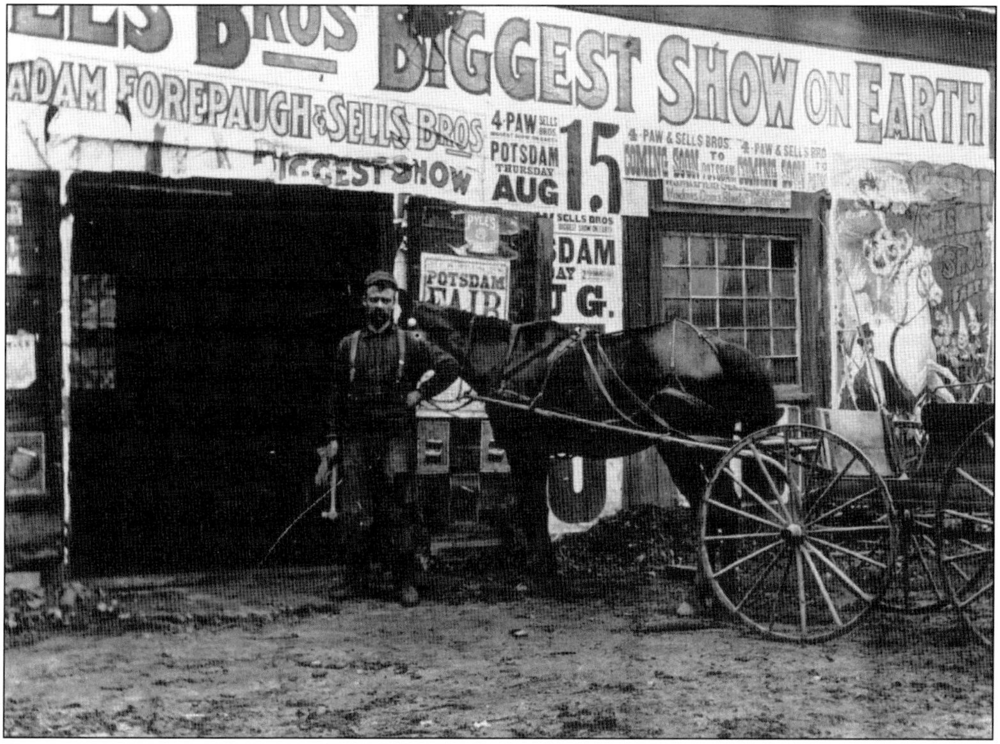

Circus Posters. At Forepaugh & Sells Brothers *c.* 1900, circus posters advertise the Potsdam performance of the "Biggest Show on Earth." (SLCHA.)

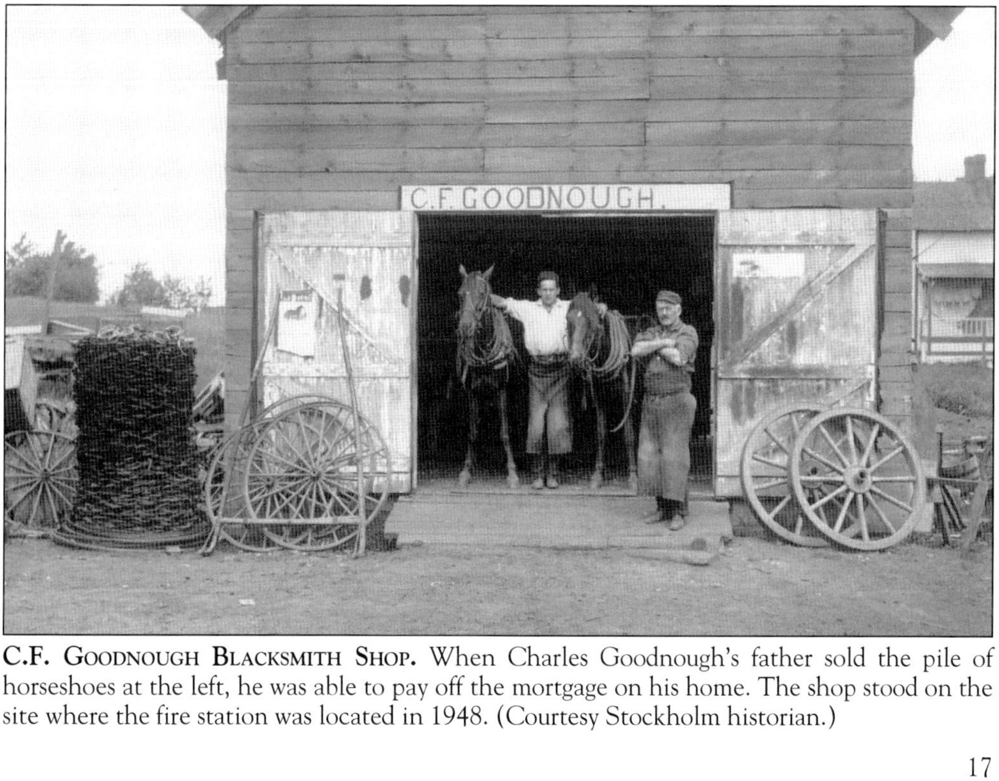

C.F. Goodnough Blacksmith Shop. When Charles Goodnough's father sold the pile of horseshoes at the left, he was able to pay off the mortgage on his home. The shop stood on the site where the fire station was located in 1948. (Courtesy Stockholm historian.)

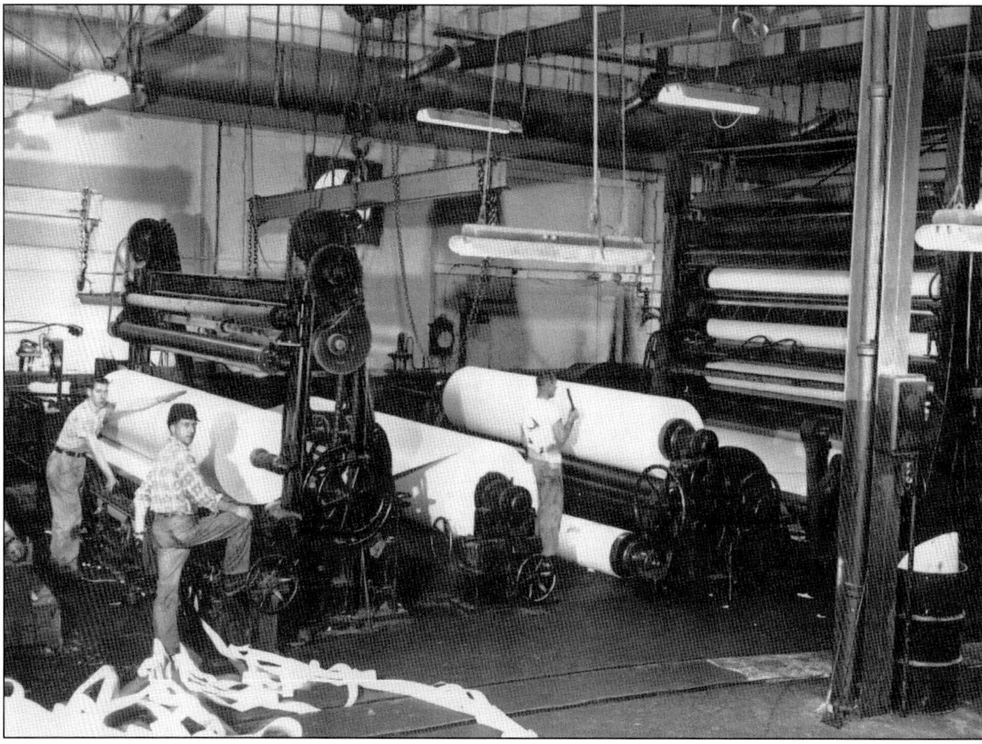

RAYMONDVILLE PAPER MILL: THE END PRODUCT. Adirondack timber was driven downstream to the mills boasted by nearly every town in the St. Lawrence River Valley. (SLCHA.)

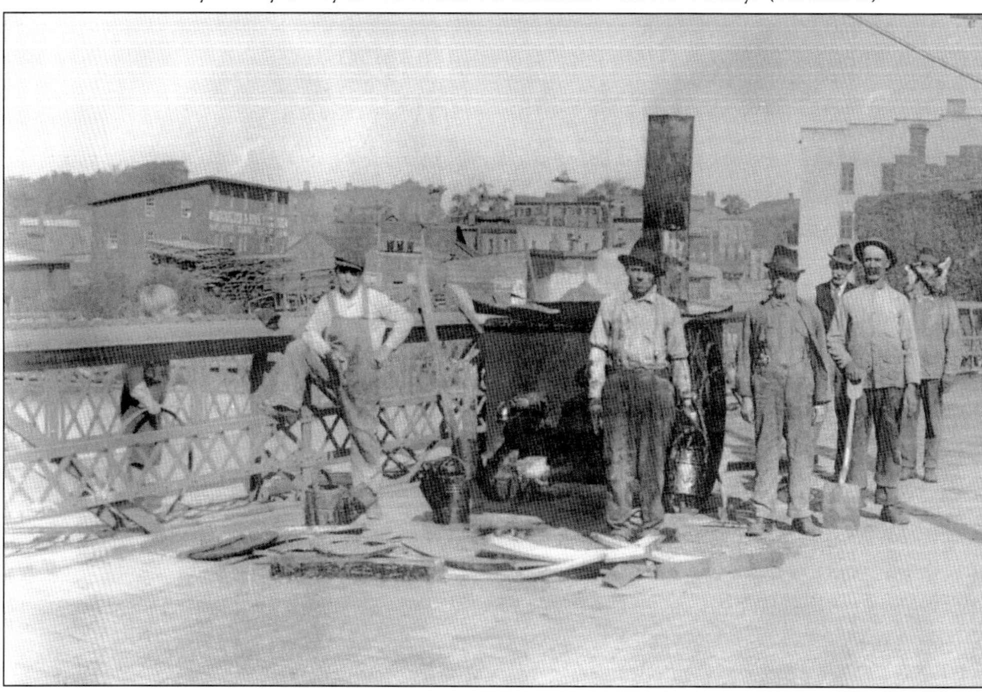

RAQUETTE RIVER BRIDGE, POTSDAM, C. 1900. Laborers have their photograph taken while working on the bridge. (Courtesy Potsdam historian.)

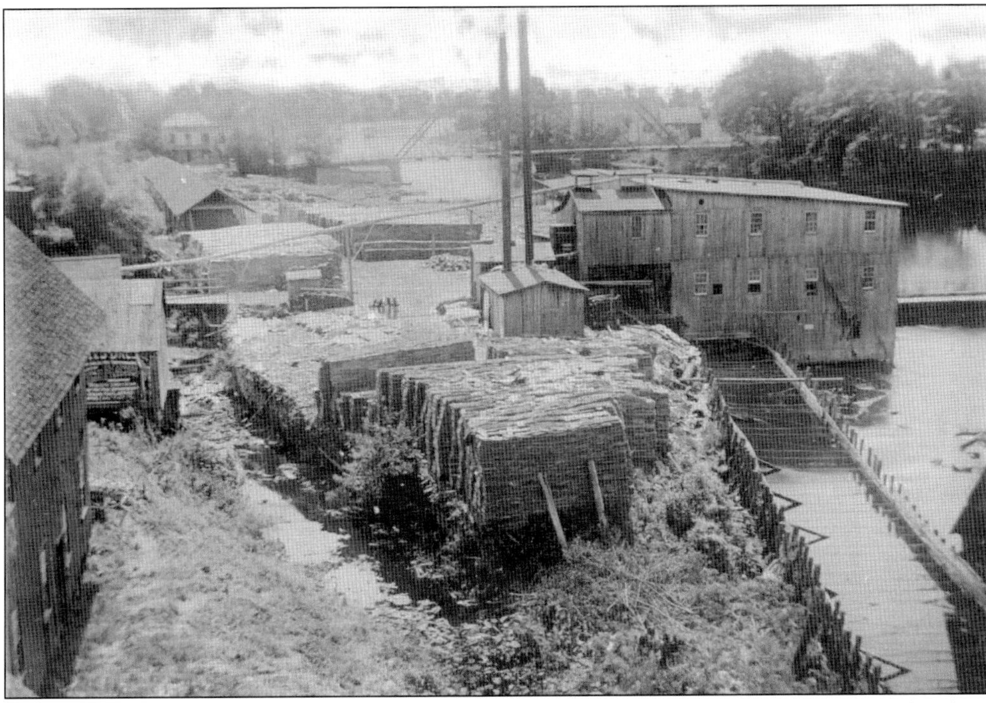

BOX FACTORY AND YARD, RENSSELAER FALLS. Agriculture has been dominated by the dairy cow throughout the county's history, and cheese factories were almost as common a sight as schoolhouses. This factory in Rensselaer Falls specialized in making cheese boxes to supply the county's cheese makers. (SLCHA.)

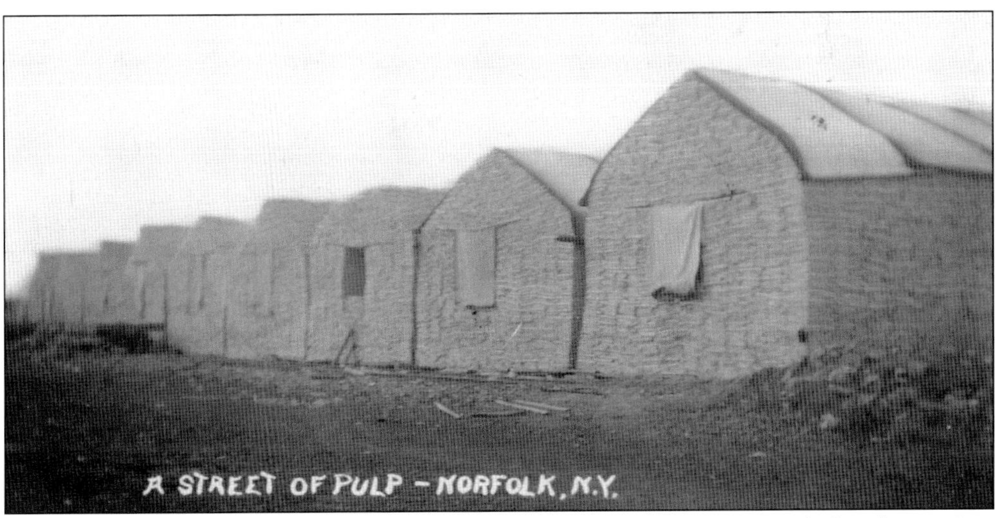

A STREET OF PULP STACKED IN HOUSE FORMS, NORFOLK. Pulp was made by chemical or mechanical means and was used to make paper and cellulose products. (SLCHA.)

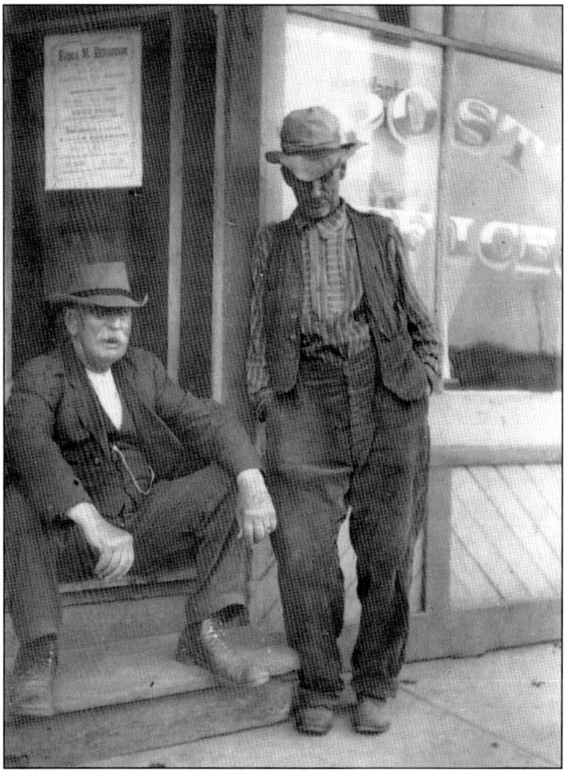

Two Old-Timers Watching the World Go By. This photograph, taken outside a store in DeKalb Junction, could date any time from the 1860s to the 1930s. (Courtesy Gouverneur Museum.)

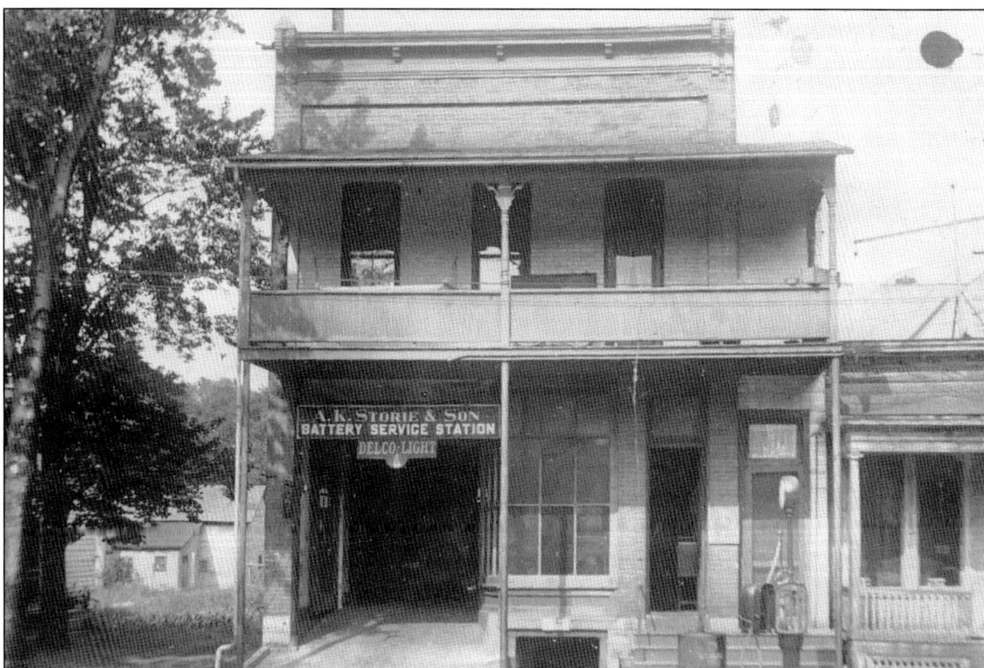

Exterior of the A.K. Storie & Son Battery Shop, c. 1920. Early service shops for automobiles show the progression of service stations and provide a glimpse into early Americana. (Courtesy Gouverneur Museum.)

AN EARLY HOT AIR BALLOON. Albert Woodward went aloft in this balloon at the Fourth of July celebration and circus at Parishville. Balloon ascents apparently were a frequent feature of 19th-century Independence Day celebrations. The archives of the St. Lawrence County Historical Association contain the following diary entry: "Tuesday, July 4, 1882. The Glorious Fourth . . . At half past four (a.m.), George, Rell, Cy and I started . . . arriving in Ogdensburg about 10:00 instead of 9:00 when we were due . . . There was a big crowd there . . . The attractions consisted of hurdle races, races between horses and Indians, . . . and a balloon ascension which proved a flat failure . . . We waited to see the balloon go up until about six o'clock (when after making two ineffectual attempts to rise they hauled it down and let the gas escape.)"—from the diary of Byron G. Parker, 19, of Parishville. (Courtesy Parishville historian.)

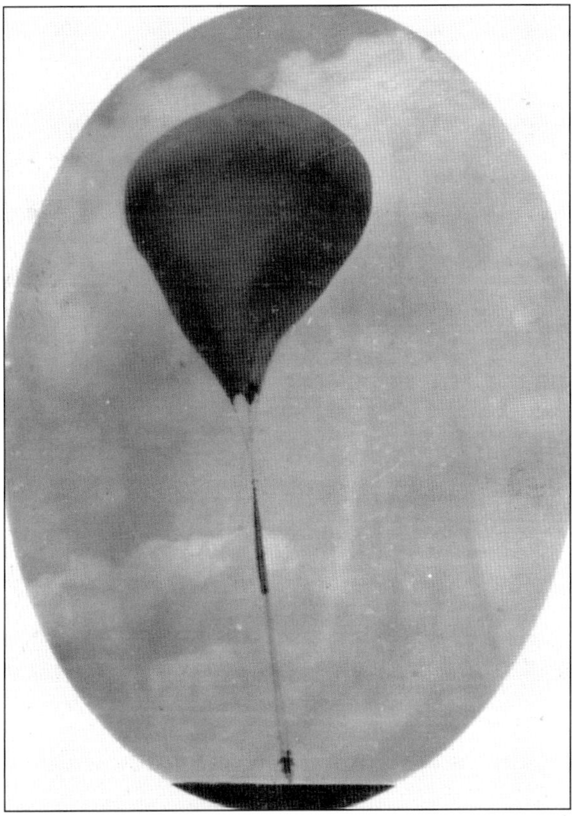

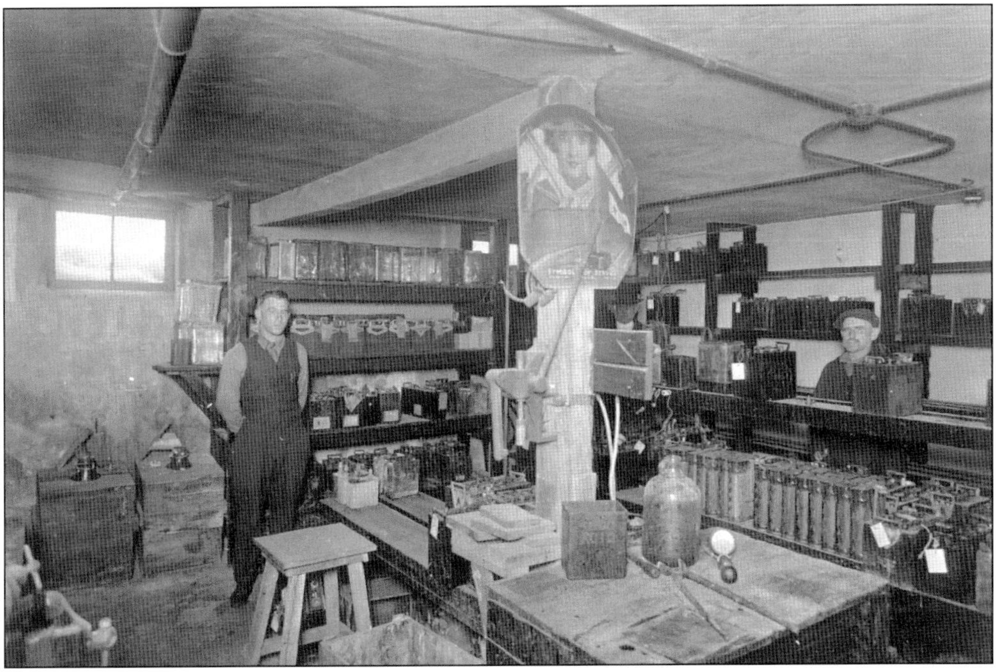

HAROLD, FRED, AND S.K. STORIE. This trio ran the battery shop at 16 John Street in Gouverneur c. 1925. (Courtesy Gouverneur Museum.)

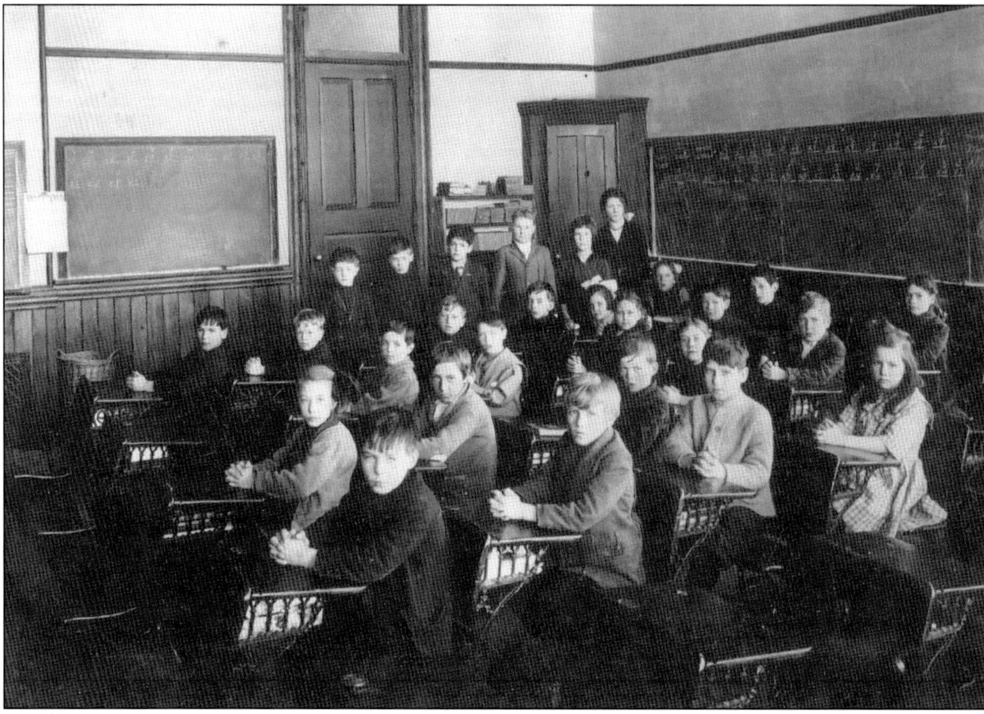

WELL-DRESSED AND EQUALLY WELL-BEHAVED. Students pose with their teacher in a Canton classroom in 1914. (SLCHA.)

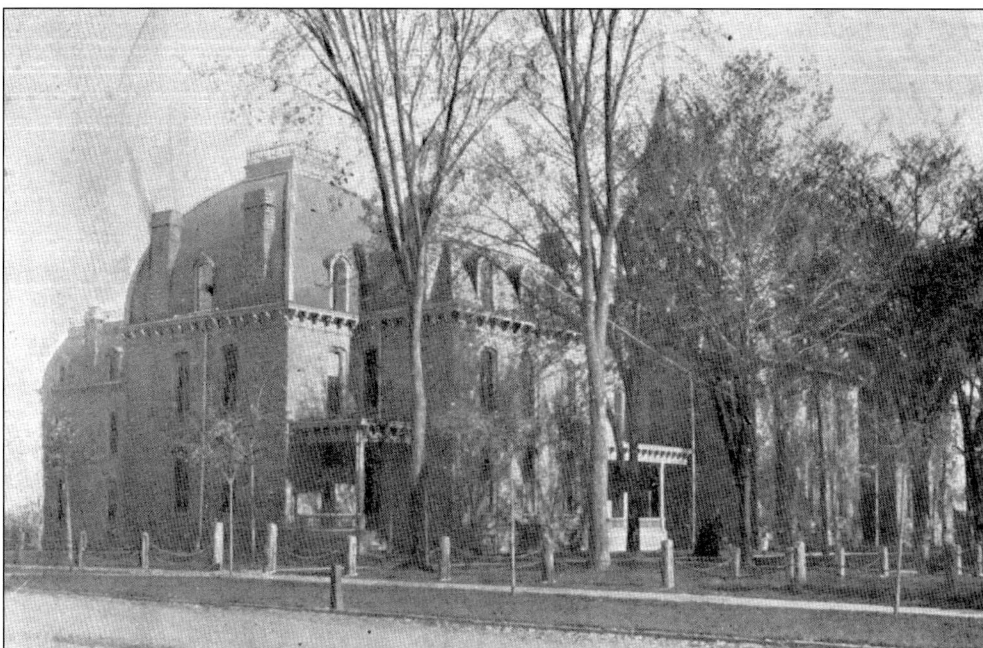

THE STATE NORMAL AND TRAINING SCHOOL, POTSDAM. Many fine buildings like this one were constructed of native Potsdam sandstone, which was widely used, including in the Ottawa Houses of Parliament. (SLCHA.)

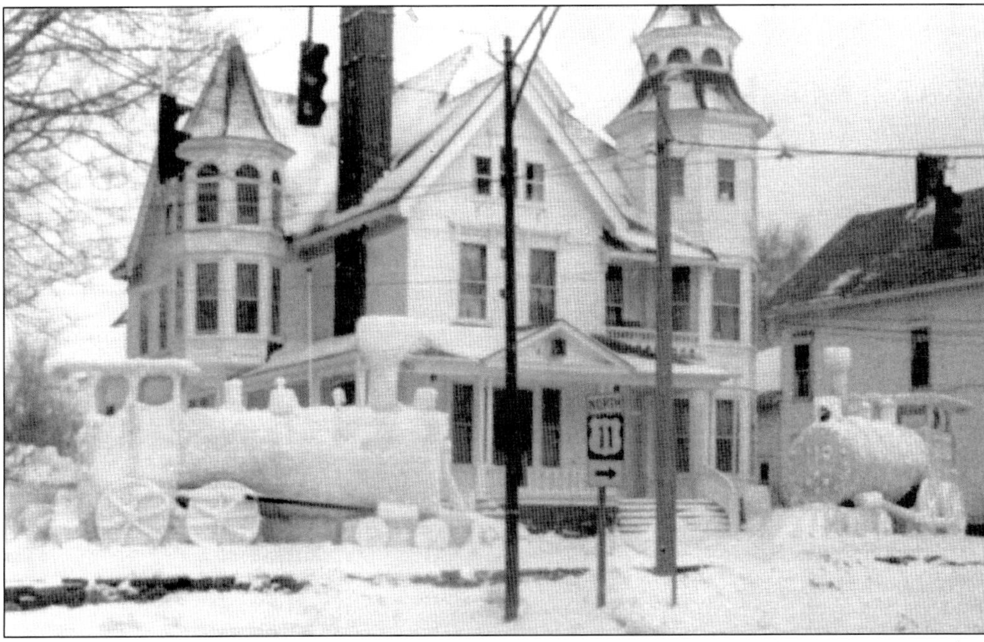

THE ICE TRAIN. With locomotive ice sculptures, this fraternity house on Elm Street in Potsdam exhibits high winter carnival form. (SLCHA.)

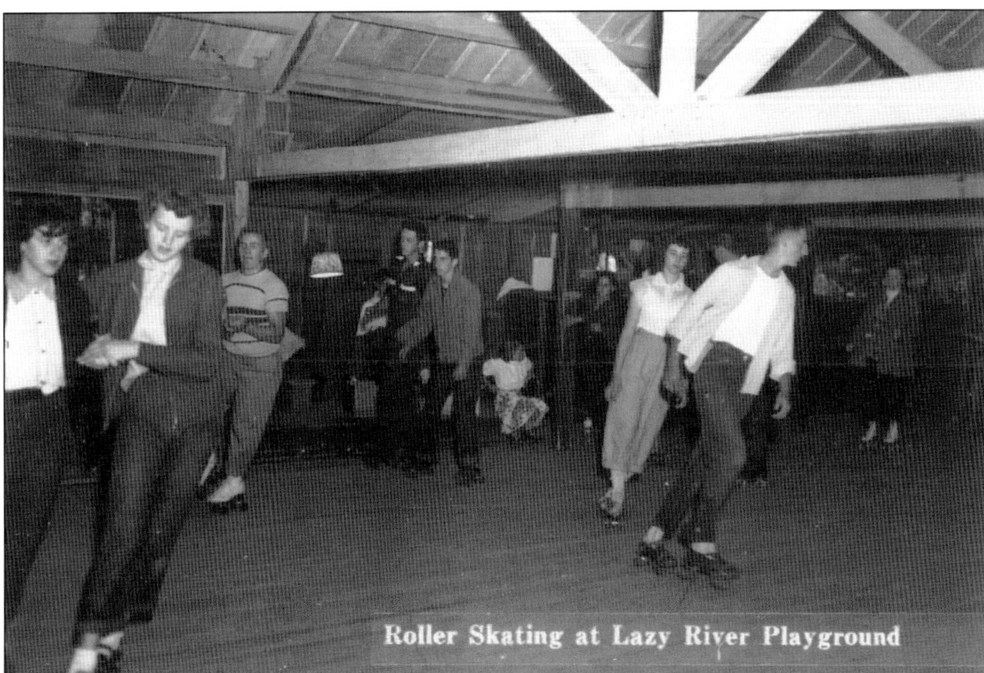

ROLLER-SKATING AT LAZY RIVER PLAYGROUND, NEAR CANTON, C. 1950. The music played, and the skaters made their rounds. (SLCHA.)

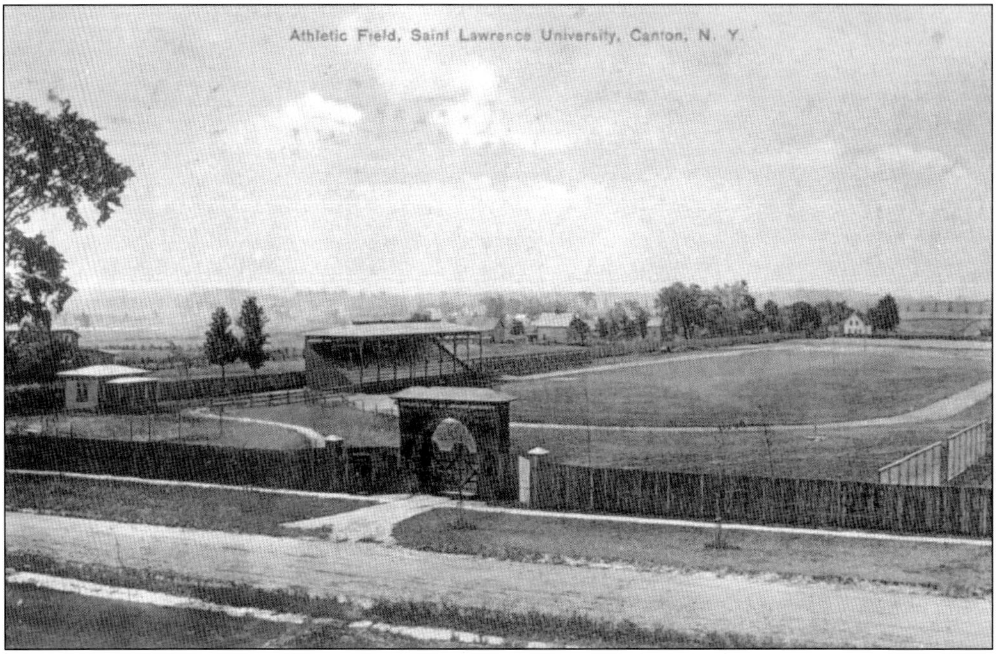

St. Lawrence University's Athletic Fields and Track, Park Street, Canton, c. 1920. There appears to be little difference between the dirt track inside the fence and the dirt highway out front. (SLCHA.)

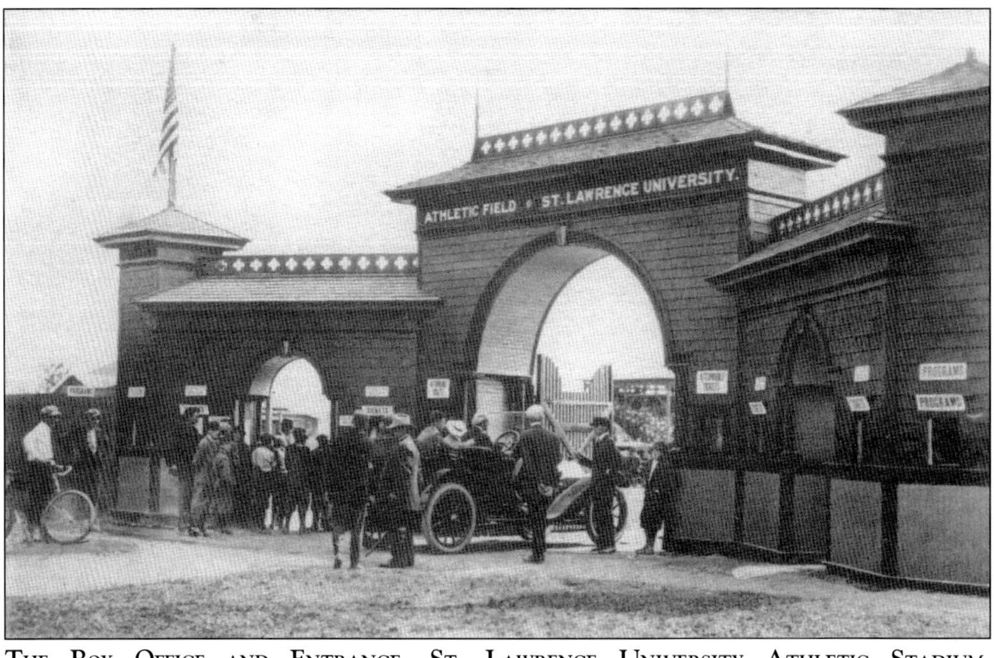

The Box Office and Entrance, St. Lawrence University Athletic Stadium, c. 1920. The university's stadiums were updated periodically over the years, including the most recent Leckonby Stadium, completed in 2000. (SLCHA.)

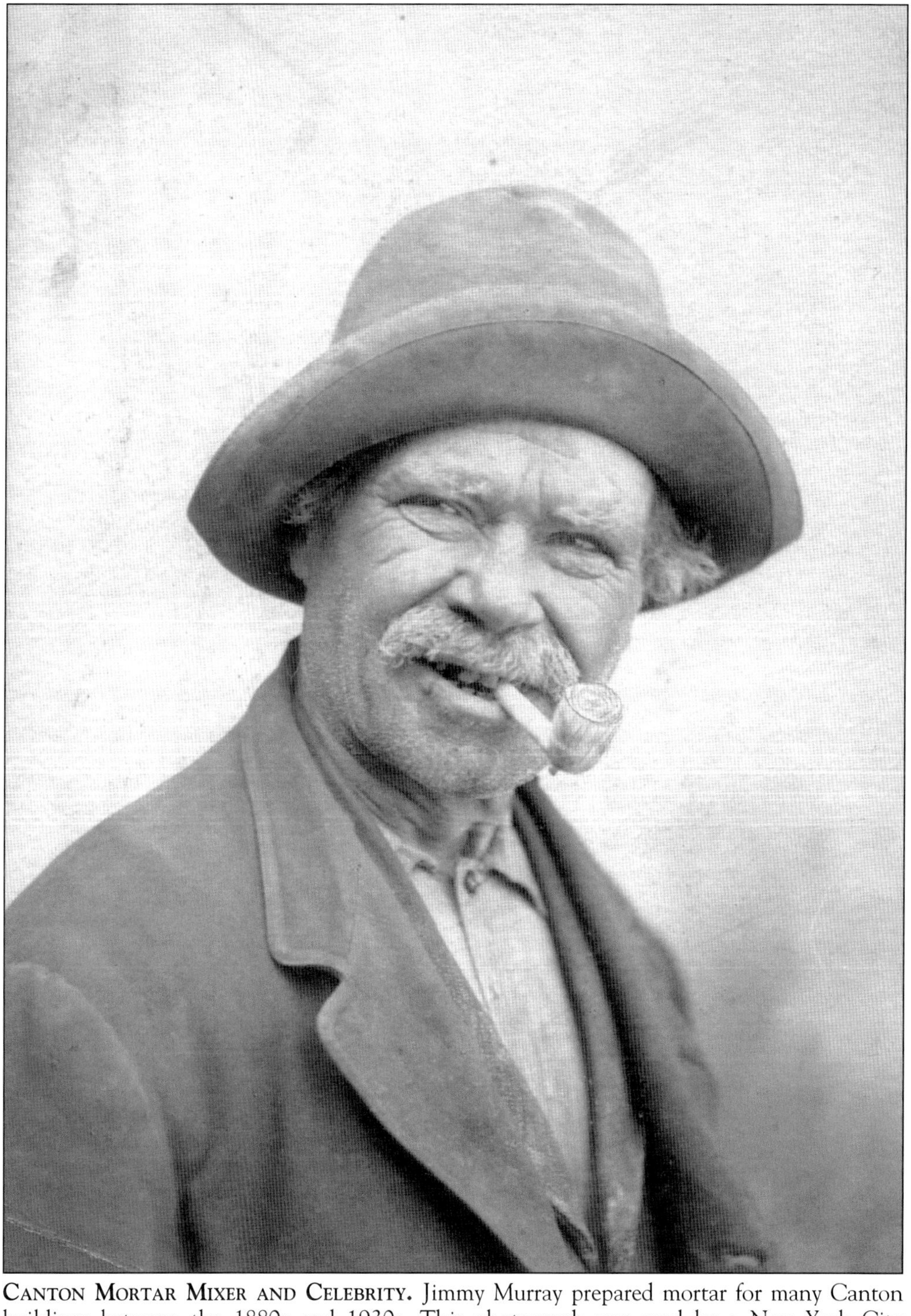

CANTON MORTAR MIXER AND CELEBRITY. Jimmy Murray prepared mortar for many Canton buildings between the 1880s and 1930s. This photograph was used by a New York City lithographer, who blew it up in full color and sold millions of copies all across the United States. Murray's face was said to be the best known in the country, surpassing even the president's. (SLCHA.)

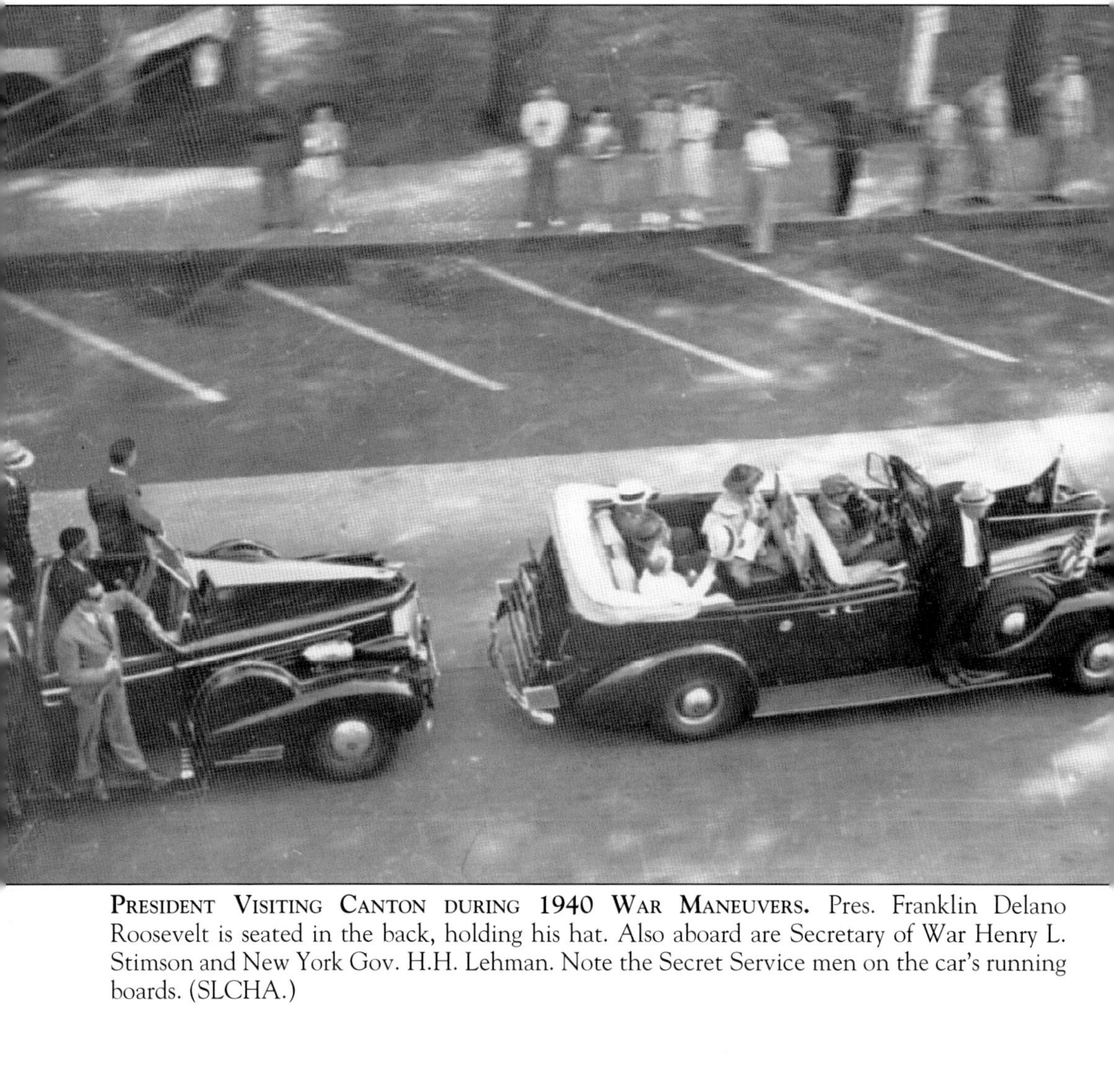

PRESIDENT VISITING CANTON DURING 1940 WAR MANEUVERS. Pres. Franklin Delano Roosevelt is seated in the back, holding his hat. Also aboard are Secretary of War Henry L. Stimson and New York Gov. H.H. Lehman. Note the Secret Service men on the car's running boards. (SLCHA.)

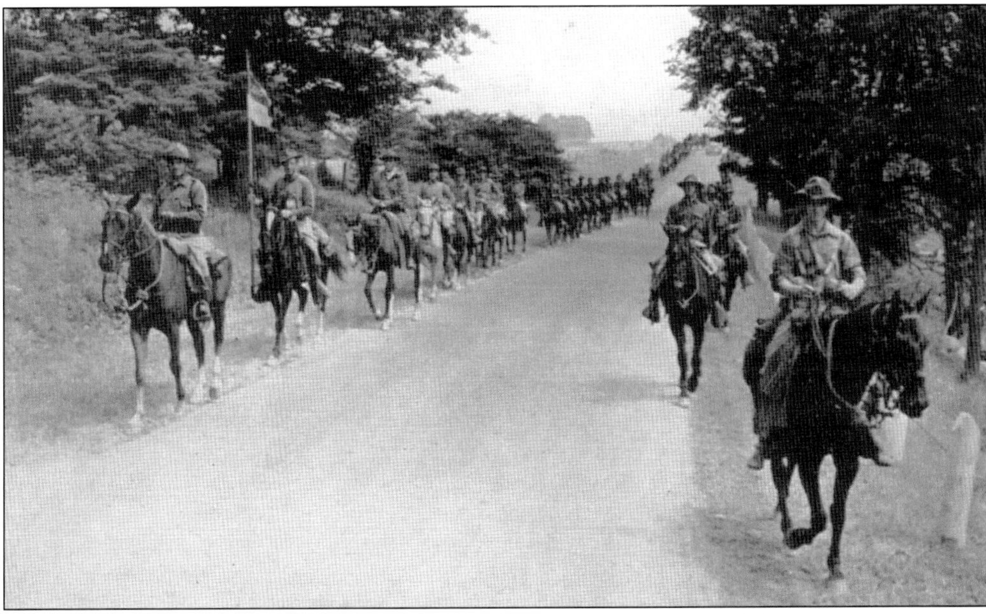

THE CAVALRY. The cavalry makes one of its final appearances in 20th-century warfare. 1st Army, St. Lawrence County, performed these military maneuvers in 1940. (SLCHA.)

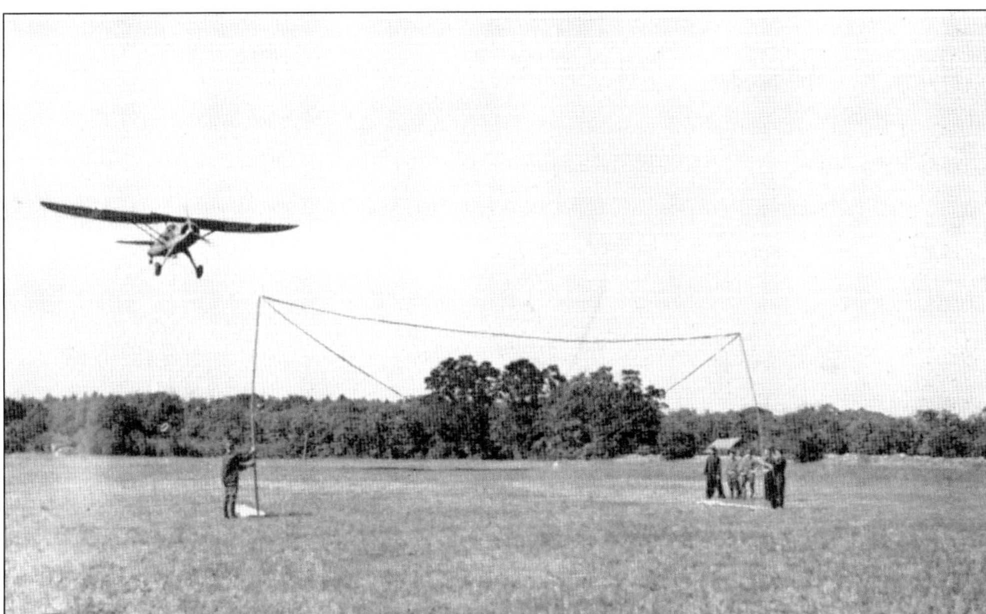

1ST ARMY MANEUVERS, ST. LAWRENCE COUNTY, 1940. Planes picking up messages tied to a rope held between poles in this manner were soon to be eliminated, as battlefield communications improved. (SLCHA.)

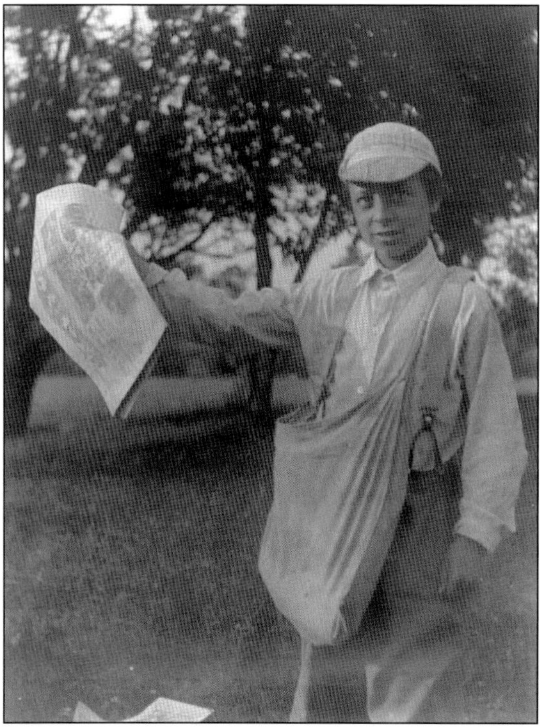

R. BARNHART, NEWSBOY. The newsboy was a firmly established tradition that would survive into the 21st century. (SLCHA.)

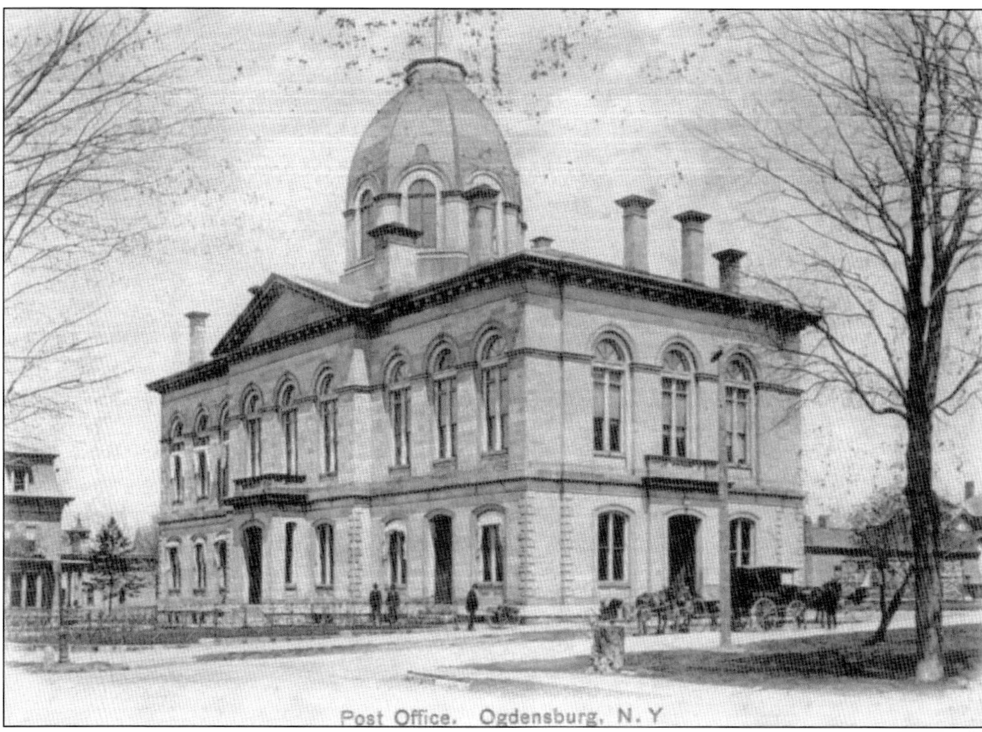

THE OLD POST OFFICE, OGDENSBURG. The cupola was later removed and the post office left the building in the 1980s, only to consider returning at the start of the 21st century. (SLCHA.)

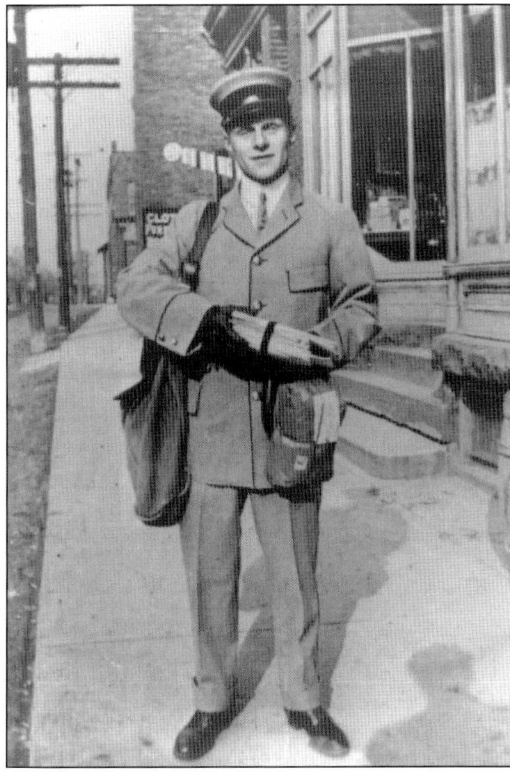

The First Letter Carrier in Norwood. Arthur Tebo served as the first letter carrier in Norwood. (Courtesy Norwood historian.)

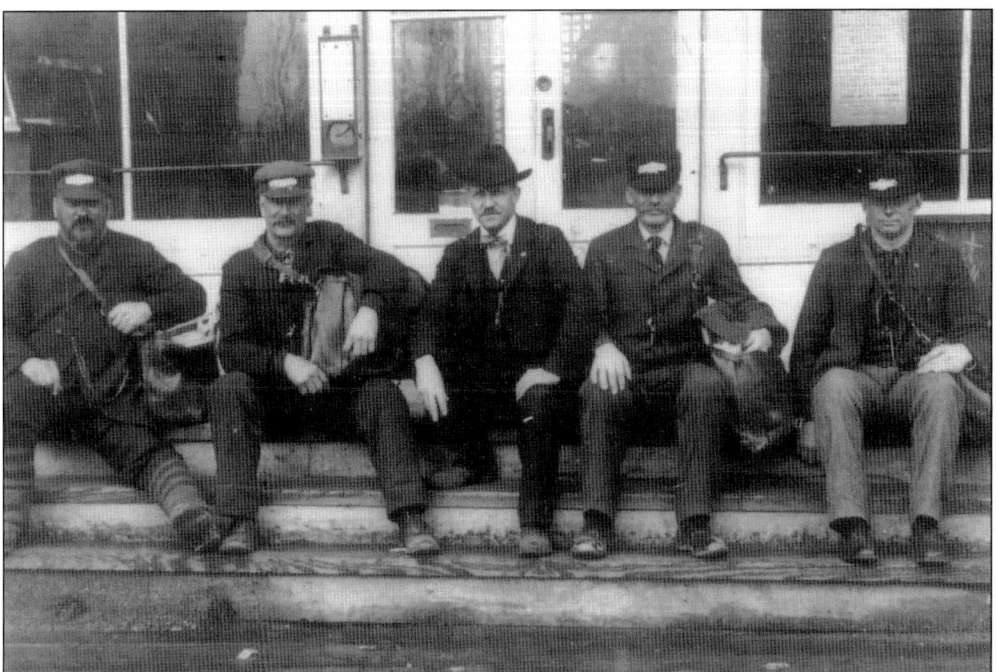

Rural Postal Deliverers, Lisbon, c. 1902. Postmaster Charles Wallace is seated in the center of this photograph. Ruth Wallace Venier is behind the door, looking through the glass. (Courtesy Lisbon historian.)

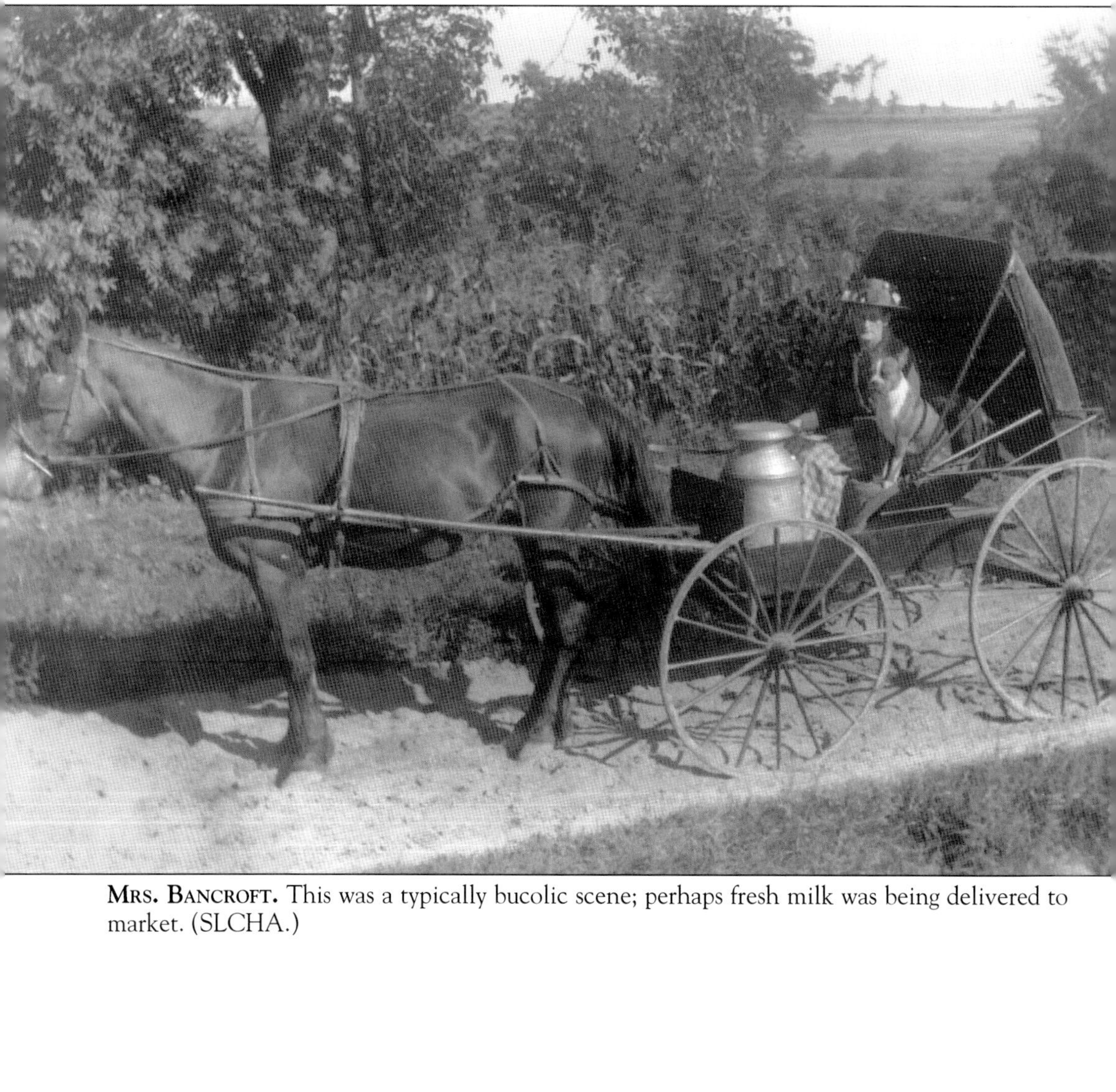

Mrs. Bancroft. This was a typically bucolic scene; perhaps fresh milk was being delivered to market. (SLCHA.)

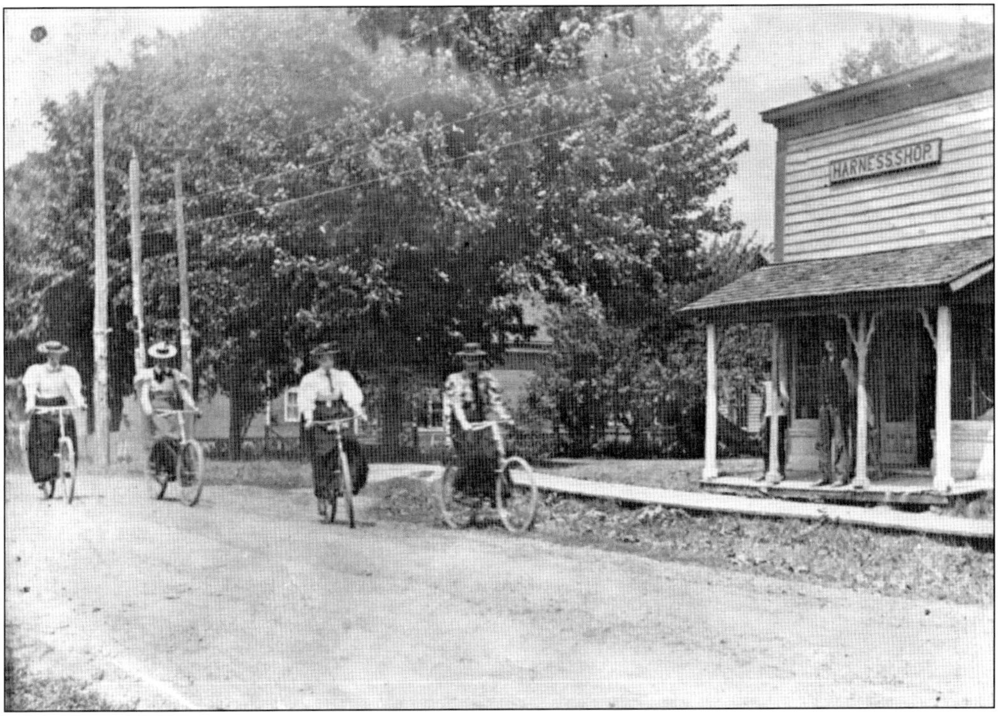

THE BRIER HILL BICYCLE CLUB. Bicycling was accepted in the late 1800s, and bike clubs and touring became popular—though road surfaces left much to be desired. (SLCHA.)

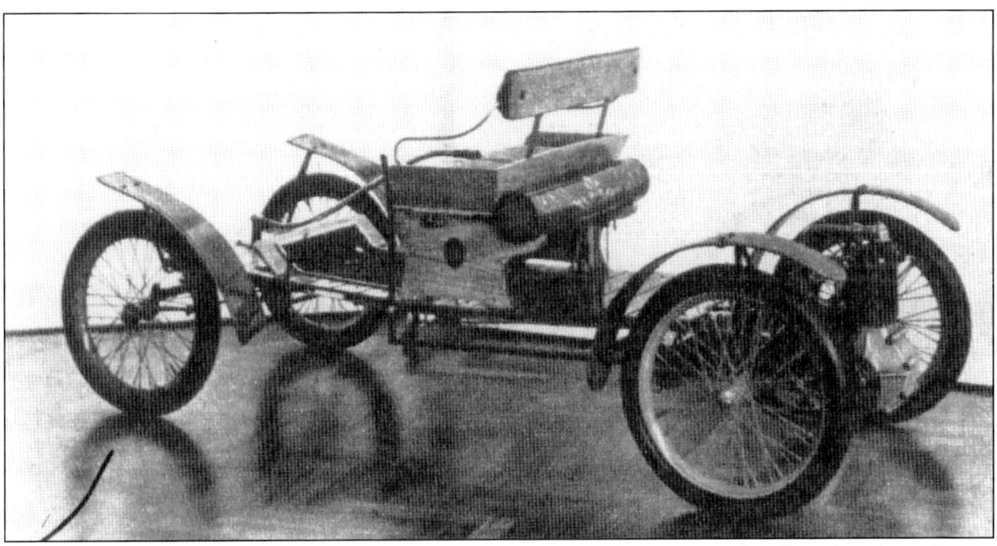

AN EVEN TRADE. *St. Lawrence Plaindealer* editor Williston Manley bought this Orient buckboard from Canton lawyer Lawrence Russell for $125 in payment for a printing bill. It had laminated wooden fenders, an oak-slat platform body, and a small air-cooled engine on the rear axle. (SLCHA.)

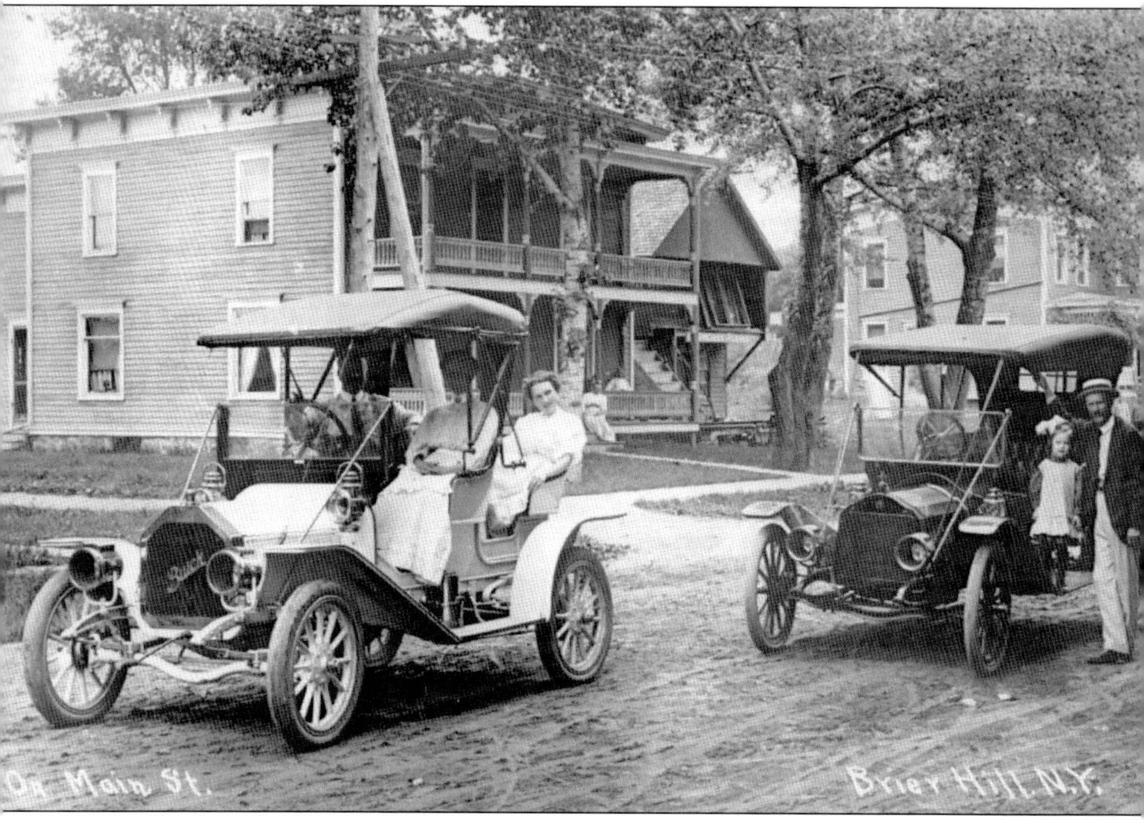

An Extra Fancy Buick and Another Early Horseless Carriage, Main Street, Brier Hill. The heyday of both the Thousand Islands and the Adirondacks occurred at the end of the 19th and the beginning of the 20th centuries—before the automobile. The car is credited with the demise of the "destination resort," causing many of the enormous hotels in such places to close. Before the automobile, transportation was difficult enough to encourage visitors to stay at a hotel for an entire season. Once the car made travel easier, visitors stopped for briefer and briefer periods. The resort hotels could not survive on weekend guests alone. Since then, tourist destinations have reinvented themselves, with the automobile an integral part of the design. (SLCHA.)

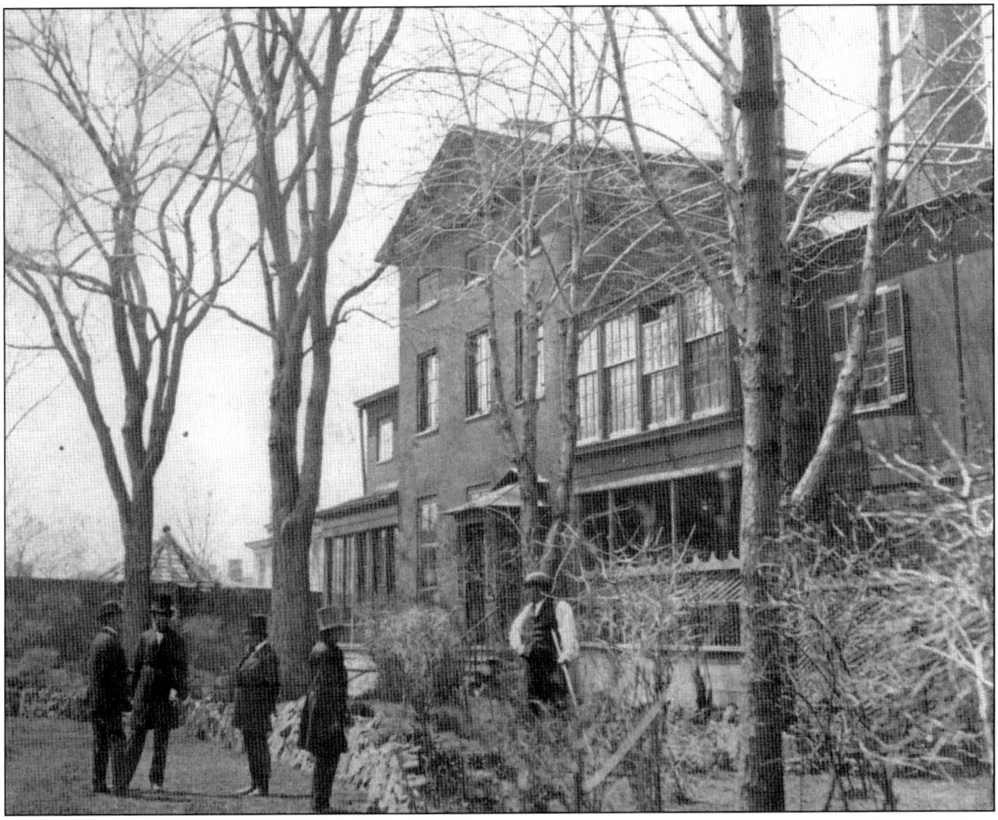

The Parish Mansion, Ogdensburg. George Parish is the man in the round-top derby hat. This building is now part of the Frederic Remington Art Museum. (SLCHA.)

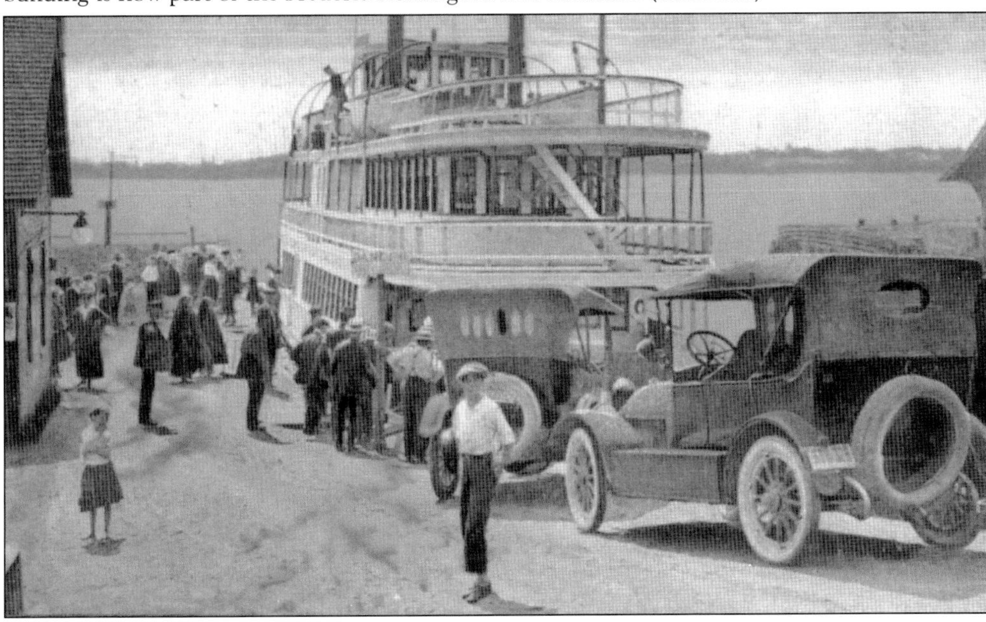

The Prescott–Ogdensburg Ferry. This view shows the Prescott–Ogdensburg Ferry docked at Prescott, Ontario. (SLCHA.)

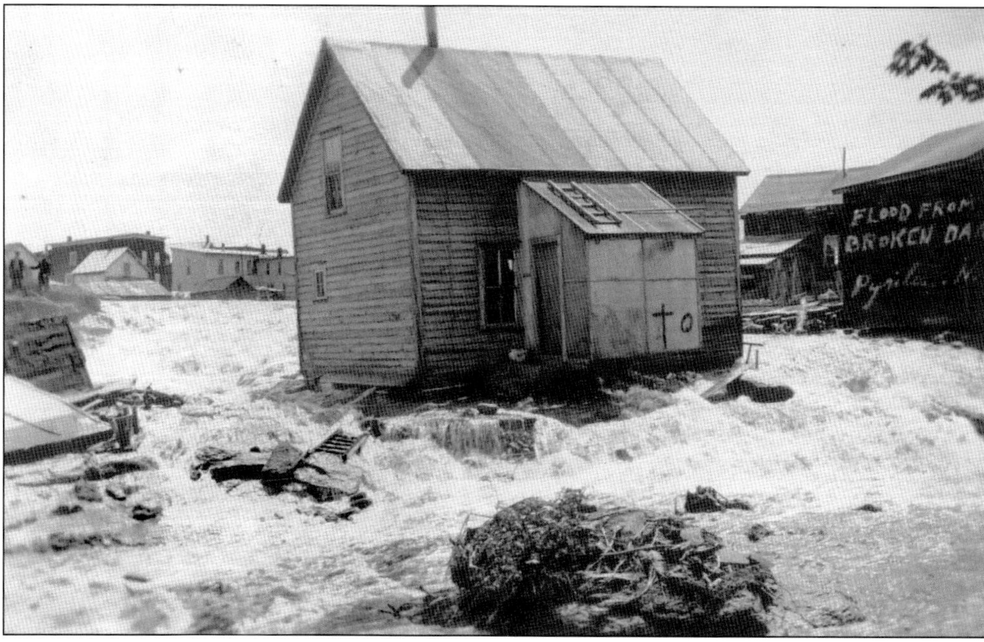

A STRANDED HOUSE. This house was stranded by a flood resulting from a broken dam in Pyrites. (SLCHA.)

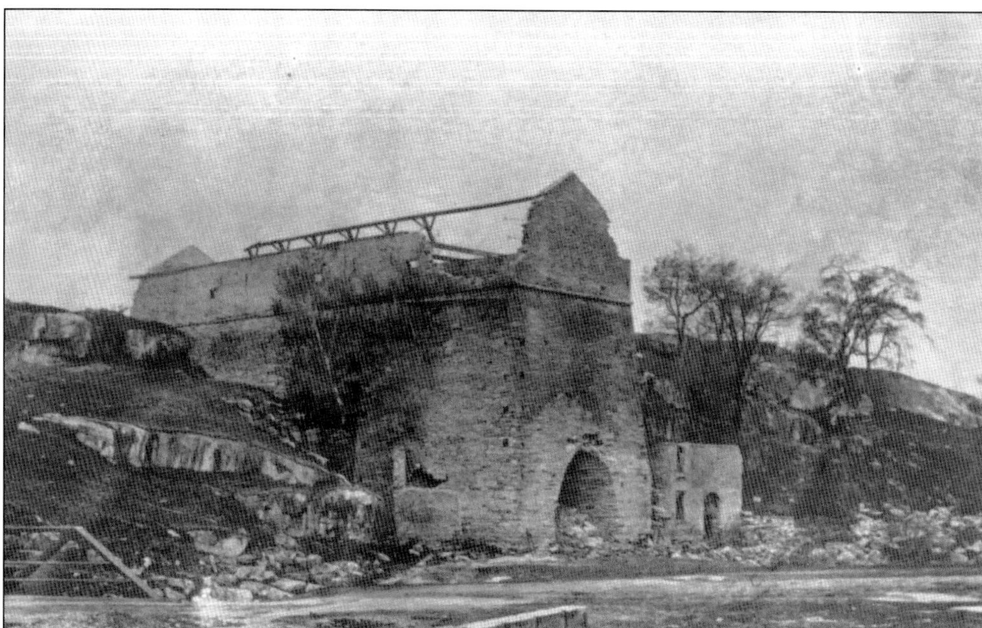

THE IRONWORKS RUINS. Rossie was the site of the first blast furnace in northern New York. Built in 1813, the ironworks were rebuilt several times and used until 1867. Ore was hauled to Rossie from the Caledonia mines, near Spragueville, for smelting. Pres. James Monroe visited the furnace as a guest of David Parish in 1817. (SLCHA.)

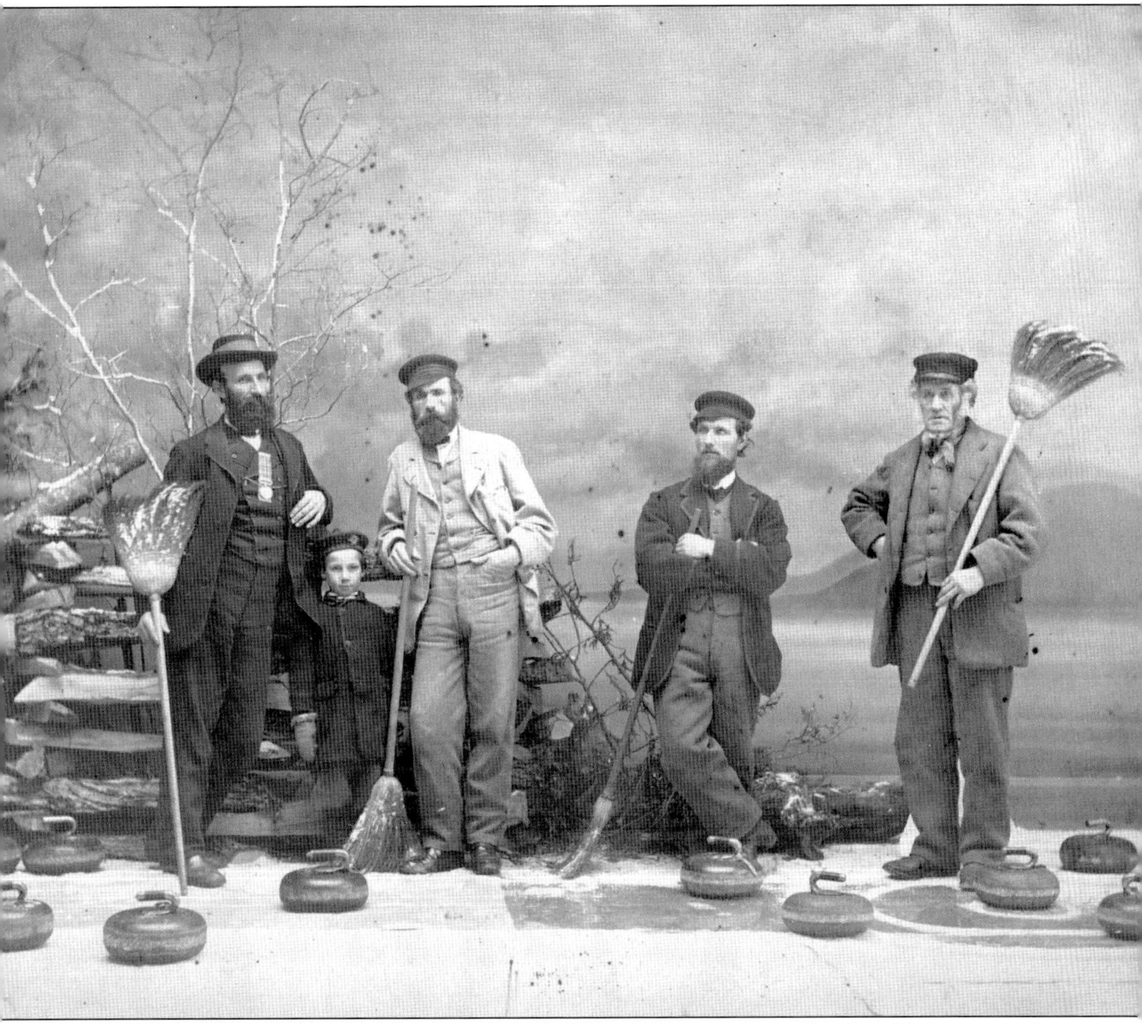

THE BURNS CURLING CLUB, OGDENSBURG. These five items on the Burns Curling Club appeared in the local newspaper:

"October 18, 1886. The Burns Curling Club of this city have closed a contract with Henry I. Proctor to erect a rink for their use on his lot on Ford St. corner of Elizabeth, which is a very convenient place to most of its members."

"January 3, 1887. Should any of your readers, on going down Ford Street, imagine when they come to a long, low building just beyond the Armory that the lunatic asylum is only the Burns Curling Club 'souping it up.'"

"January 10, 1887. The Burns Curling Club of this city, or three rinks of it, goes to Toronto Canada to be held there on the 12th."

"February 23, 1887. The Burns Curling Club of our city played an interesting game with the Cornwall Club on Friday last, each side scoring 32 points."

"March 21, 1887. The Burns Club of our city are doing considerable loud chinning these days, having taken into camp the crack players of the Cornwall and Brockville clubs."

Curling grew in popularity throughout the 20th century, and it eventually became an Olympic sport. (SLCHA.)

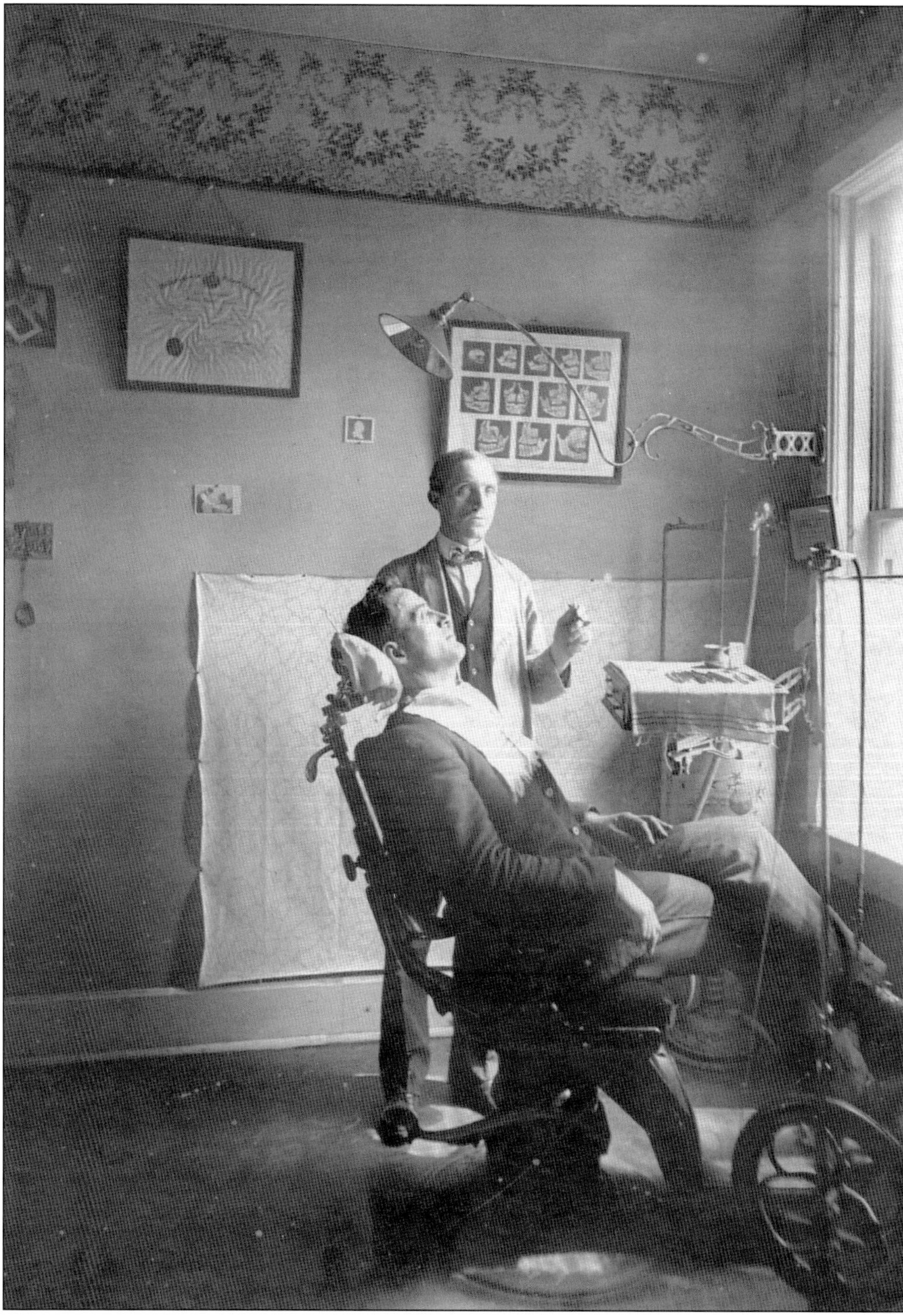

WESLEY STOUR OF KENDREW CORNERS, 1907. Wesley Stour sits in the chair, awaiting Dr. Austin's ministrations. (SLCHA.)

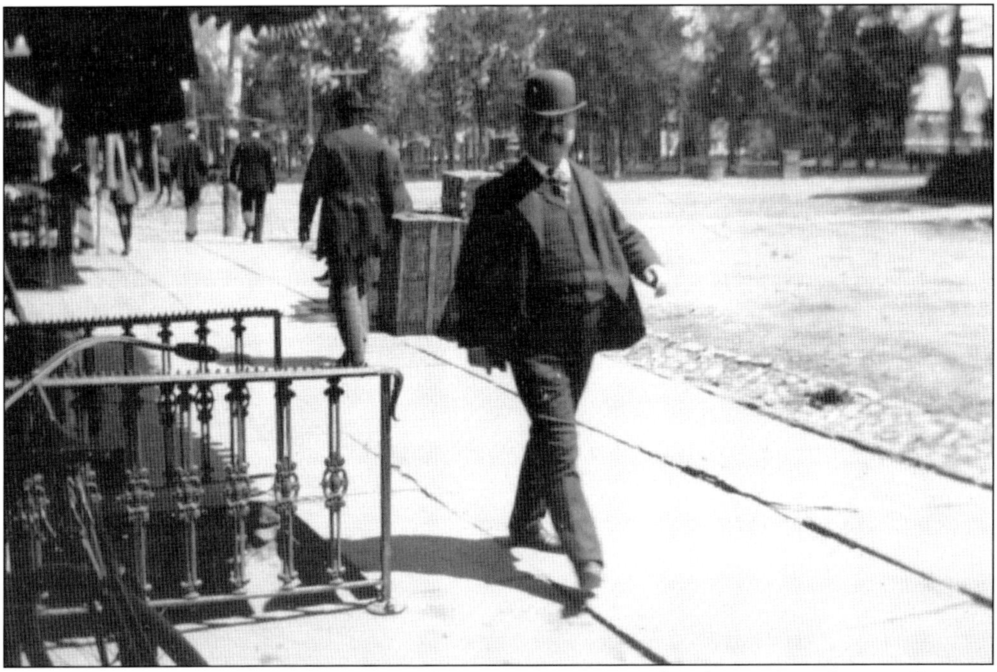

DAPPER MAN. Bowler-hatted artist Frederic Remington strolls along Main Street, Canton, *c*. 1900. (SLCHA.)

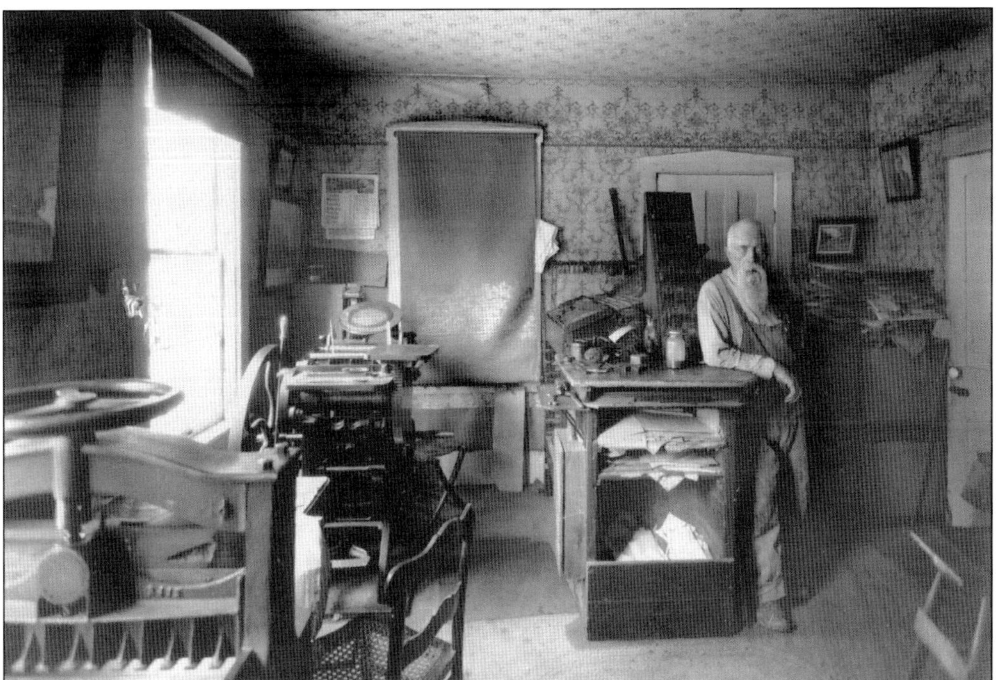

GEORGE T. MANLEY, FORMER FOREMAN OF THE *ST. LAWRENCE PLAINDEALER*. George T. Manley worked at the paper from 1873 to 1908. They say that he went into a print shop in 1863 at the age of 13 and never came out. (SLCHA.)

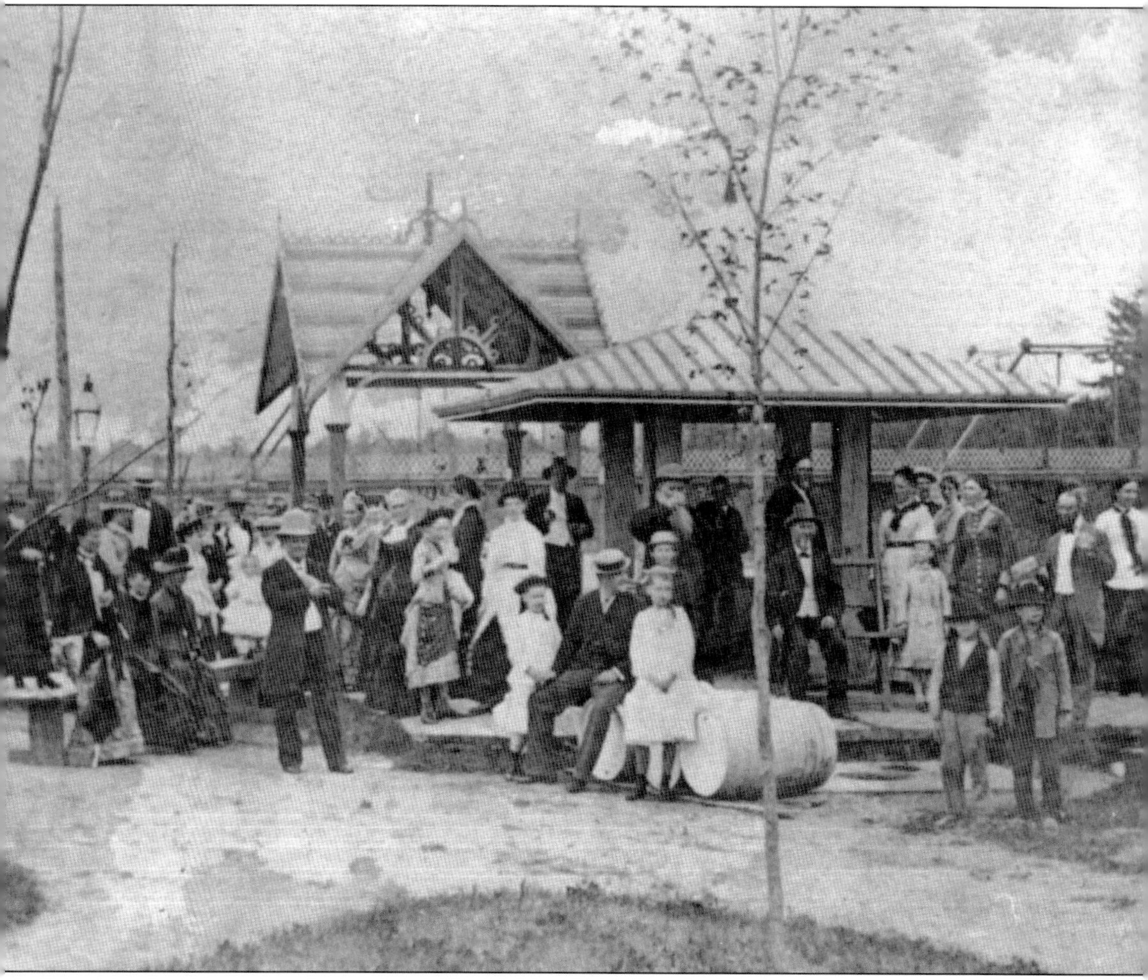

MASSENA MINERAL SPRINGS, C. 1890. Guests at hotels and boardinghouses came by the thousands to bathe in and drink the waters to cure rheumatism. The baths were made from heavy slate. The water stained the towels, and the bathers' clothes reeked of the sulfur-laden springs. (Courtesy Massena historian.)

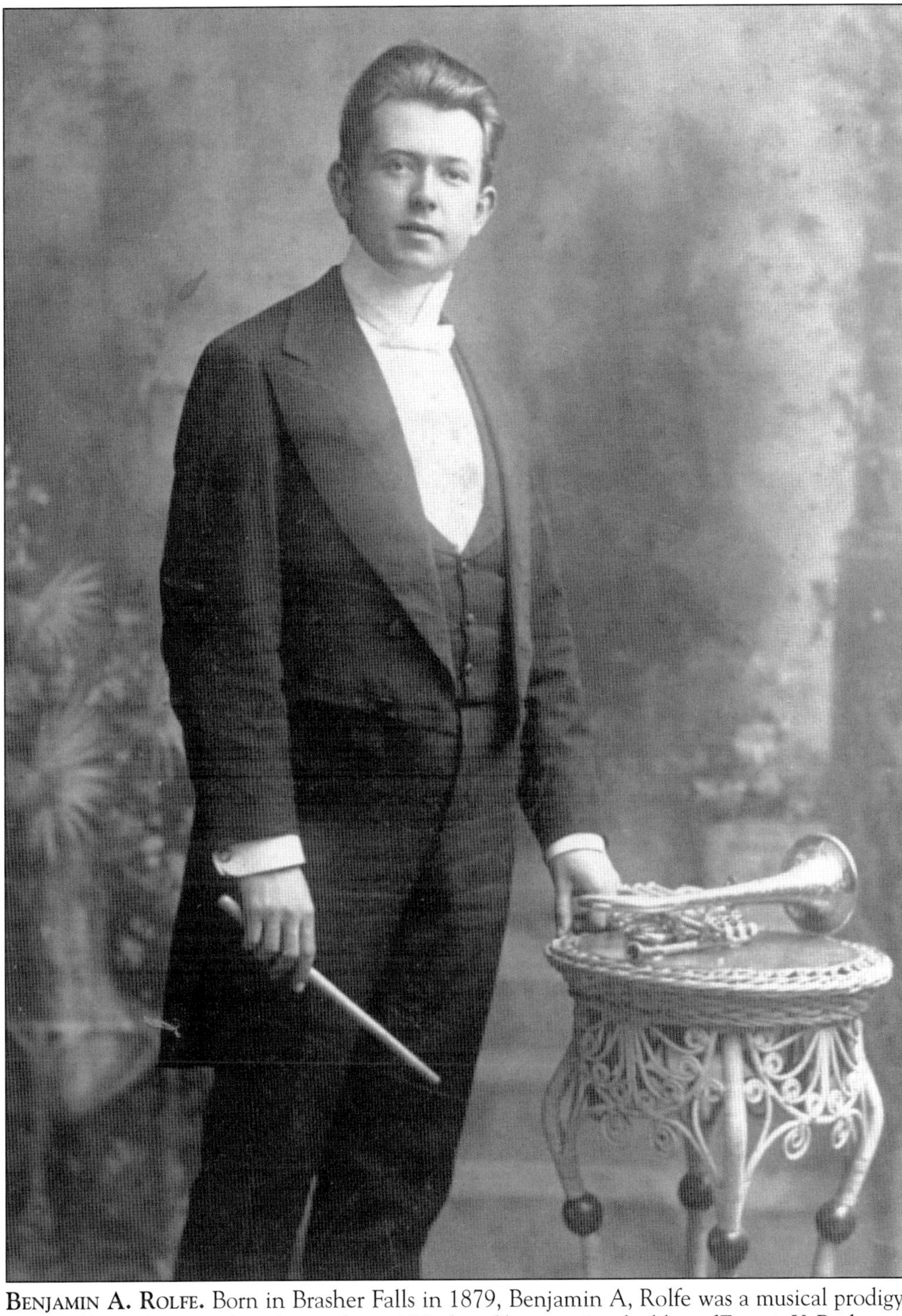

Benjamin A. Rolfe. Born in Brasher Falls in 1879, Benjamin A, Rolfe was a musical prodigy, vaudeville producer, and producer of over 100 silent films starring the likes of Francis X. Bushman, Beverly Bayne, and June Mathis. He is reputed to have performed with John Philip Sousa and the U.S. Marine Band as a 10-year-old soloist. Rolfe contracted with Harry Houdini to make films of the escape artist at work, but the two had a falling out over money. (SLCHA.)

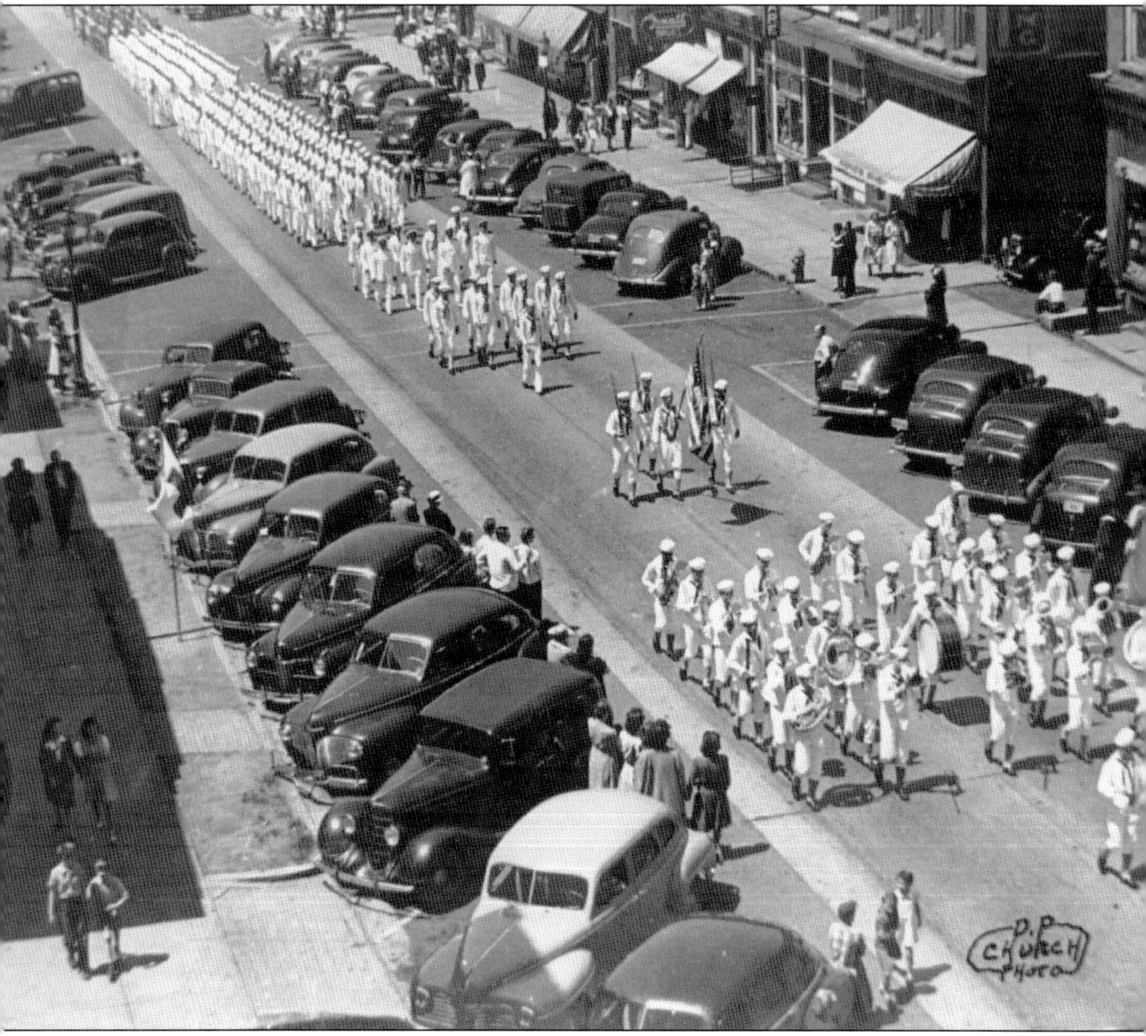

THE 1944 MEMORIAL DAY PARADE. A navy V-12 unit marches along Main Street, Canton, in the Memorial Day parade of 1944. (Dwight Church photograph, SLCHA.)

Two

Living on the Land

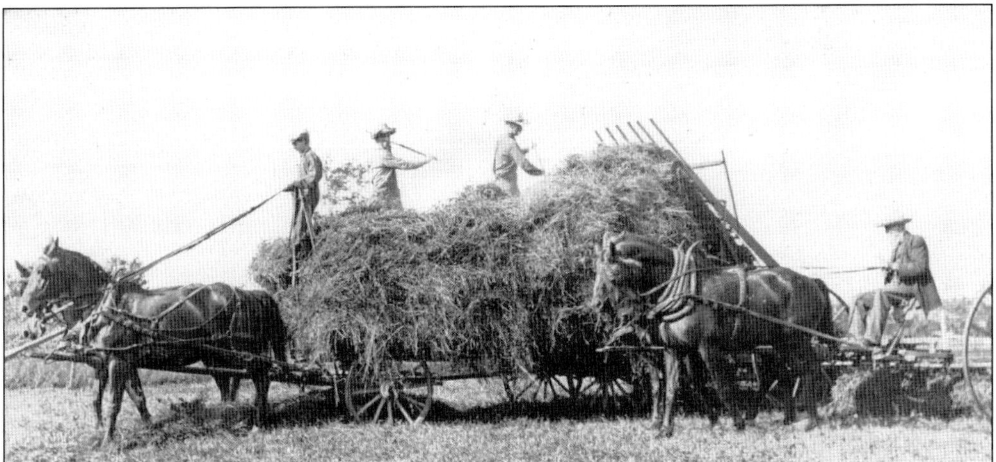

Madrid Farmers. Agriculture has always been the foundation of the county's economy. The dairy farmers of the North Country have made New York State cheddar cheese famous. (Courtesy Chris Angus.)

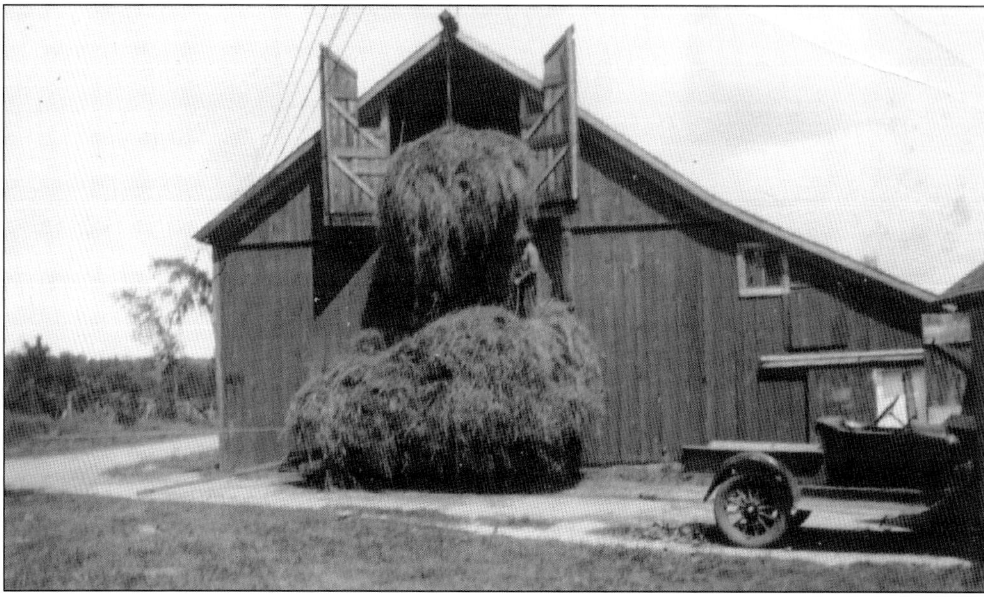

Loading Hay by Hand. While most farmers now use mechanical balers, Amish farmers in the county still do it by hand. (SLCHA.)

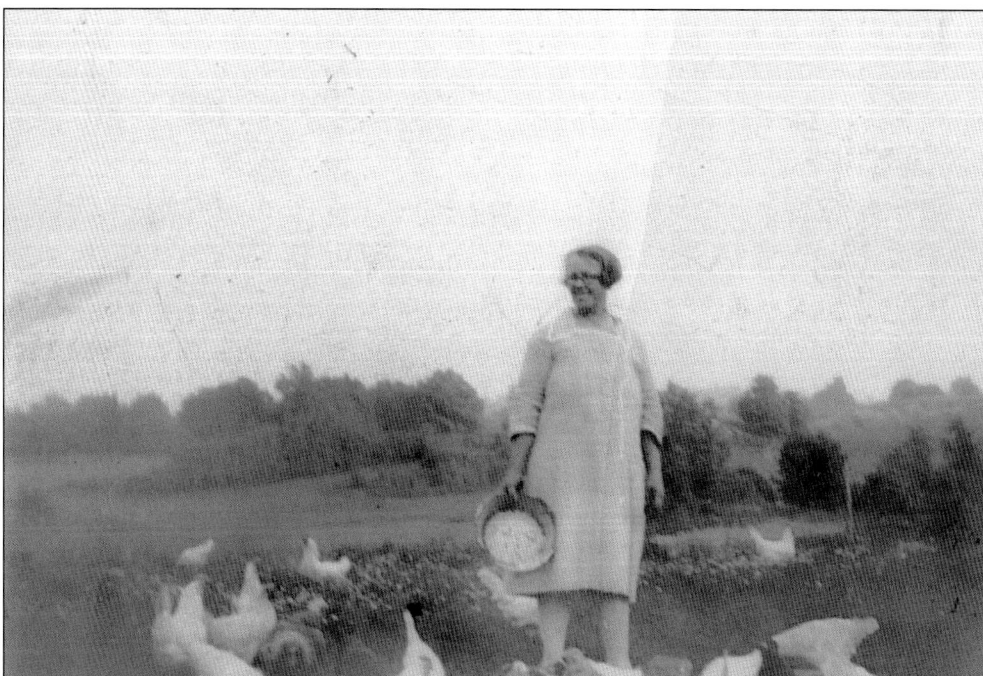

Adeline Hurlbut Thompson Feeding Her Chickens, c. 1920. This photograph was taken in Osbornville, in the town of DeKalb. (Courtesy DeKalb historian.)

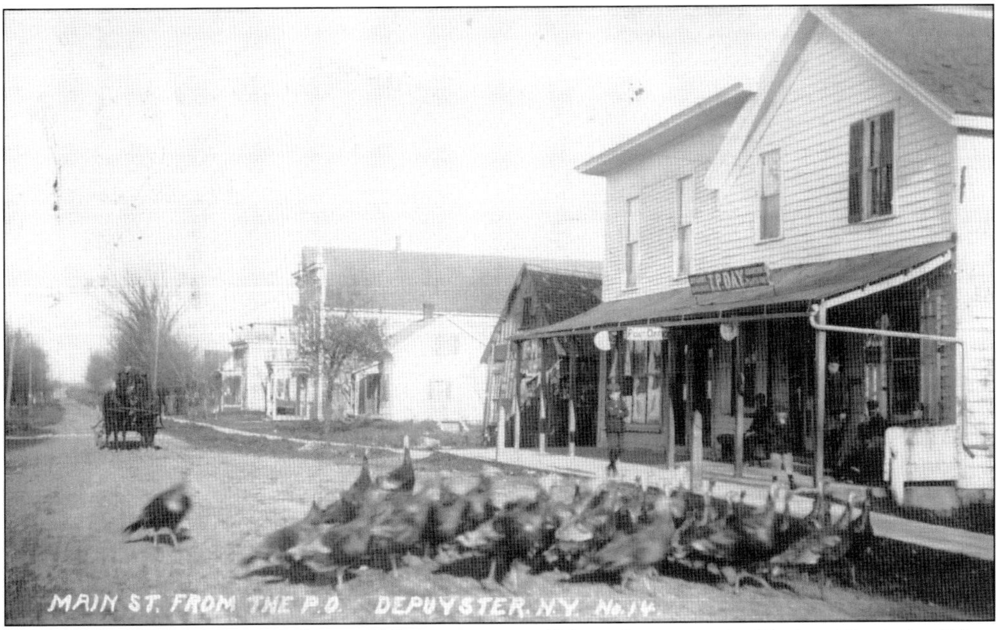

MAIN STREET, DEPEYSTER. The neighboring town of Heuvelton was the Turkey Capital of New York from 1853 to 1926 and was recognized as the world's largest dressed turkey market between 1893 and 1928. (SLCHA.)

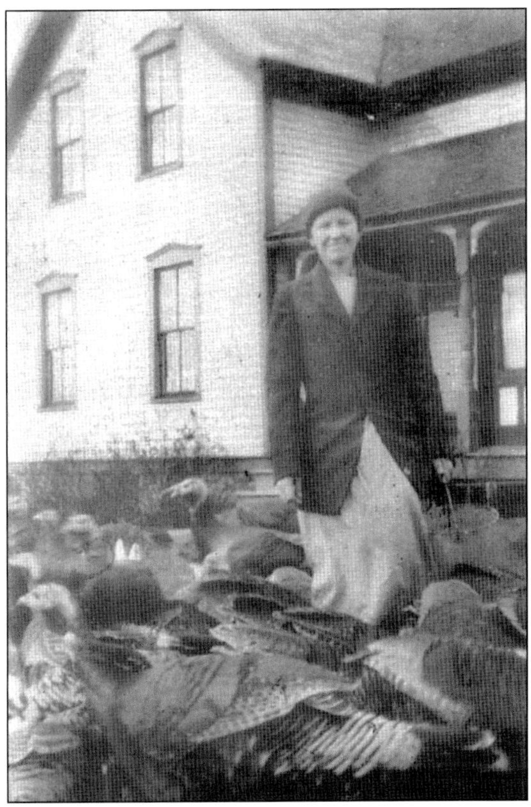

TURKEY FEEDING TIME. Adeline Hurlbut Thompson feeds her turkeys c. 1920. (Courtesy DeKalb historian.)

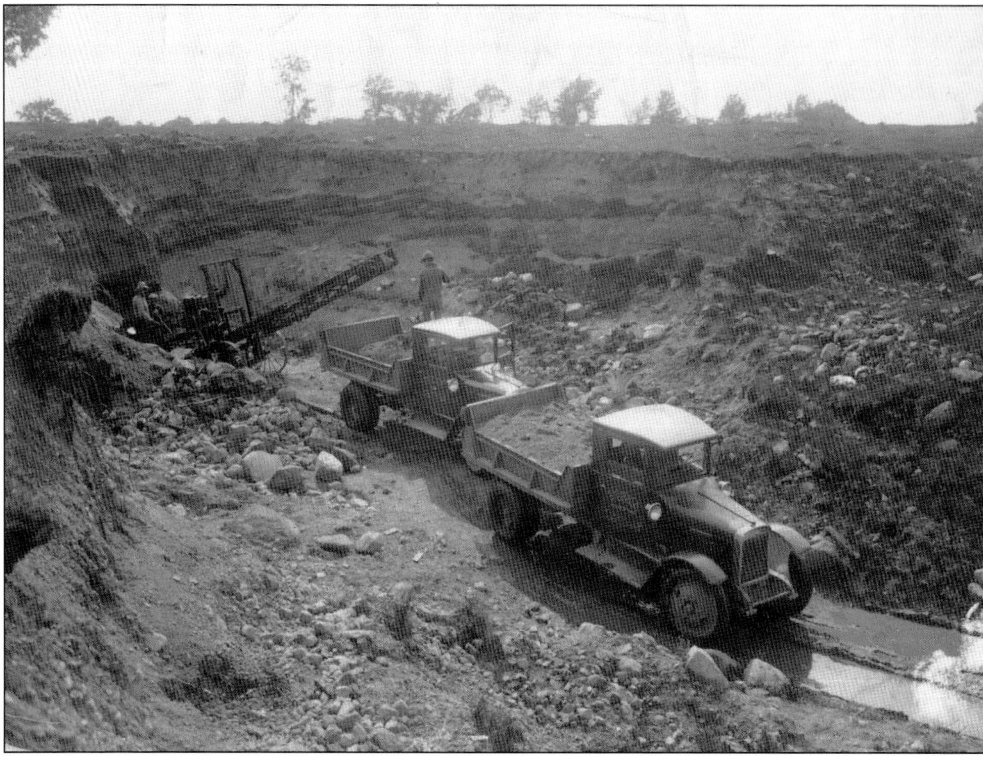

The Town of Lisbon Highway Crew and Equipment. The Lisbon highway crew works in Aldrich Pit, on Pray Road, in the 1920s. (Courtesy Lisbon historian.)

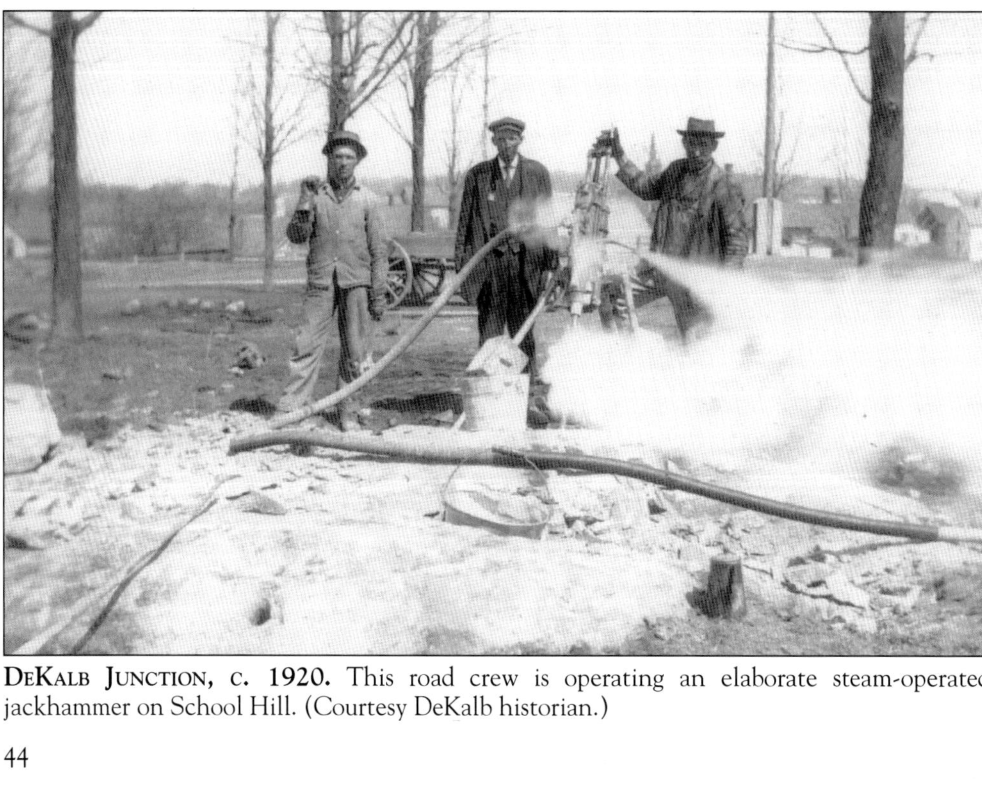

DeKalb Junction, c. 1920. This road crew is operating an elaborate steam-operated jackhammer on School Hill. (Courtesy DeKalb historian.)

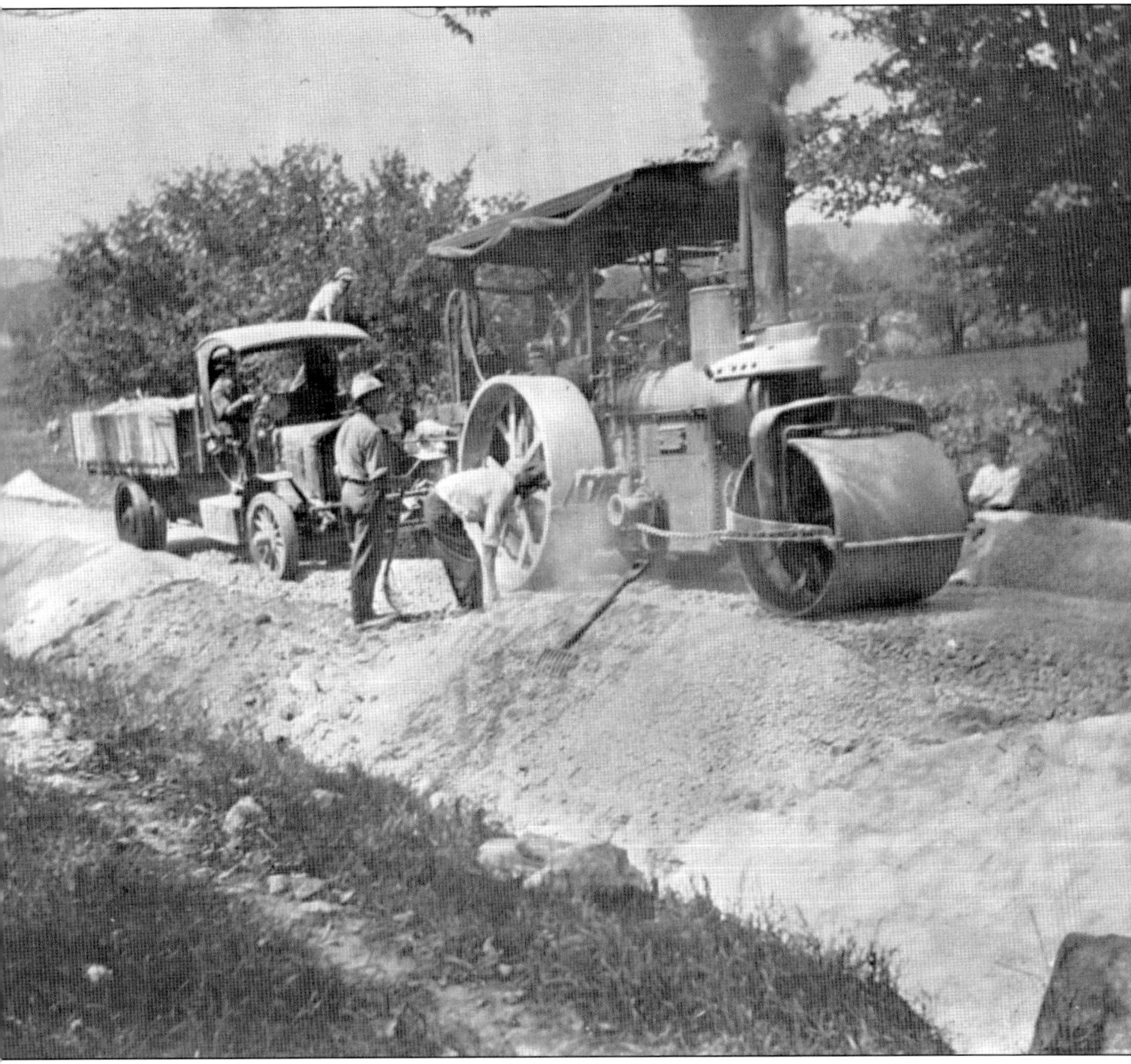

ROAD BUILDING. Workmen build a road in Pierrepont in the 1930s. (SLCHA.)

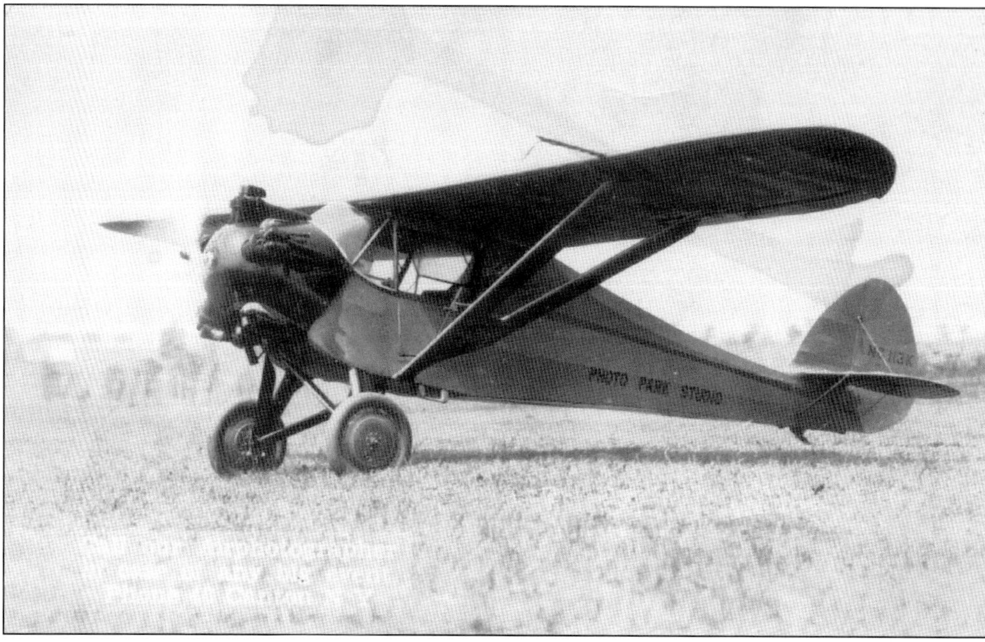

Possibly the First Plane Owned by Dwight Church, c. 1930. Dwight Church was a well-known aerial photographer from Canton. (Courtesy Chris Angus.)

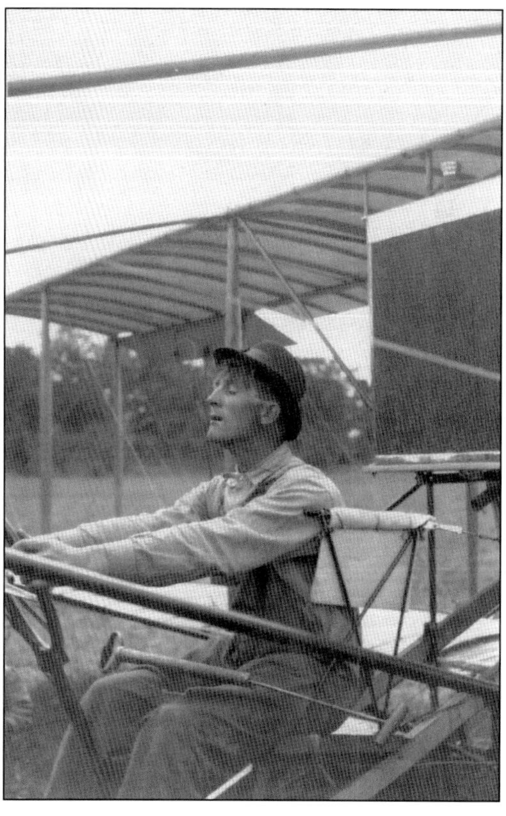

Timothy Thomas at the Controls. Timothy Thomas was forced down between Richville and Gouverneur on September 12, 1912. (SLCHA.)

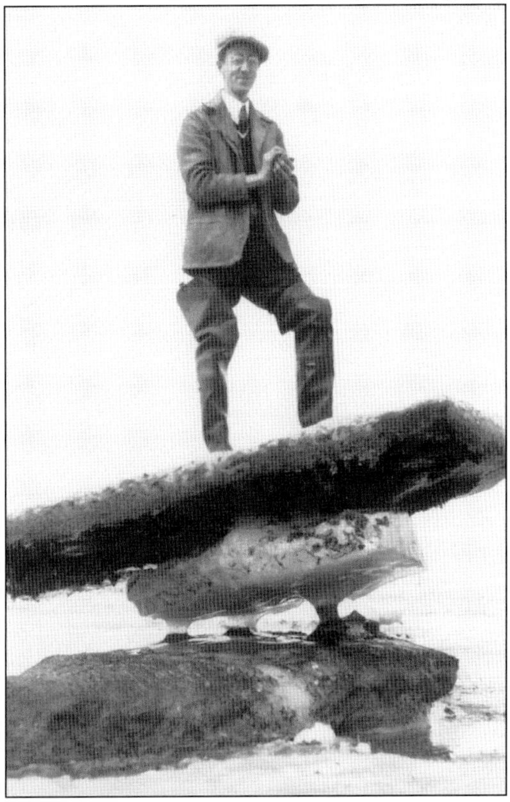

Dwight Church. This pioneer in the art of aerial photography was born in Canton in 1891. His daughter describes working as his assistant: "Once he had the camera and had arranged its settings, we would spiral slowly toward earth as he clicked pictures straight down. The pull of the gravity put my heart in my mouth, but the exhilaration was extraordinary."—from "A Wing and a Prayer" by Neal Burdick, July/August 1992 *Adirondack Life*. (SLCHA.)

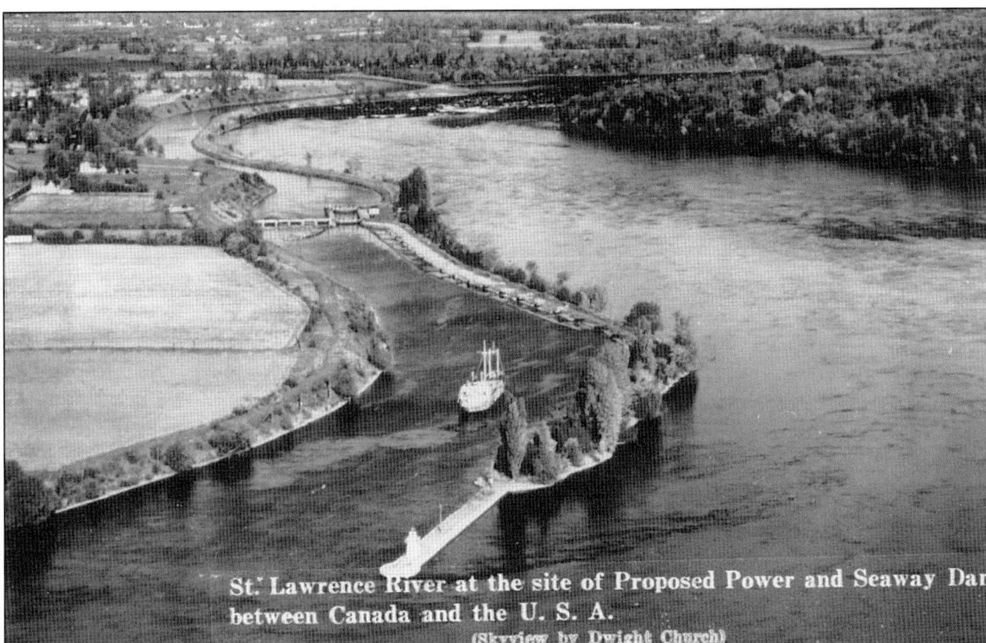

The Proposed Dam Site. This aerial view shows the St. Lawrence River at the site of the proposed Power and Seaway Dam between Canada and the United States. (Skyview by Dwight Church, SLCHA.)

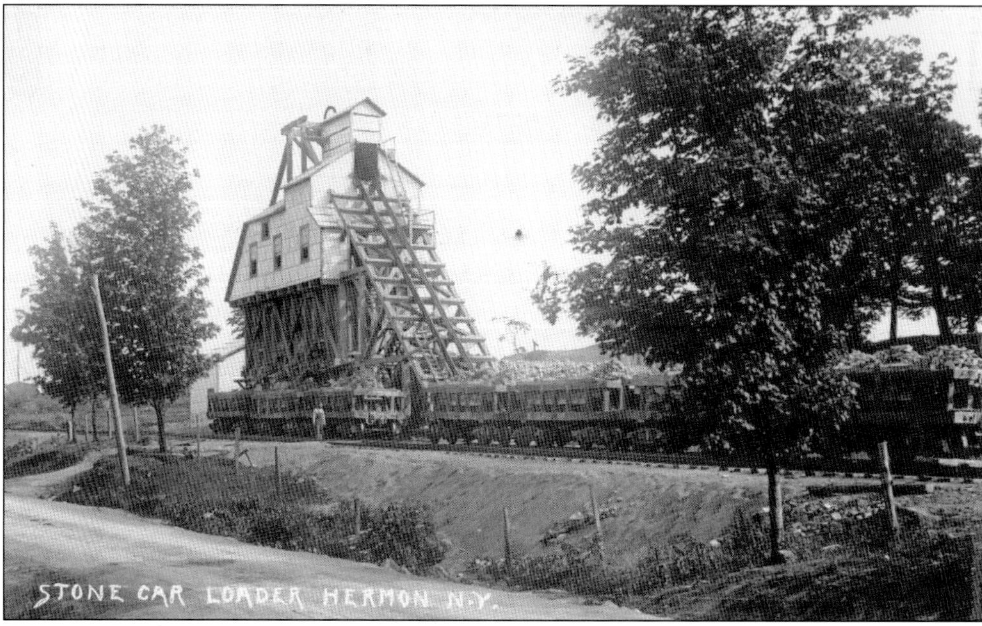

The Stone Car Loader. Shown near Hermon is the stone car loader for St. Lawrence Pyrites Company, Stellaville. (SLCHA.)

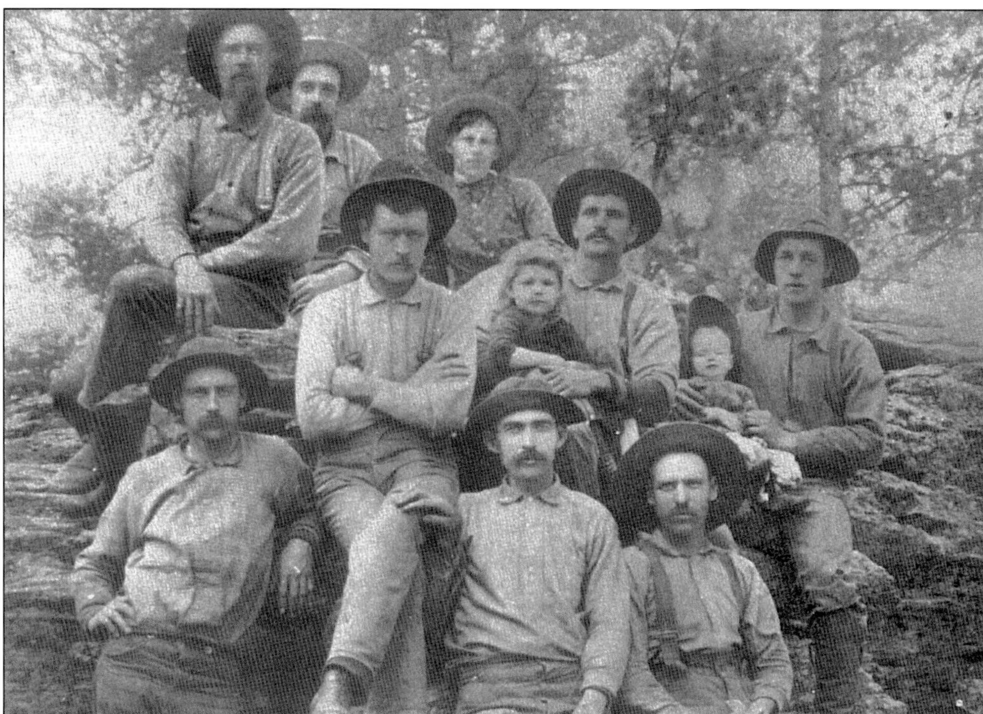

Some Stone Quarry Cutters with Family Members, 1903. These men cut the bridge abutment stones at Brasher Center. (Courtesy Brasher historian.)

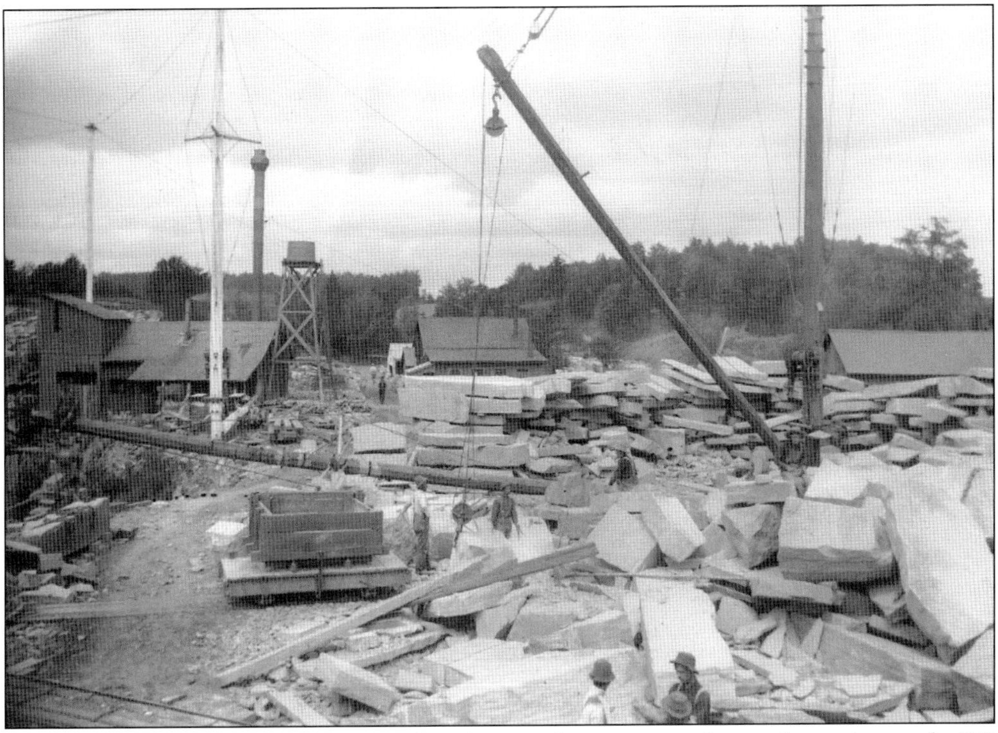

The Potsdam Sandstone Company. Potsdam sandstone comes from a formation made 500 million years ago that stretches across northern New York from the Thousand Islands to Lake Champlain. It is an excellent building material due to the unusual quantity of quartz in its makeup. (SLCHA.)

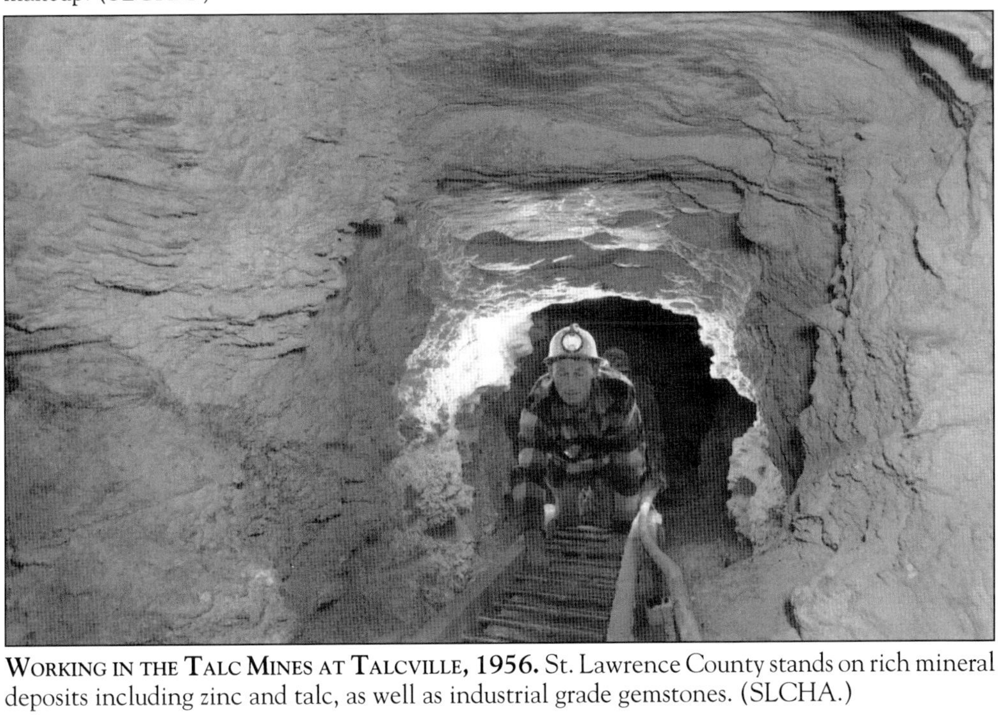

Working in the Talc Mines at Talcville, 1956. St. Lawrence County stands on rich mineral deposits including zinc and talc, as well as industrial grade gemstones. (SLCHA.)

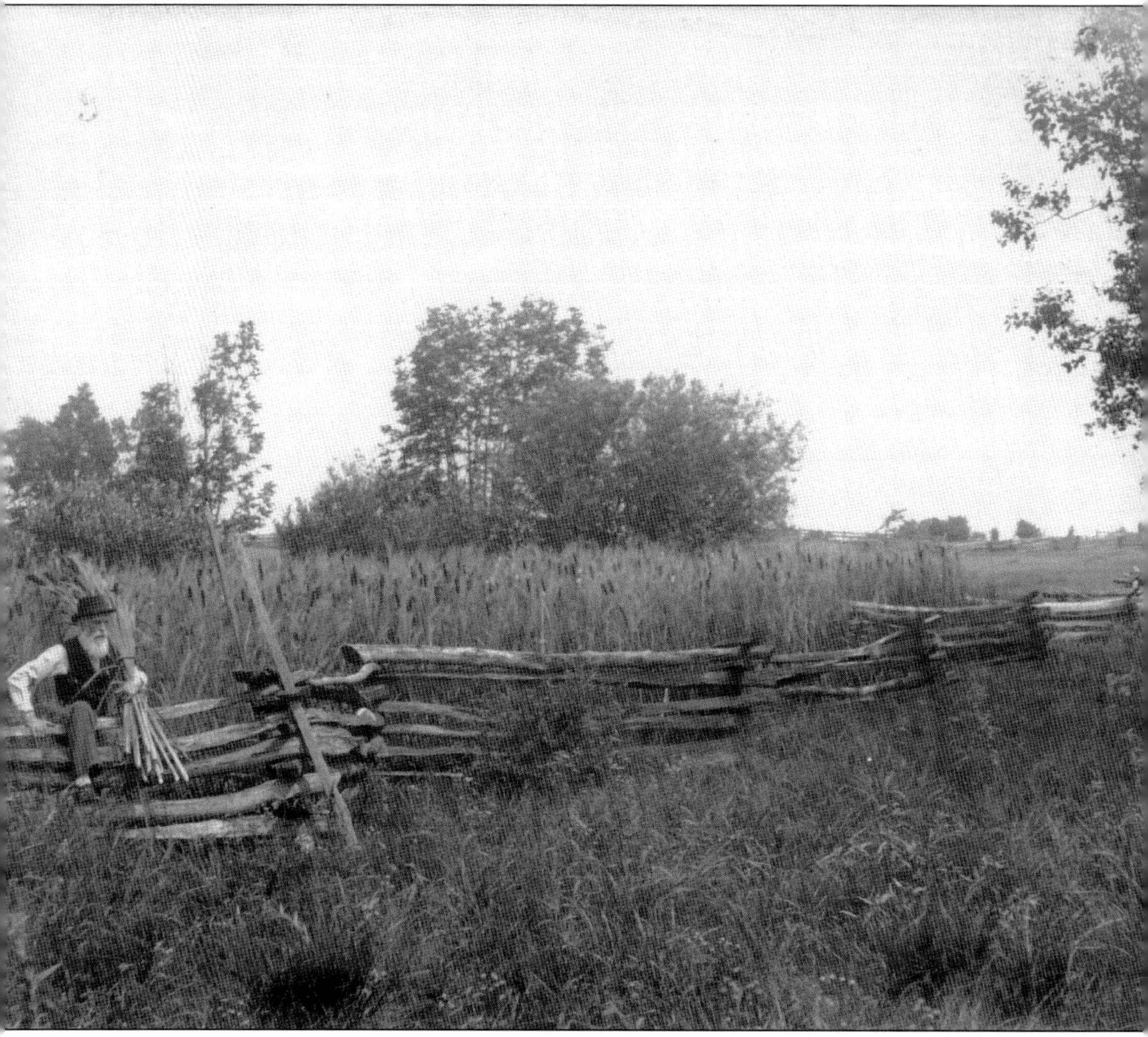

H.D. KIP, CLIMBING OVER A SPLIT RAIL FENCE. The father of Canton photographer Benjamin Kip, H.D. Kip was also a respected artist. He operated a family furniture business in Canton until it burned in the 1870 fire. He then returned to his "hobby" of painting, and he designed and painted frescoes for local churches and public buildings. (SLCHA.)

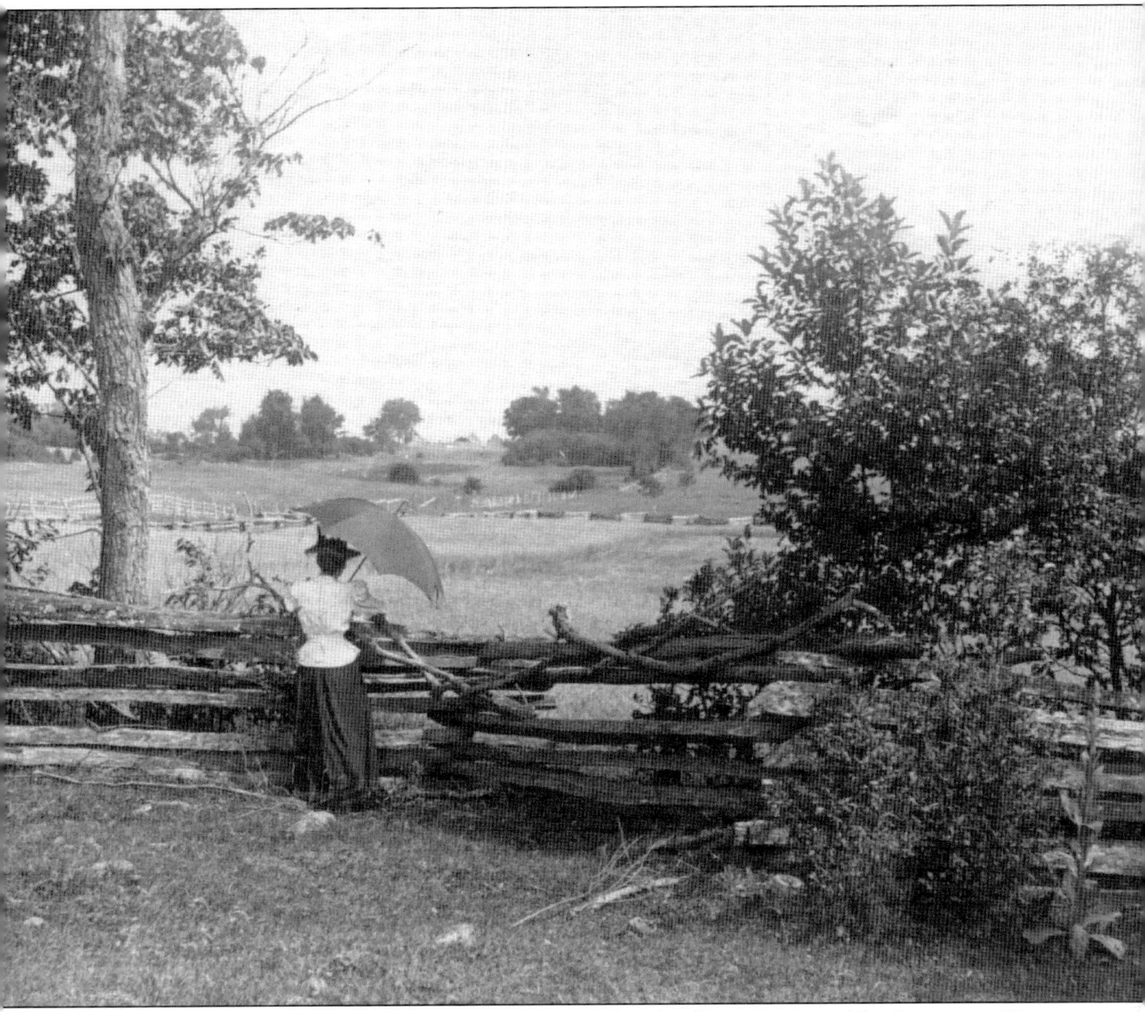

A Moment of Reverie. This is a scene from the Kip family album. Presumably, Benjamin Kip was the photographer. (SLCHA.)

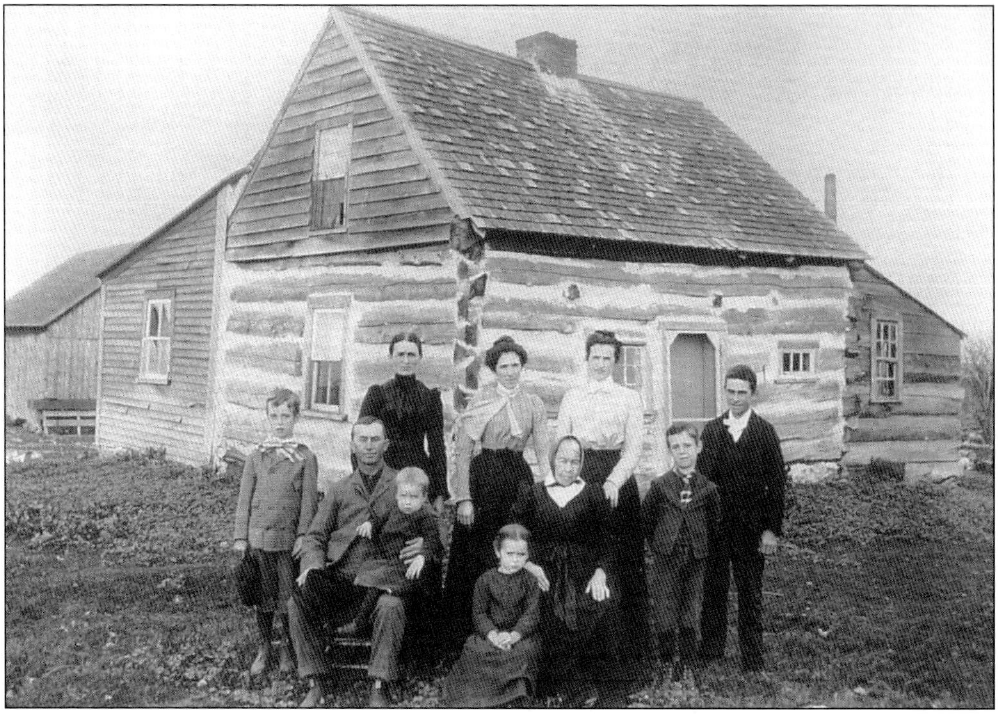

The Foley Family. Members of the Foley family pose for this photograph, taken outside their log home, located on Keenan Road in the Helena area. (Courtesy Brasher historian.)

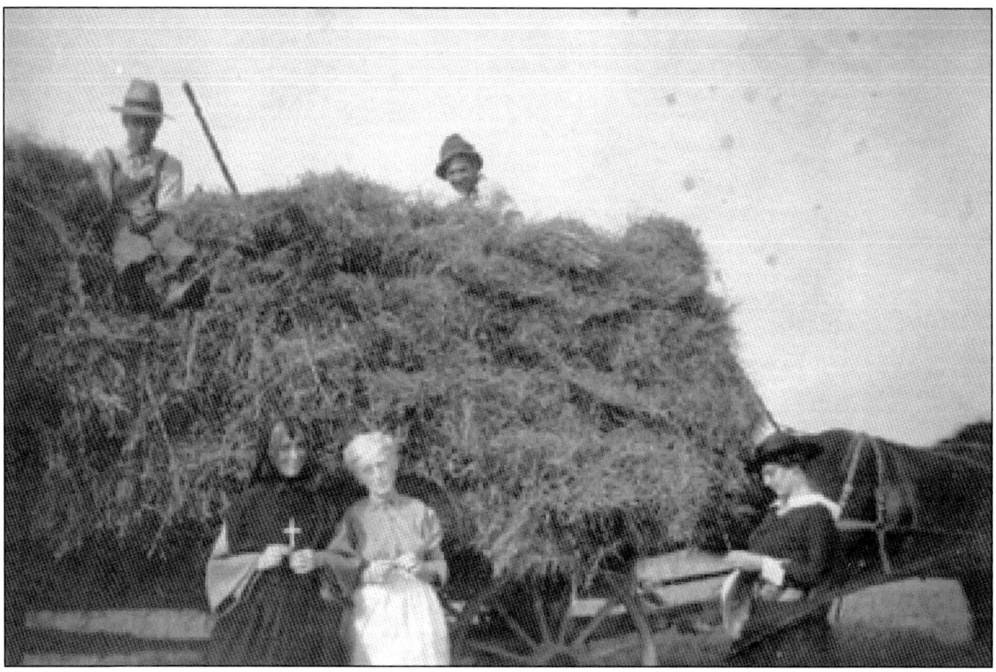

A Good Hay Crop. Every member of the family contributes to and celebrates the harvest. (SLCHA.)

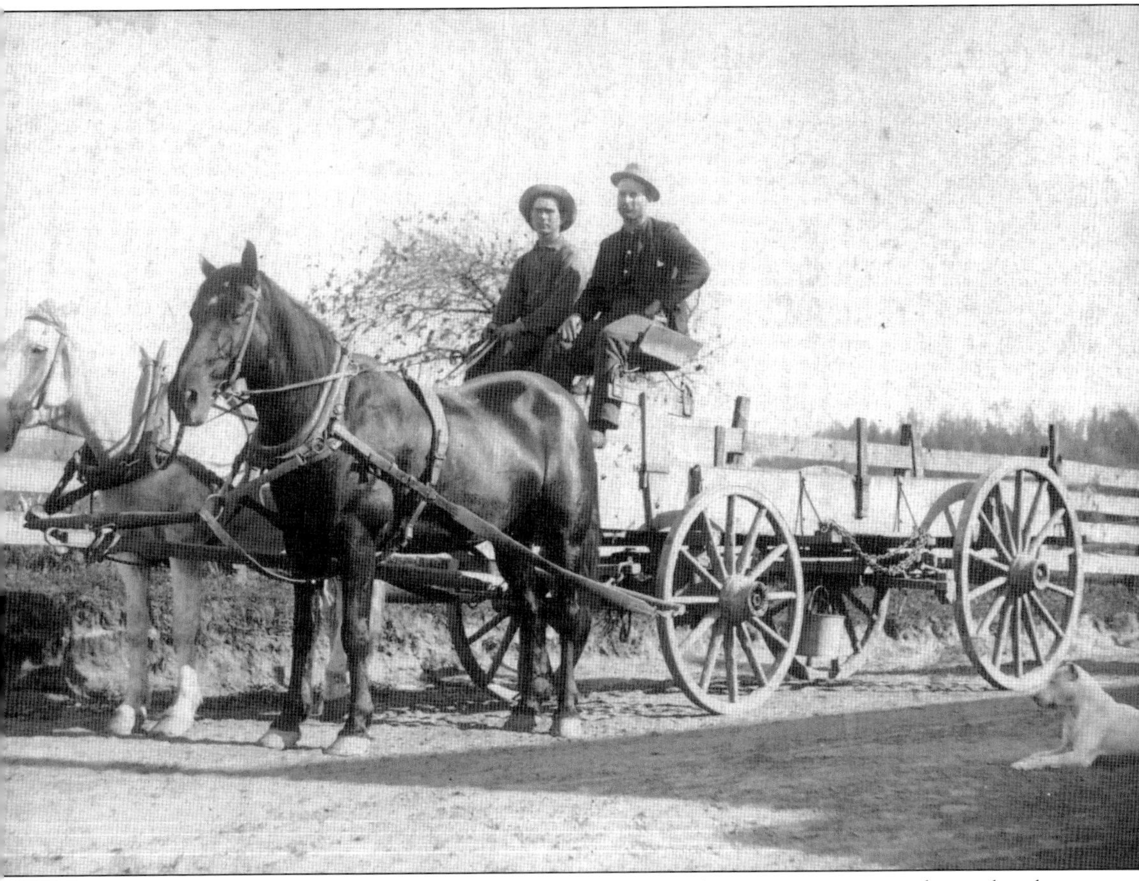

A WORKING TEAM. A team of horses pulling a wagon is no longer a common sight on local roads. However, such teams are still at work in hayfields and woodlots both in the Amish and non-Amish communities throughout the county. There will always be some circumstances that a horse can handle better than a machine.. (Courtesy Clare historian.)

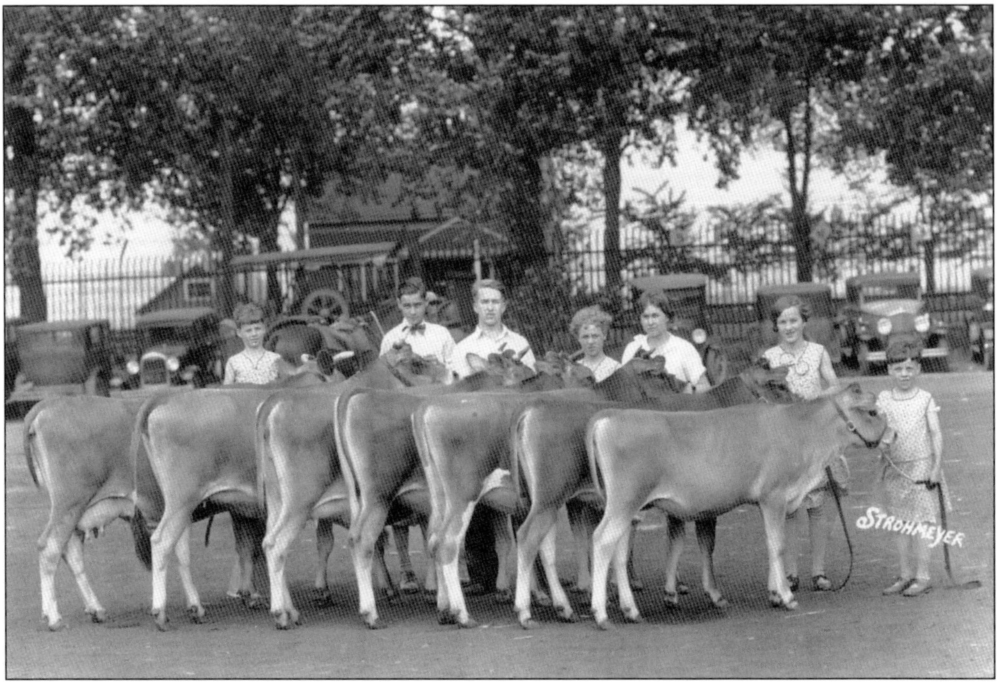

The County Fair. These St. Lawrence County Jerseys were entered in the 1932 New York State Fair. (SLCHA.)

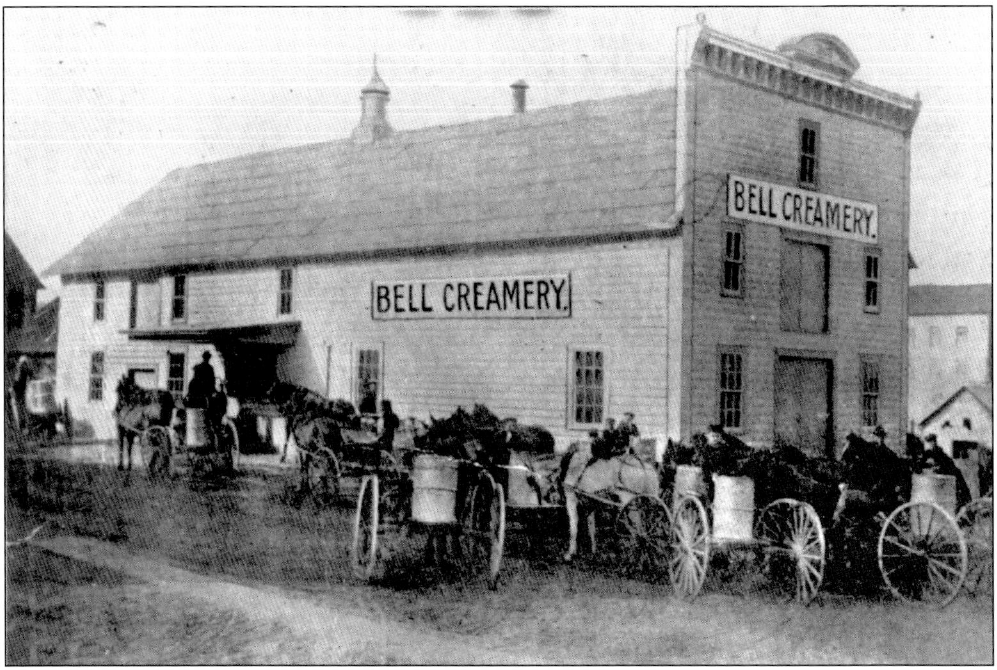

Bell Creamery. This creamery was established in 1896 by Warren E. and William J. Bell, sons of Oliver Bell. By 1902, the brothers had three branch receiving stations for patrons, sometimes taking in 30,000 pounds of milk a day. The creamery was located in Brasher Falls. (Courtesy Brasher historian.)

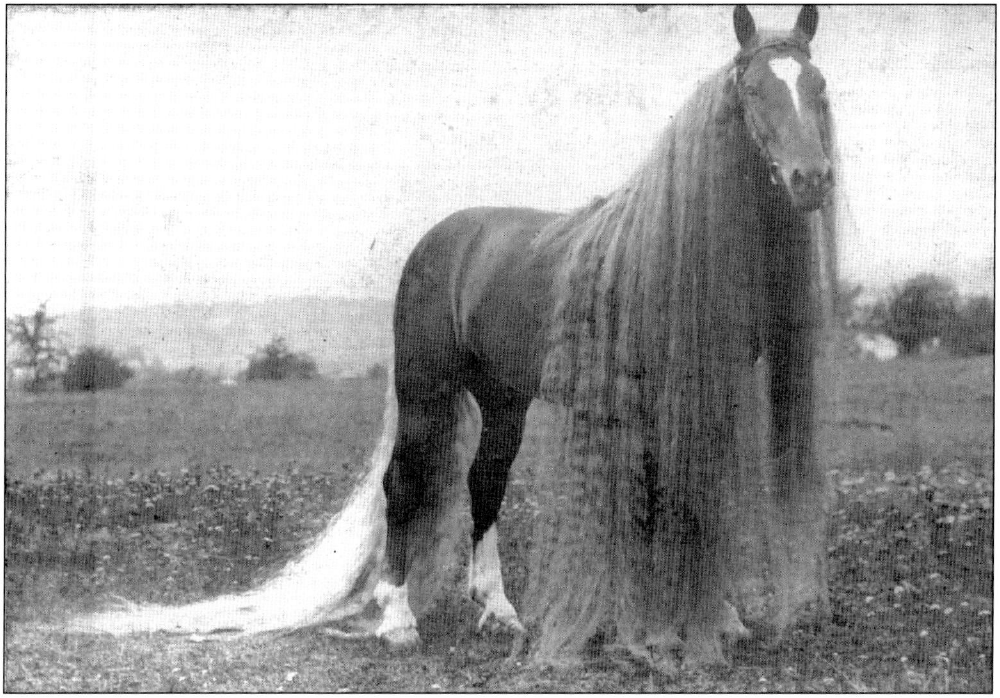

AURELIUS, THE WONDER HORSE. L.A. Cole and J.K. Rutherford, both of Waddington-on-the-St. Lawrence, owned a two-thirds interest in this horse, which toured through the county in 1895. He was foaled in Oregon in June 1890. His mane was seven feet long and his tail, eight feet long, spread out three feet on the ground when he was standing still. (Courtesy Waddington historian.)

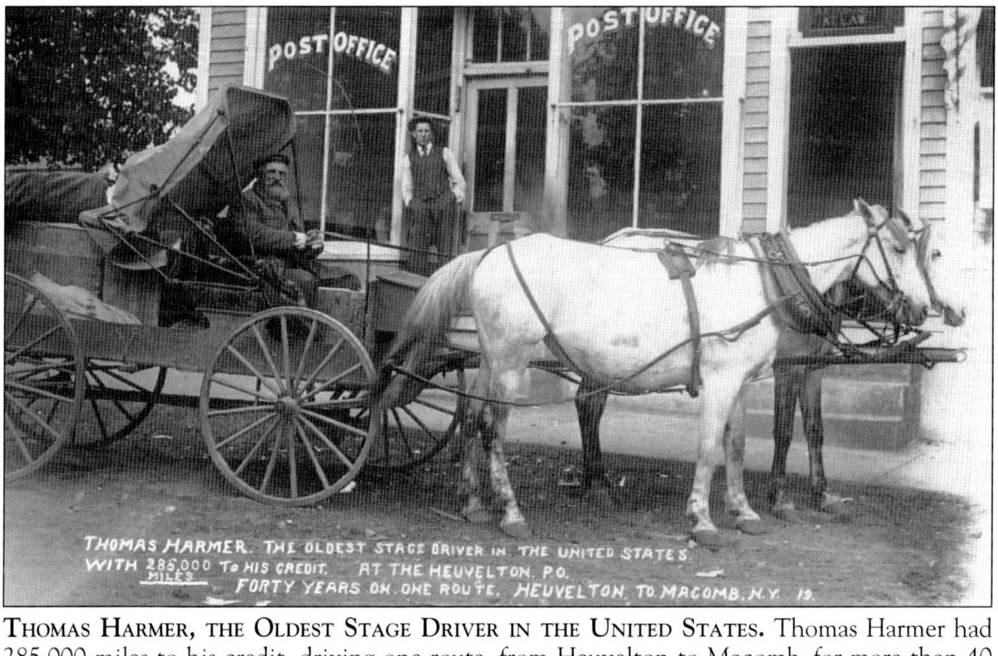

THOMAS HARMER, THE OLDEST STAGE DRIVER IN THE UNITED STATES. Thomas Harmer had 285,000 miles to his credit, driving one route, from Heuvelton to Macomb, for more than 40 years. He is pictured here at the Heuvelton Post Office. (SLCHA.)

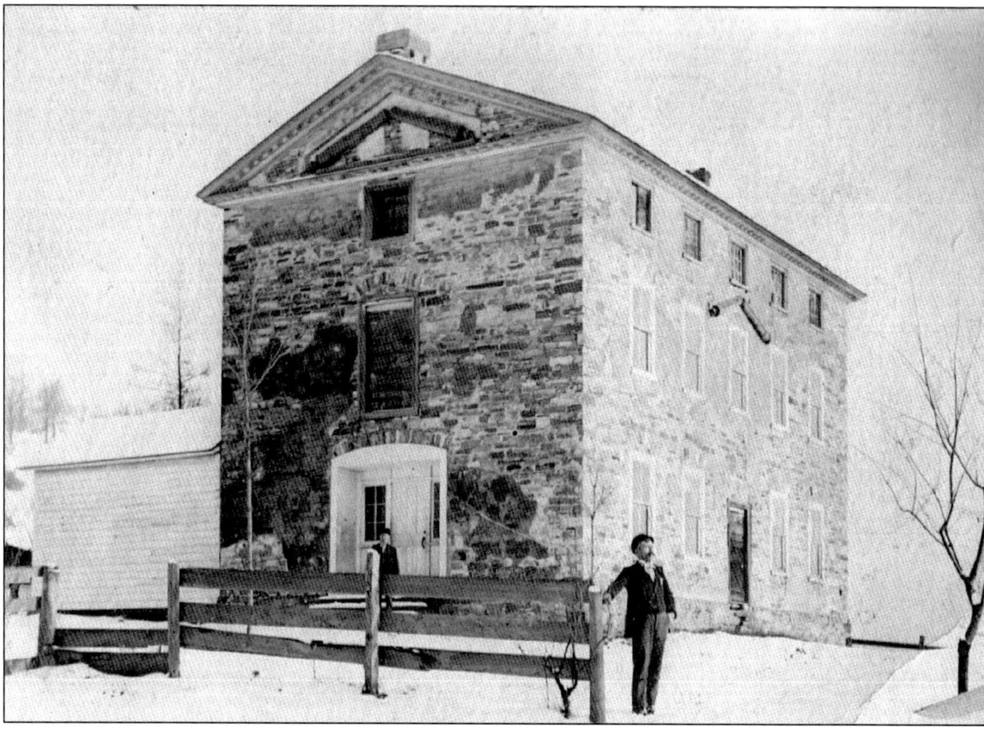

The Old Arsenal, Russell. The arsenal was built during the War of 1812 as a storehouse for artillery and small arms and ammunition. It was later used as the Russell village schoolhouse. (SLCHA.)

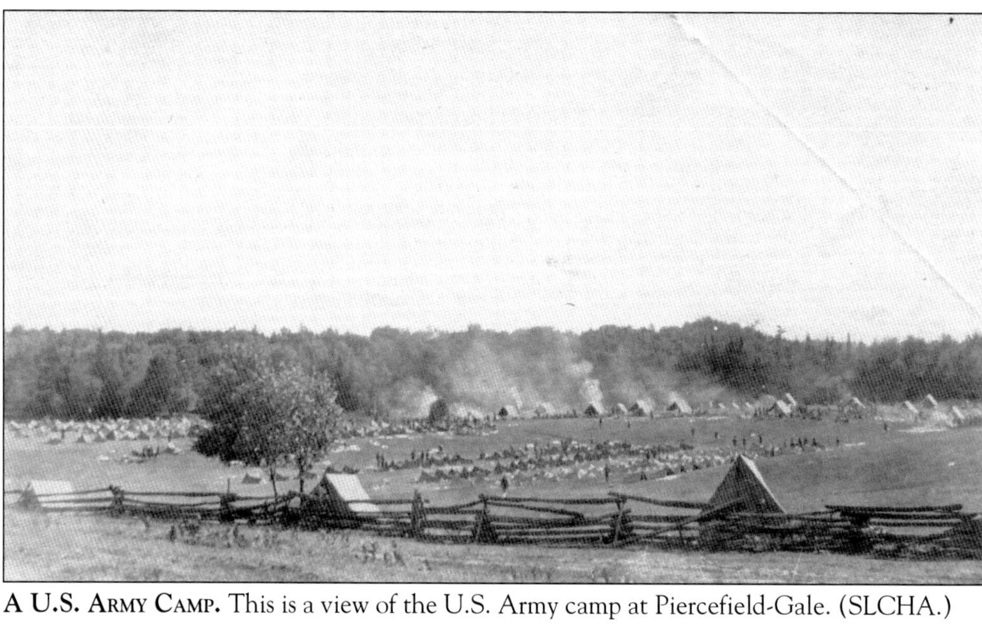

A U.S. Army Camp. This is a view of the U.S. Army camp at Piercefield-Gale. (SLCHA.)

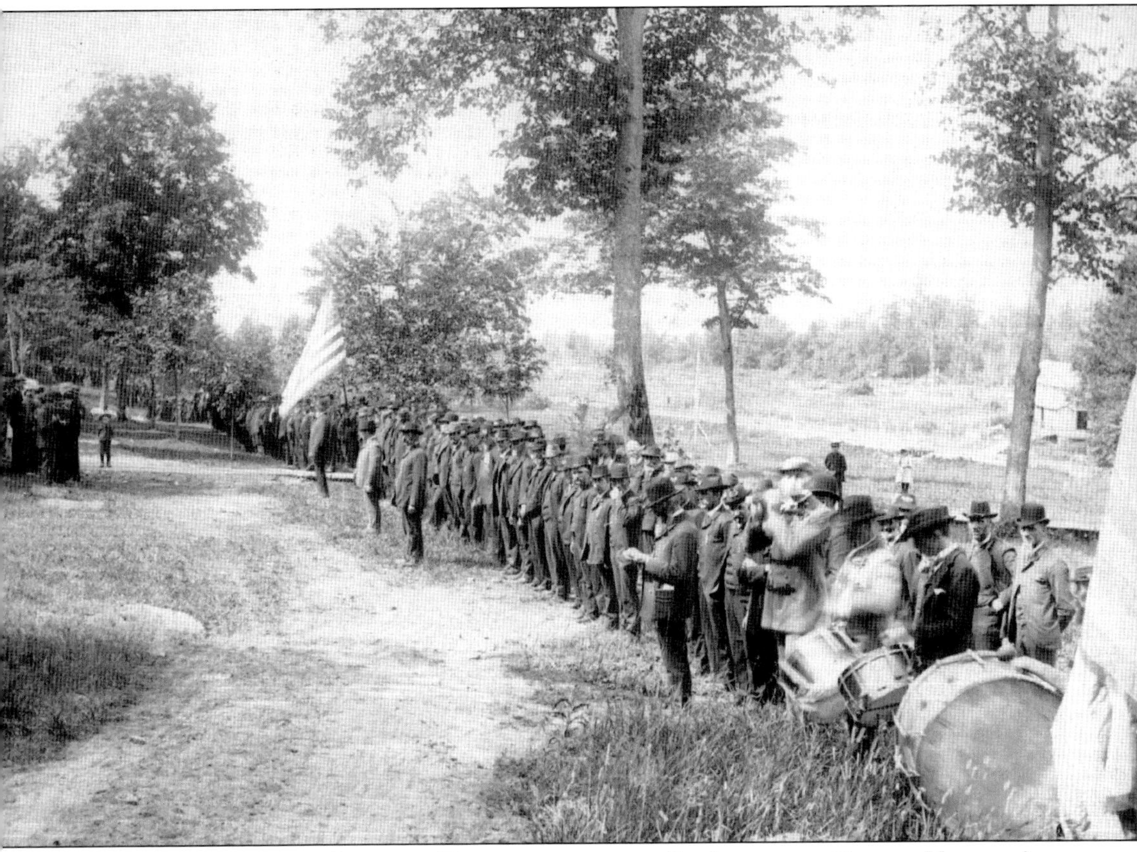

The Grand Army of the Republic Encampment of the St. Lawrence County Veteran's Association, at Terrace Park, Morristown. The 24-acre park property was purchased to provide camp meeting grounds for the Methodist Episcopal Church in the Ogdensburg and Potsdam districts. The land was "hilly and wooded and was laid out in lots and platforms for tents were erected and camp meetings of giant proportions were held. August was the special month for large gatherings with the GAR reunions held for two weeks then." (SLCHA.)

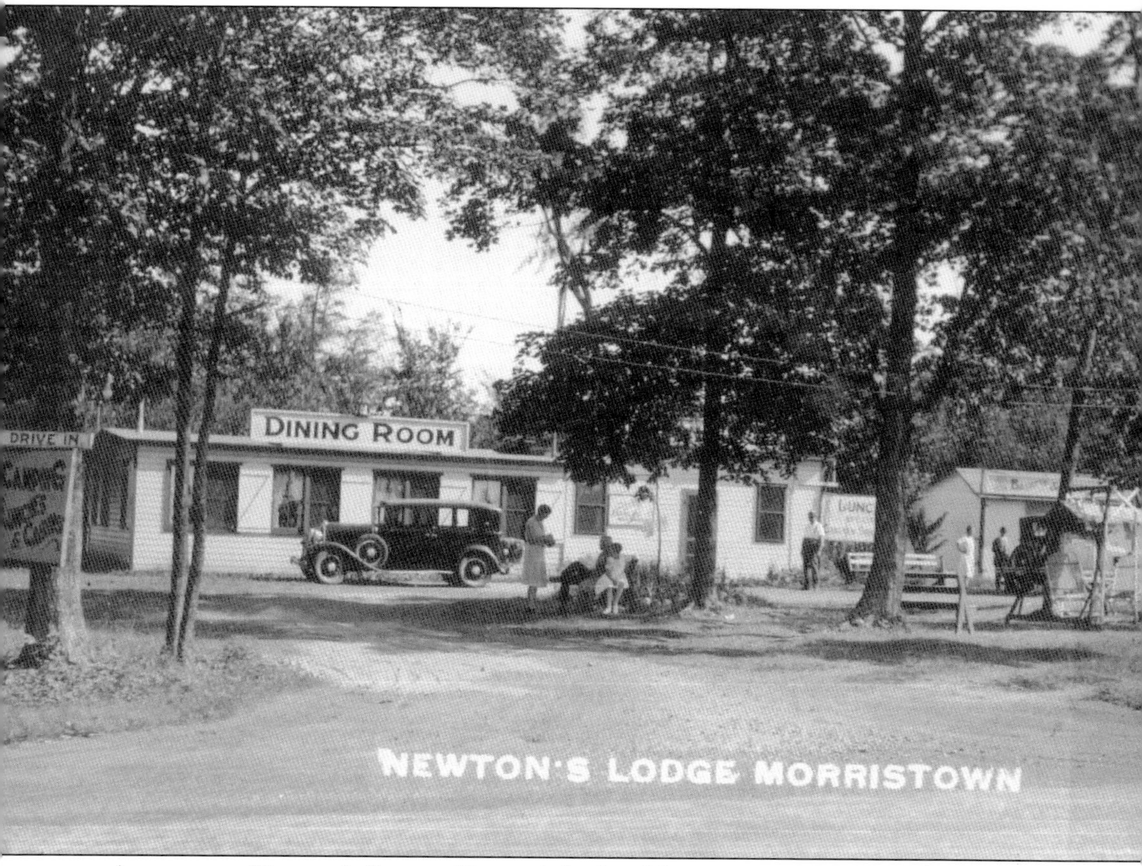

Americana: Newton's Lodge. Newton's Lodge, Morristown, conjures up the pre-interstate days when motels and roadside diners began to replace the larger hotels and restaurants in town and city centers. The automobile changed forever the way Americans vacationed, sealing the doom of many destination resorts in the Thousand Islands and in the Adirondacks. (SLCHA.)

Three

Living in the Mountains

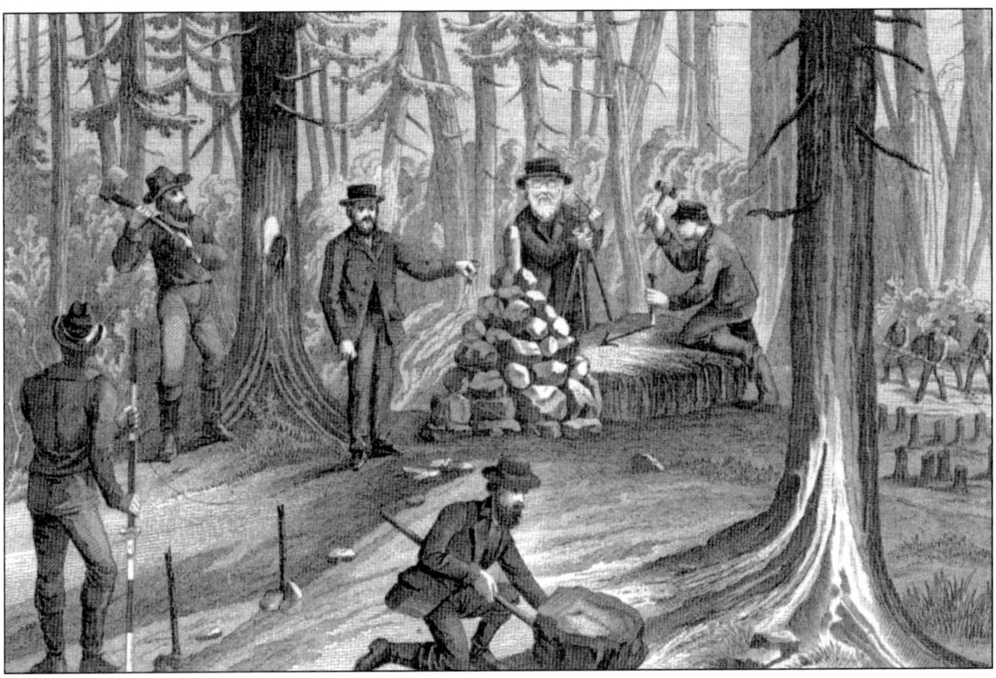

The Great Corner. This is the point from which the lines of the patents of the Totten & Crossfield and Macomb land purchases part, dividing millions of acres of land. This drawing by Verplanck Colvin was part of the State of New York Adirondack Survey. Verplanck Colvin was the superintendent.

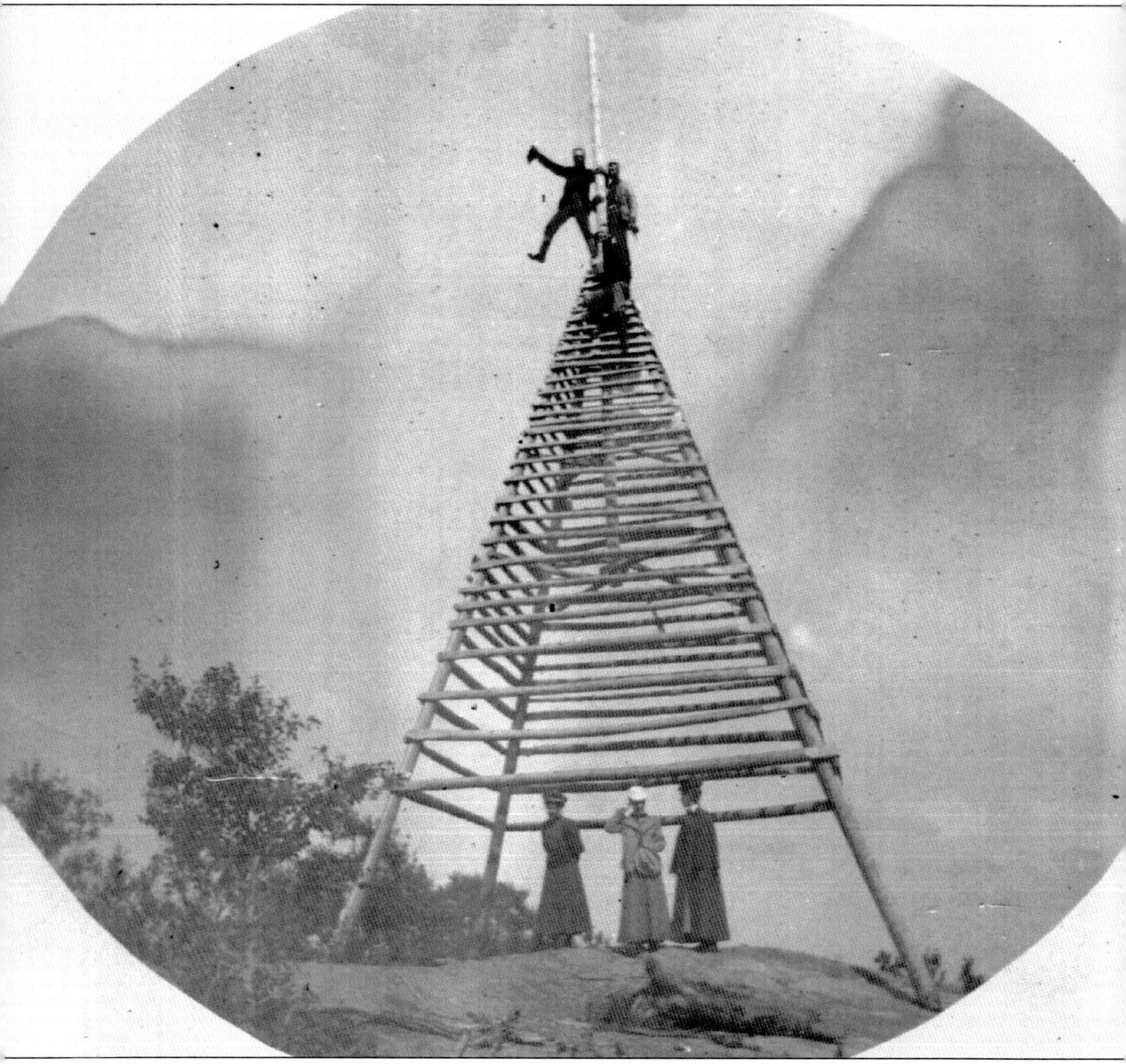

Williston Manley on Top of Graves Mountain. This is the highest point in St. Lawrence County. Adirondack surveyor Verplanck Colvin constructed towers such as these for taking his measurements, often clear-cutting the mountaintop to gain clear sightings. (SLCHA.)

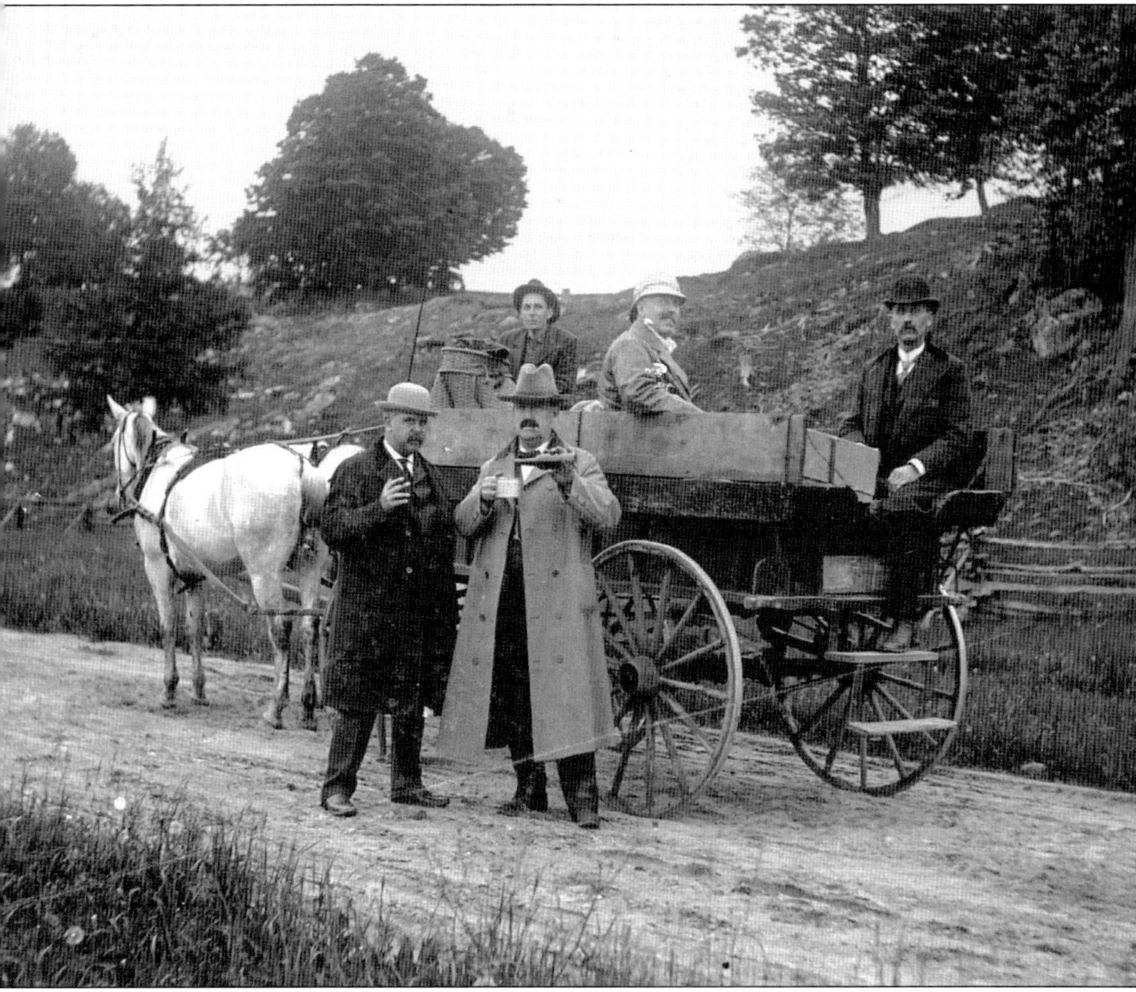

Sporting Party en Route to Cranberry Lake. On June 9, 1900, these sporting men went on their 17th annual outing. (SLCHA.)

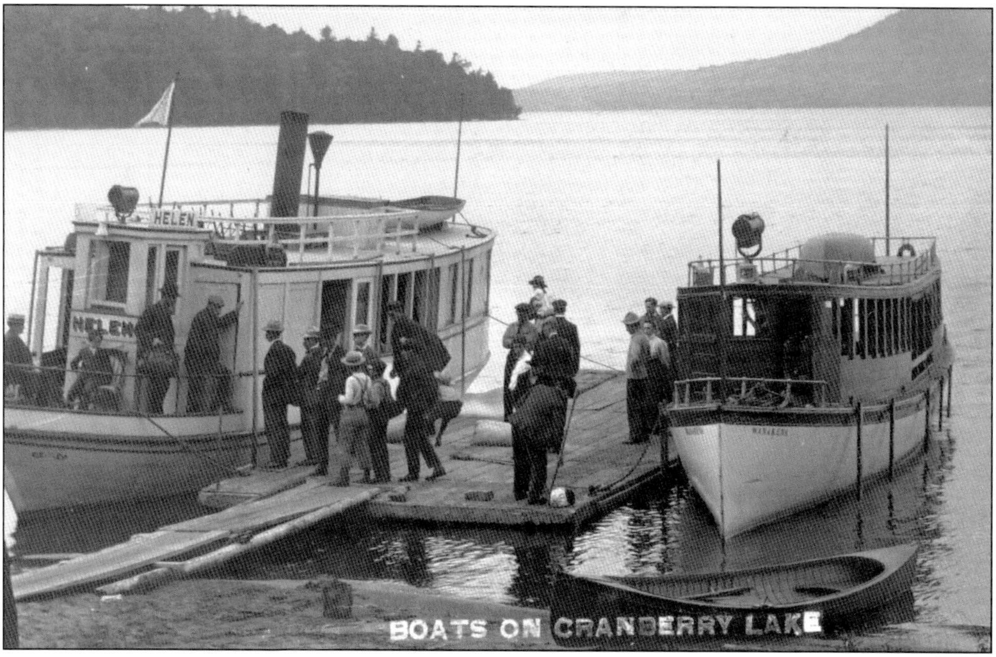

EARLY STEAMBOATS *HELEN* AND *WANAKENA*, DOCKED AT NUNN'S INN, AT THE HEAD OF CRANBERRY LAKE. Both boats plied the lake in the early 1900s, carrying passengers and mail to and from Wanakena and Cranberry Lake villages and summer cottages. (Courtesy Clifton historian.)

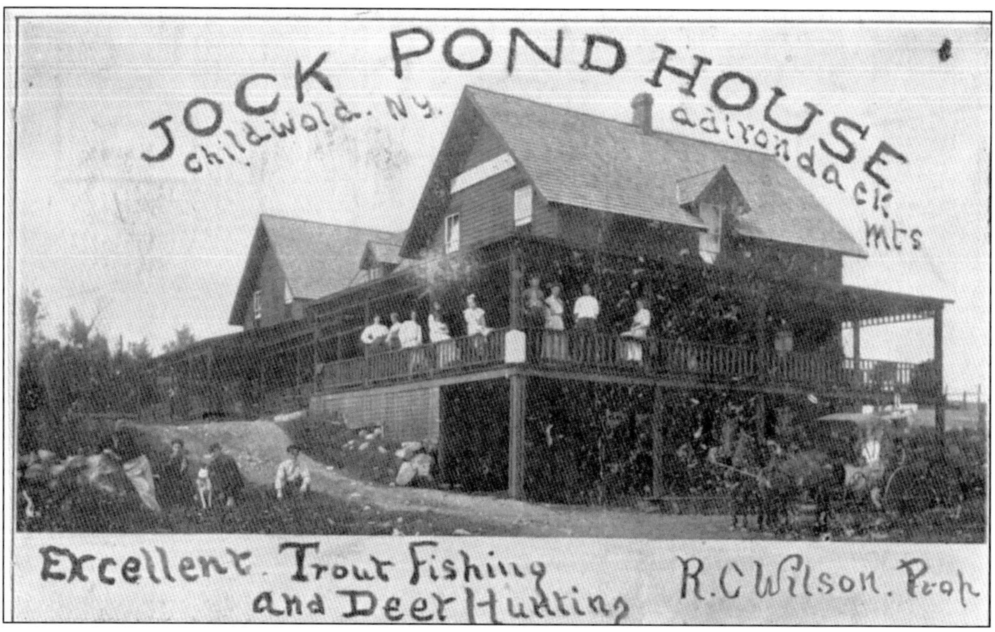

JOCK POND HOUSE, CHILDWOLD. This was one of many hotels that sprang up in the late 1800s and early 1900s to serve the sporting public. The huge influx of such sports led to the decimation of many animals in the Adirondacks, including the moose, wolf, panther, lynx, and beaver. (SLCHA.)

Paddling on Star Lake, 1905. Emma is out for a paddle on Star Lake in 1905. (SLCHA.)

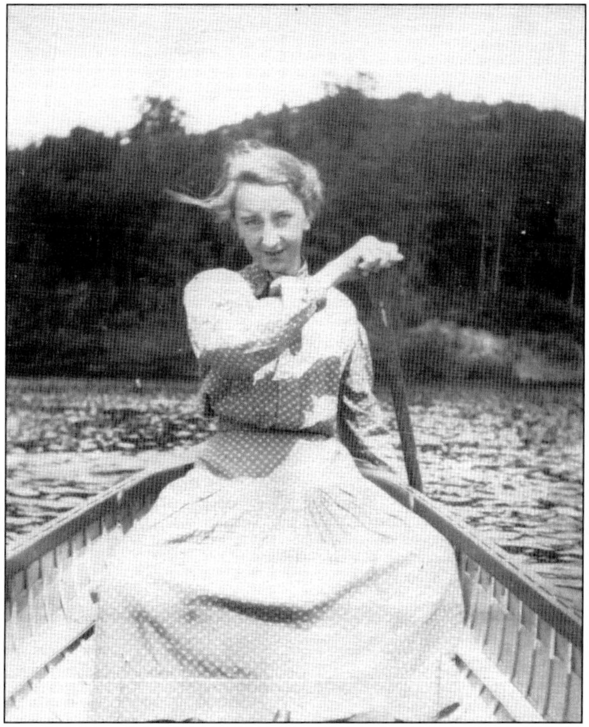

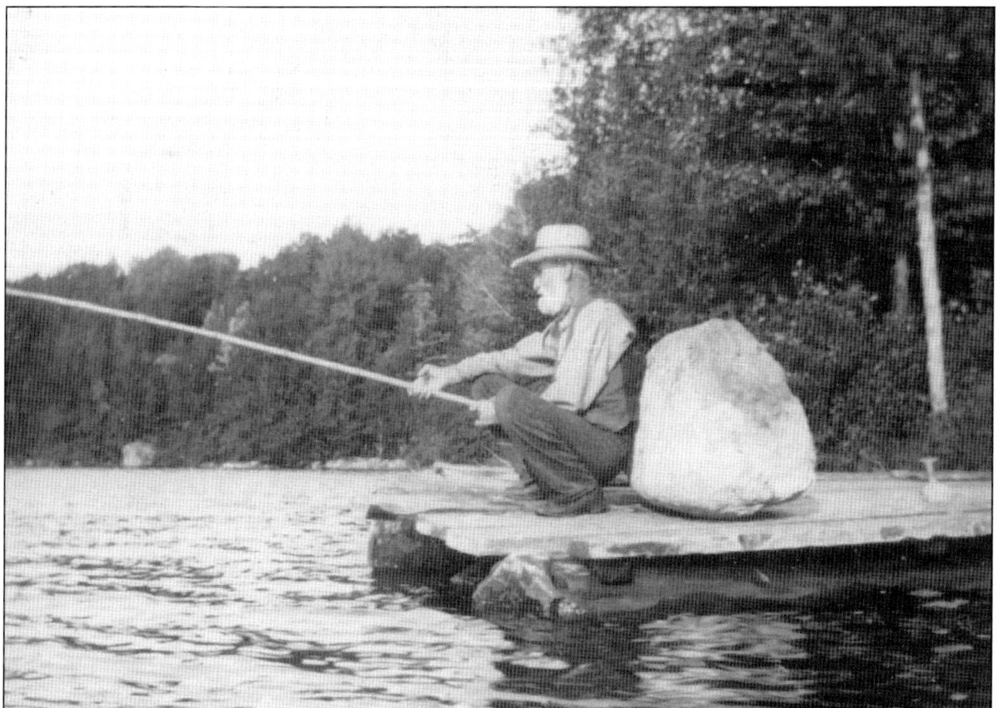

Fishing on Lake Ozonia. Is he a guide catching dinner for his swells, a lonely hermit, or simply a rustic-looking tourist? (SLCHA.)

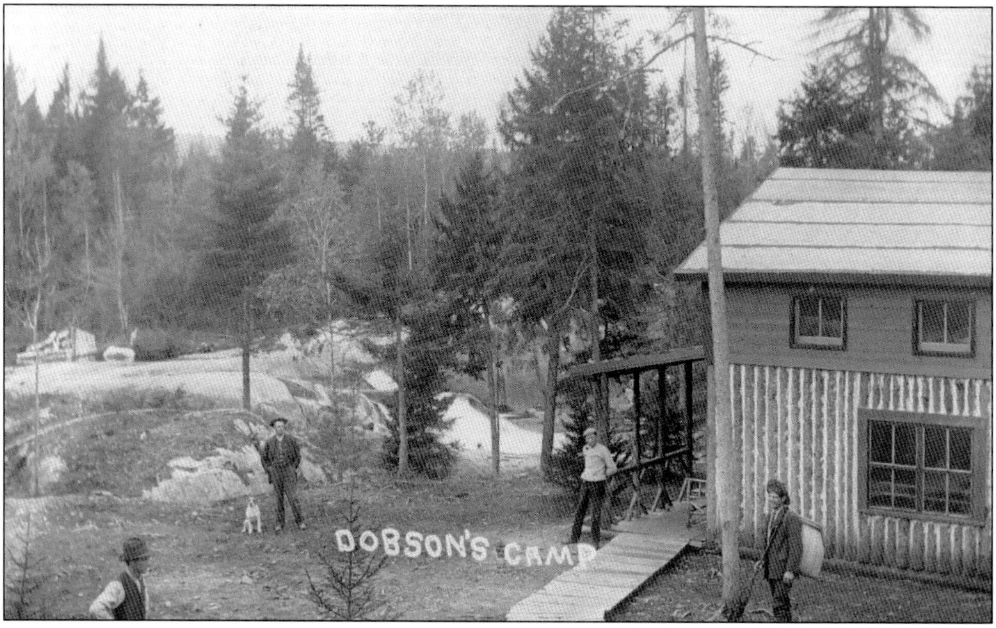

A SPORTSMAN'S CAMP AT HIGH FALLS ON THE OSWEGATCHIE. Dobson's Camp was popular among many well-known adventurers. Dobson's magnificent pines were cut down by a disgruntled logger, leading ultimately to the closing of the camp. (SLCHA.)

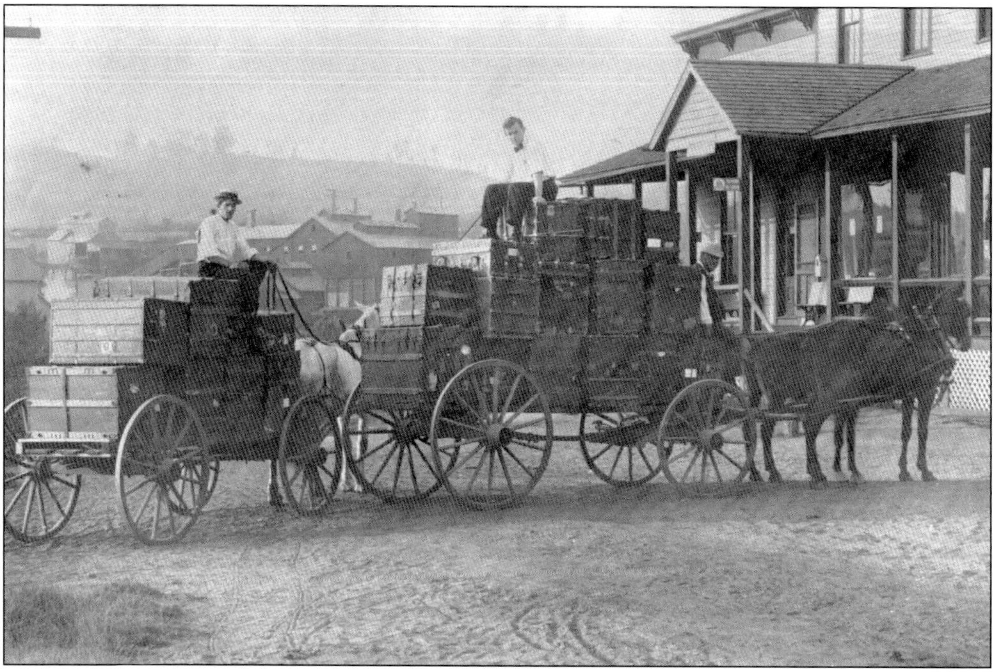

THE SUMMER PEOPLE ARRIVE. Often staying for the season, summer visitors to the county *c.* 1900 arrived, not with backpacks, but with steamer trunks. (SLCHA.)

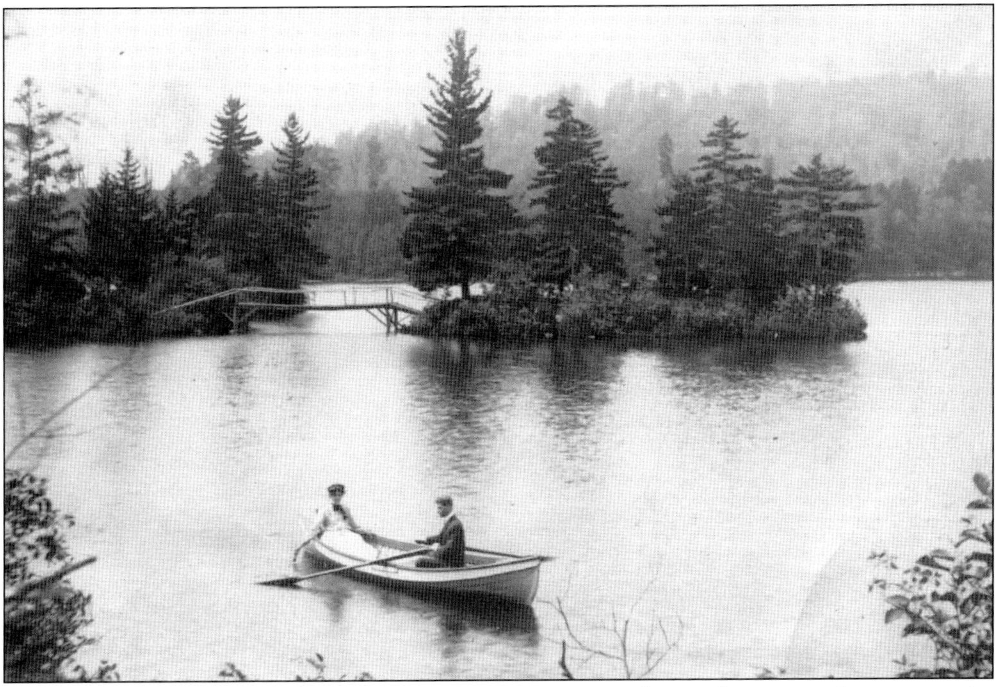

Star Lake. There is no better way to woo your sweetheart than in a boat on quiet water. (SLCHA.)

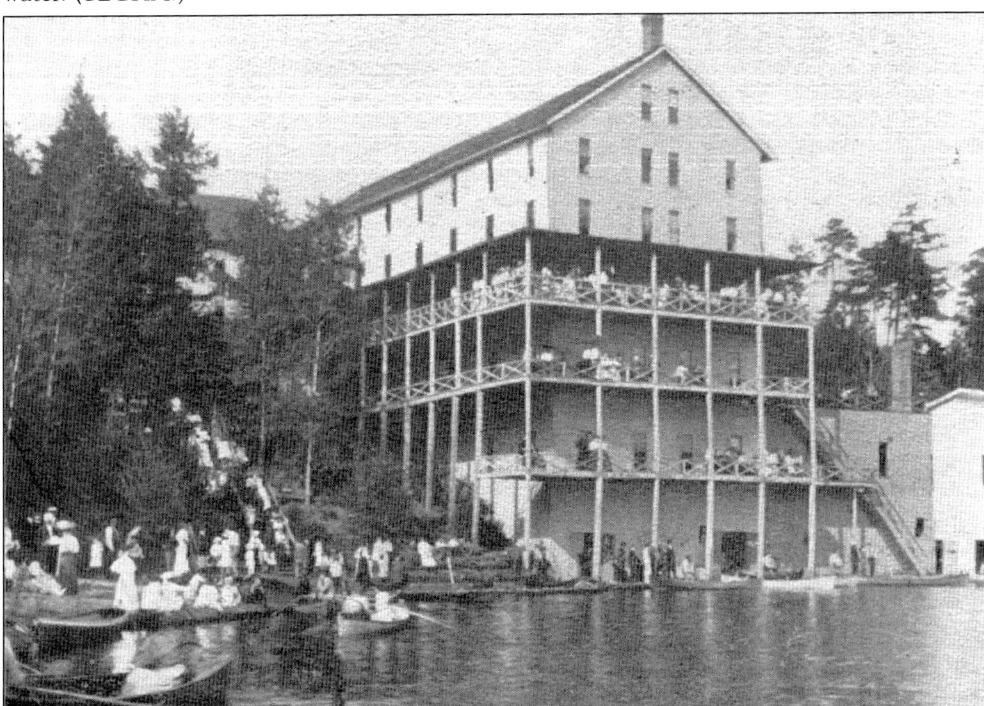

The Star Lake Inn on Field Day. The inn was famous for its magnificent wraparound porches. Morning competition for veranda chairs was fierce, with some guests attempting to reserve chairs with name tags. (SLCHA.)

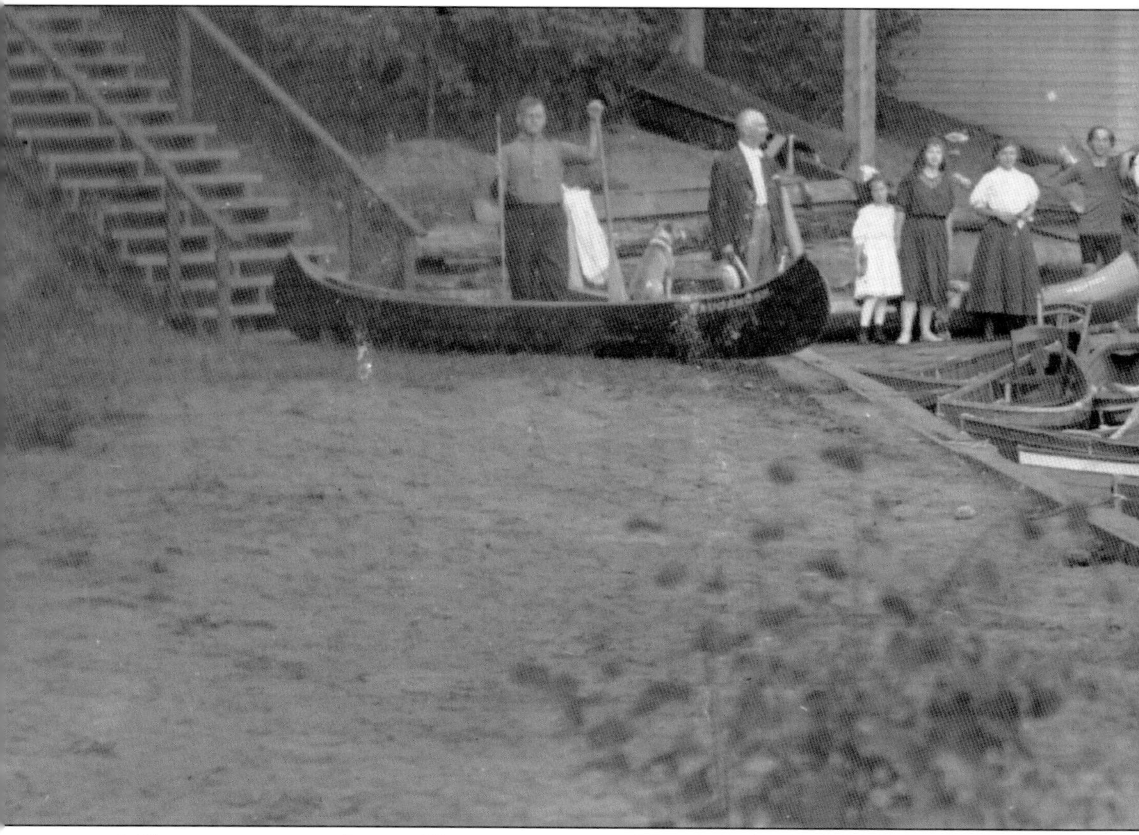

A GATHERING AT THE LOWER VERANDA, C. 1900. This group has gathered at the lower veranda

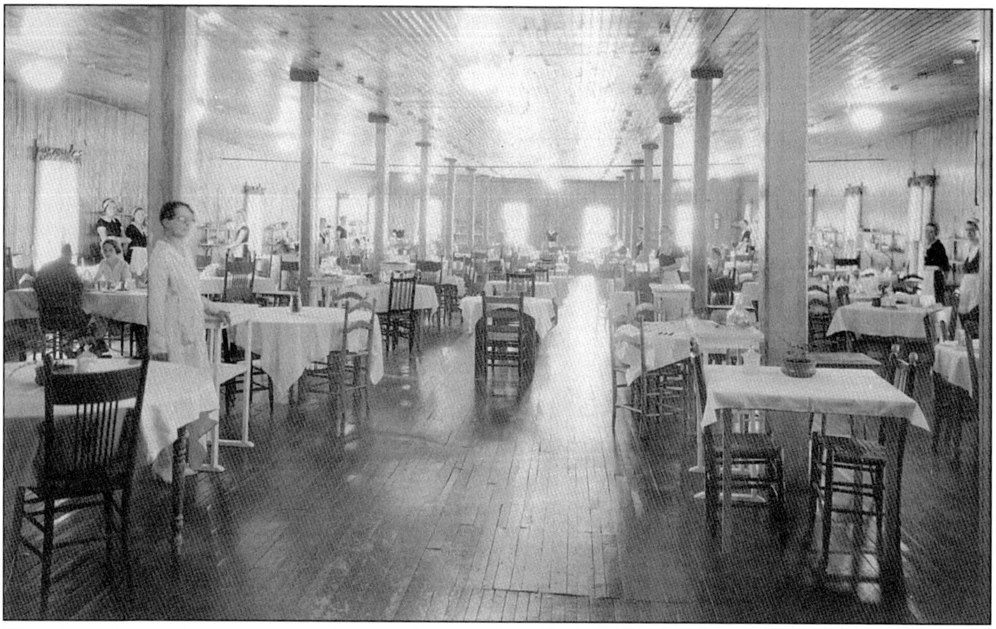

THE STAR LAKE INN DINING HALL. Note the hardwood floors and the waitresses waiting to serve. (SLCHA.)

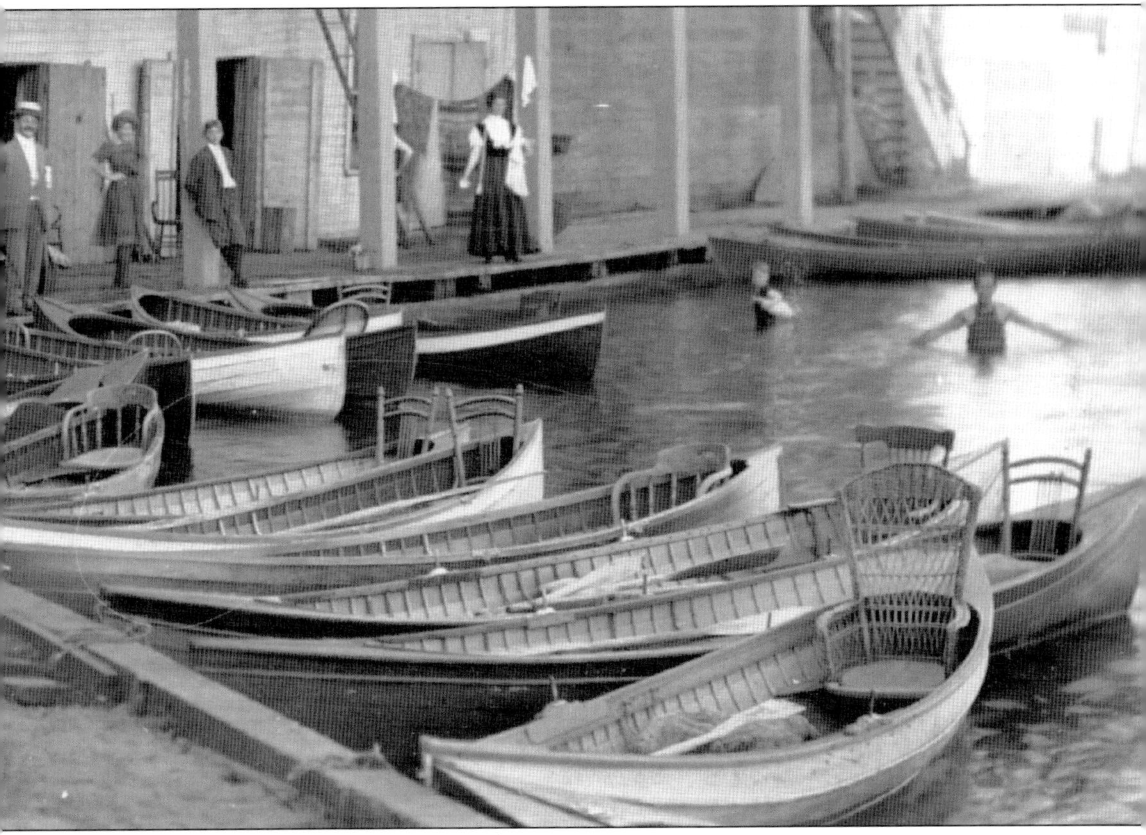

of the Star Lake Inn for boating. (SLCHA.)

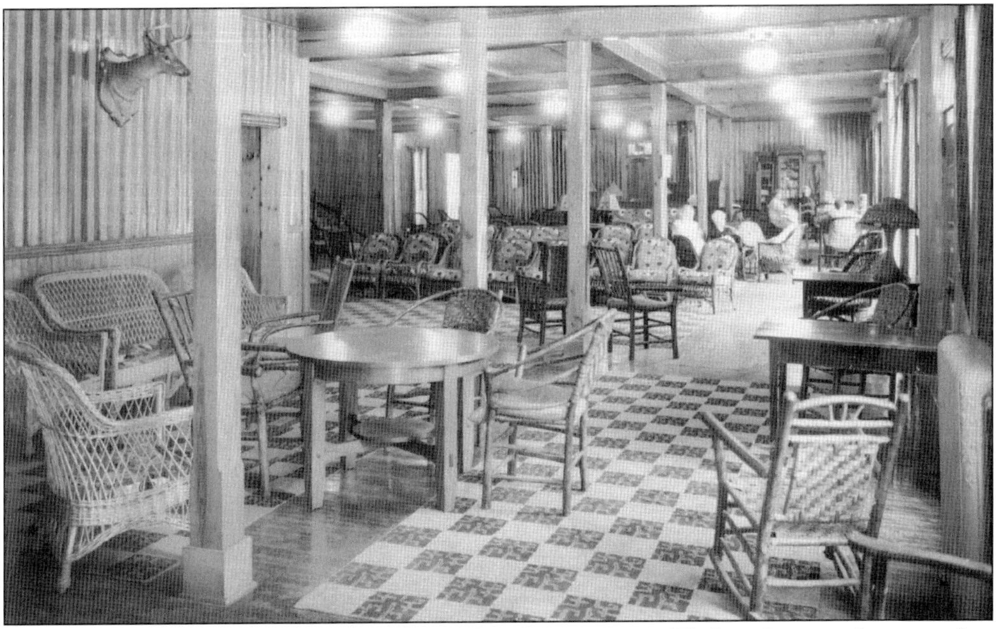

PUBLIC ROOMS AT THE STAR LAKE INN. These rooms were filled with magnificent wicker furnishings. (SLCHA.)

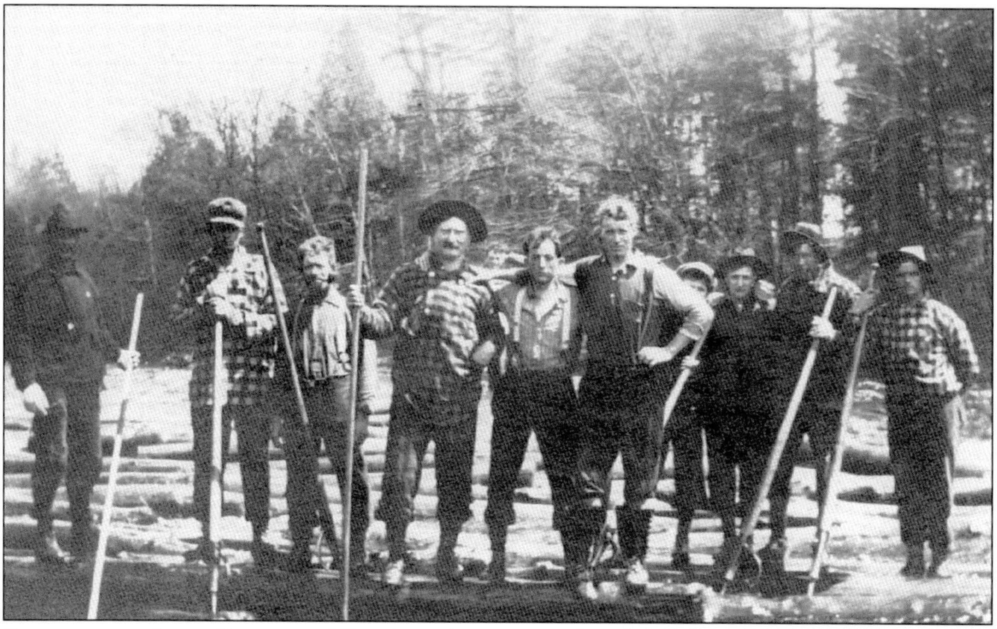

PARISHVILLE LOG DRIVERS. The log drivers in this May 12, 1917 photograph are, from left to right, Homer Walker, Henry Santimaw, Arthur Remington, Bill Delosh, Mart Cassidy, unidentified, Oral "Pete" Smith, George Dailey, and Nick Planty. (Courtesy Parishville historian.)

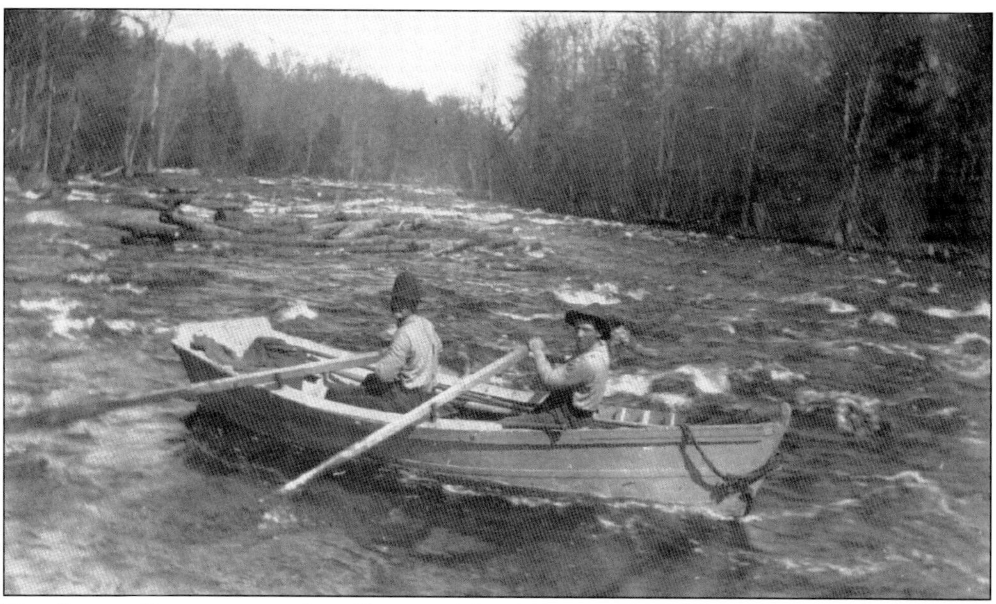

THE RESCUE BOAT FOR THE LOG DRIVERS. The drivers are seen here with Arthur Remington and Bill Delosh on the St. Regis River on April 18, 1917. (Courtesy Parishville historian.)

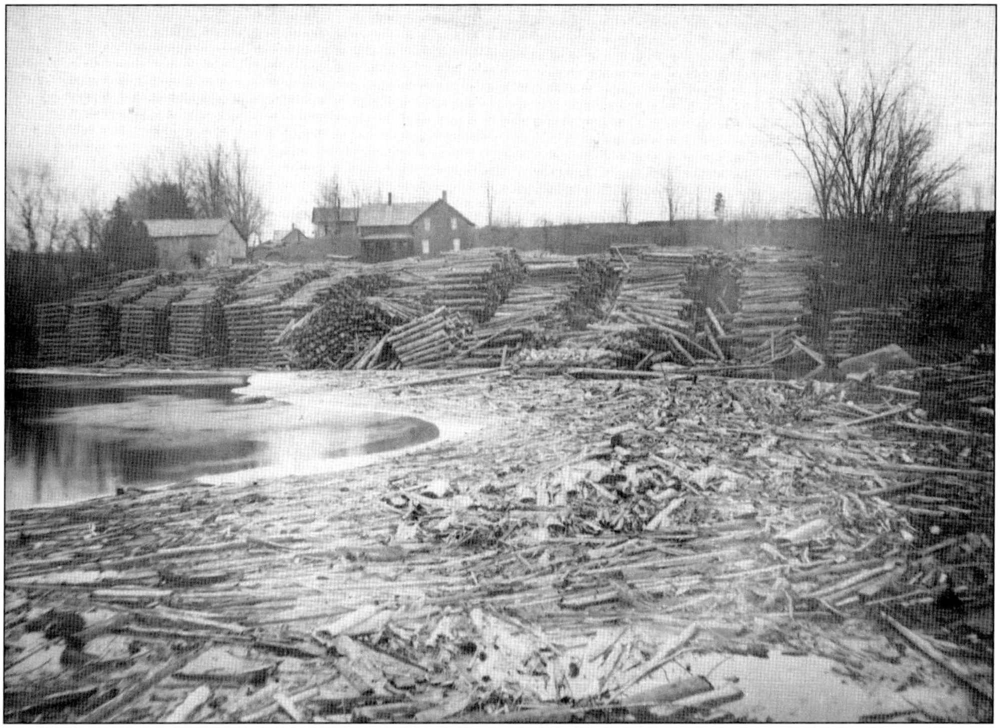

Day's Mill, Hopkinton, 1902. Shown is part of a half-million board feet at Day's Mill in Hopkinton. This illustrates the organized chaos of a timber operation. (SLCHA.)

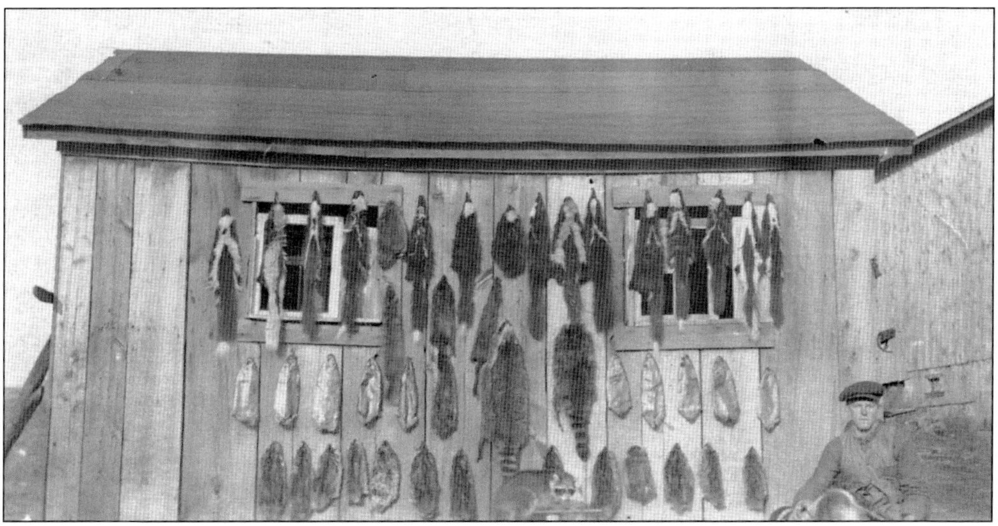

Displaying His Wares. Earning a living in the mountains has always required ingenuity and adaptability. A trapper might also guide hunters and fishermen, or log, or operate a lodge, or teach school . . . (SLCHA.)

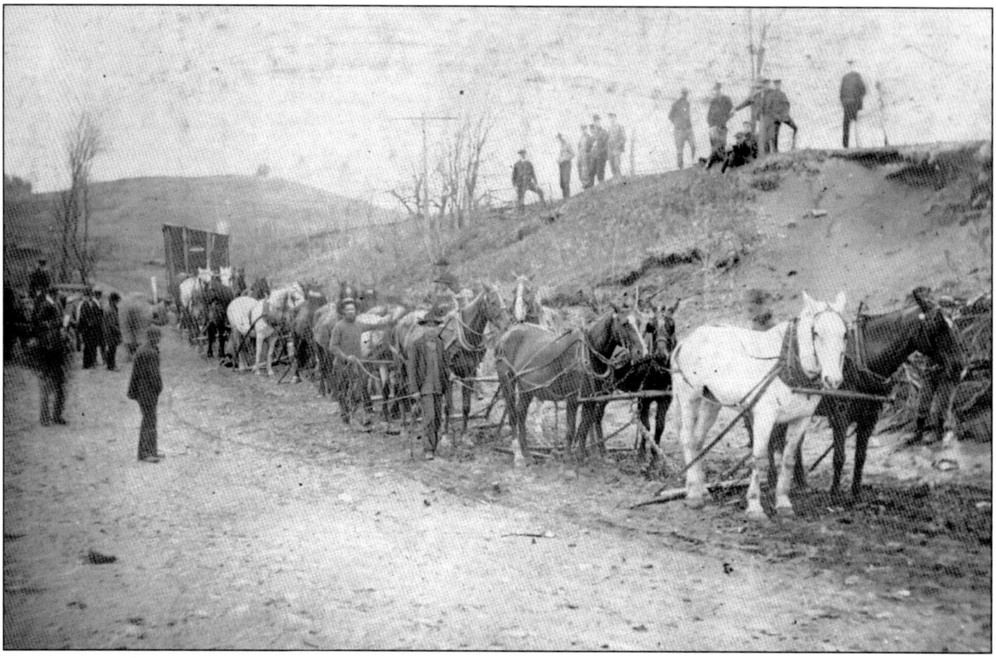

NICHOLVILLE ELECTRIC LIGHT COMPANY'S NEW DYNAMO. This machine required nine teams of horses to haul it to its new location near Eagle Rock *c.* 1905. (SLCHA.)

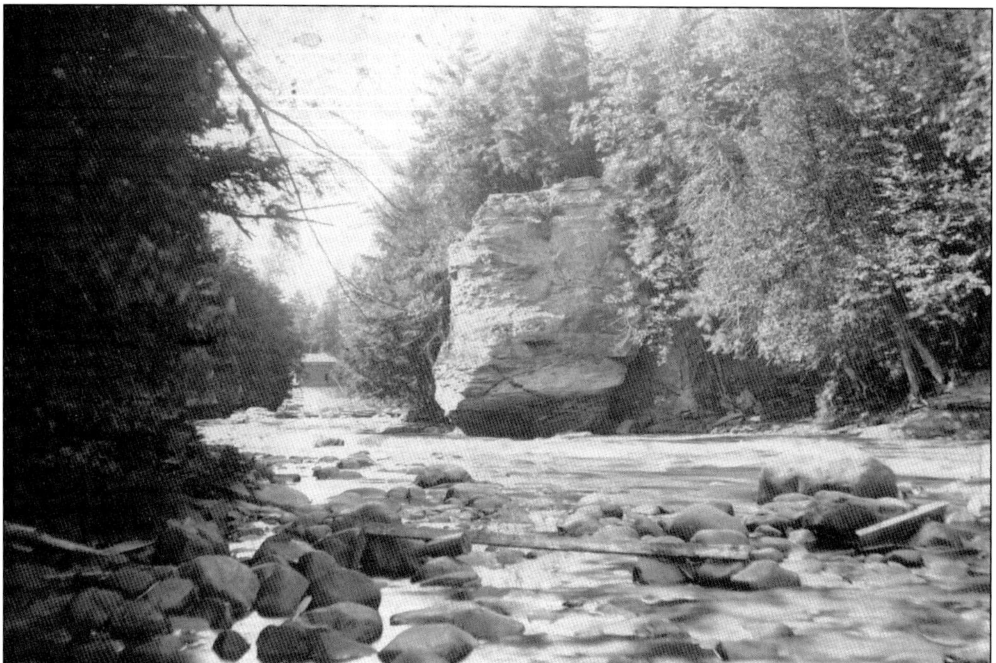

EAGLE ROCK. "The Nicholville Electric Light Company . . . have commenced preparations for the erection of a dam on the river at what is known as Eagle Rock, some three-fourths of a mile above this village. The river at this point passes through a deep narrow gorge with bottom and sides of solid rock and is one of the best natural locations for a dam and development of power on the river."—from the *Courier-Freeman*, October 25, 1905. (SLCHA.)

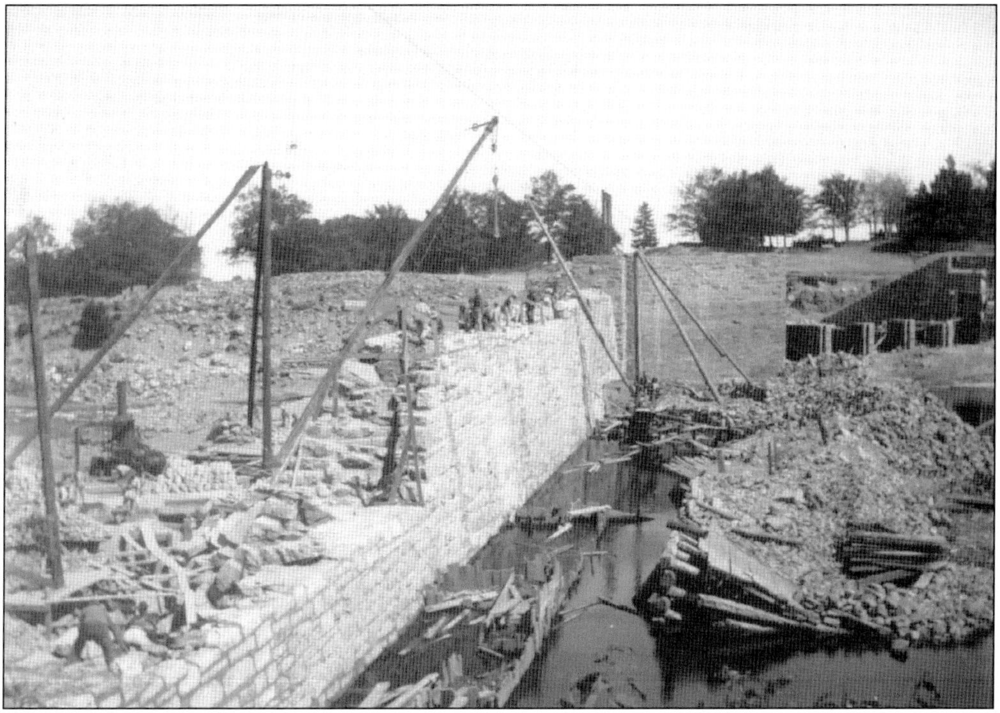

The Dam at Hannawa Falls Power Plant. This photograph shows the dam under construction *c.* 1900. (SLCHA.)

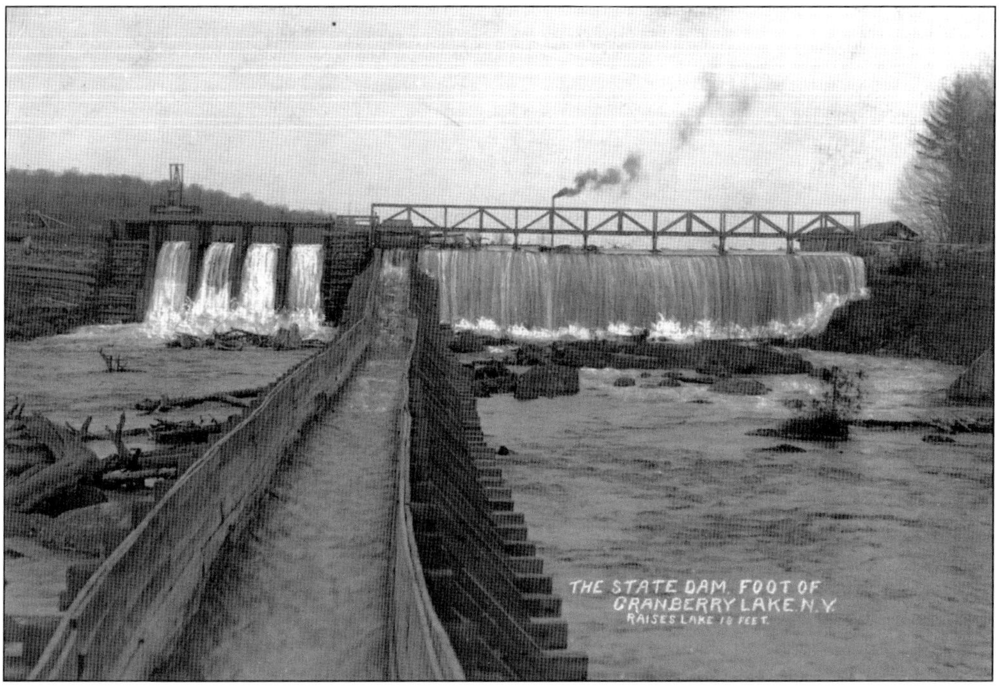

The Cranberry Lake Dam, 1890s. Built in 1865–1867, this was the first of several dams at the site. A log flume carried logs down the Oswegatchie River to mills downstream. (Courtesy Clifton historian.)

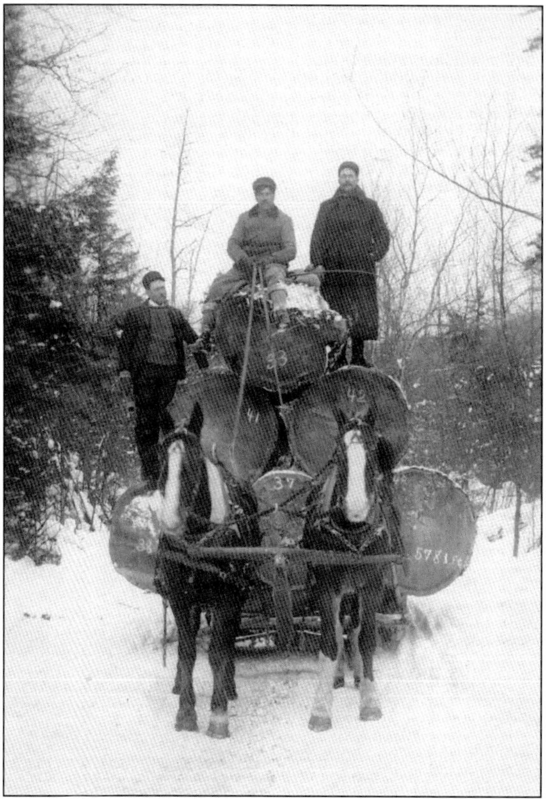

A LOGGING TEAM. These loggers worked for the mill owned by the Woodcock brothers, in Edwards. (SLCHA.)

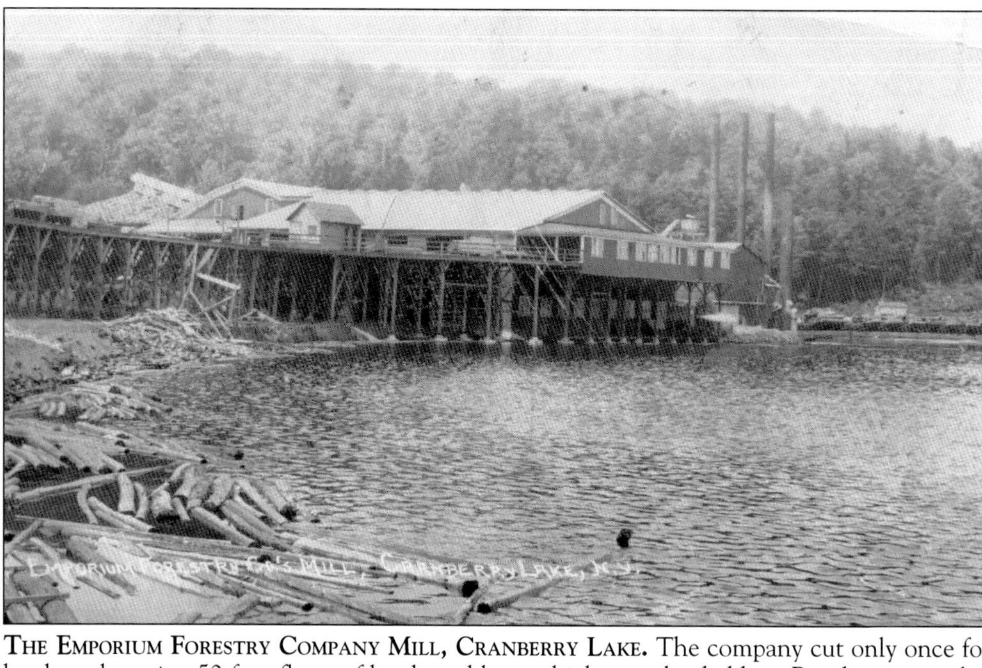

THE EMPORIUM FORESTRY COMPANY MILL, CRANBERRY LAKE. The company cut only once for hardwood, towing 50-foot floats of hardwood logs, which were loaded by a Barnhart steam log loader, to the railroad pier at Cranberry Lake village. (SLCHA.)

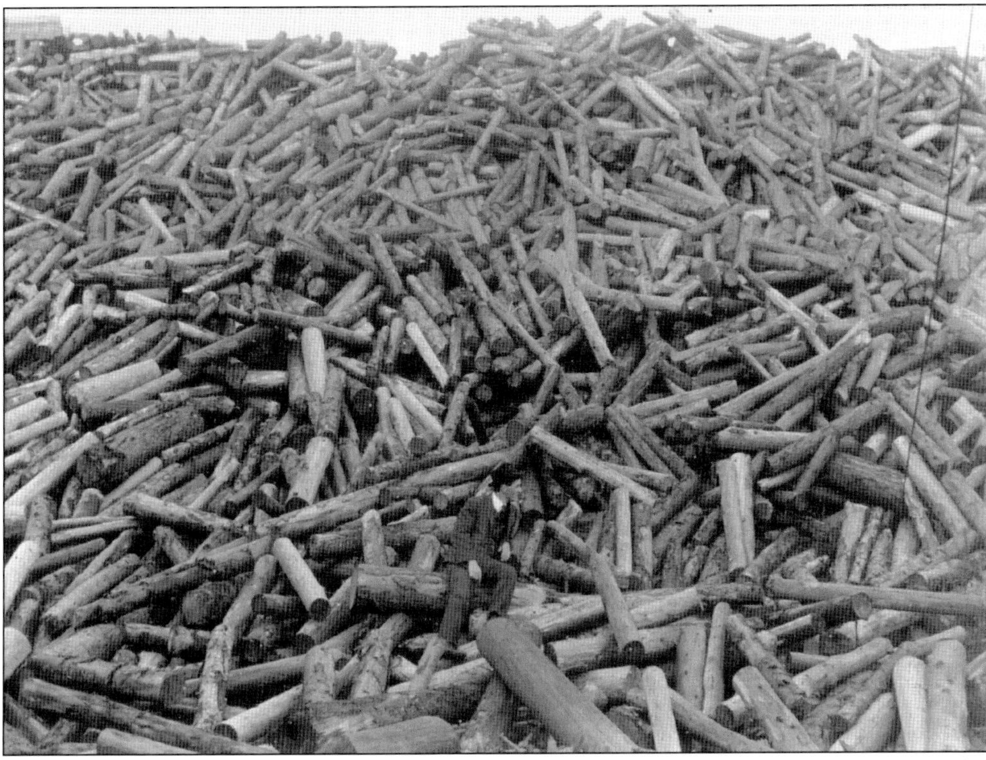

Ill Prepared. A man, definitely not dressed for logging, examines an enormous logjam. This c. 1910 photograph is from the Kip family album. Benjamin Kip was a well-known Canton photographer. (SLCHA.)

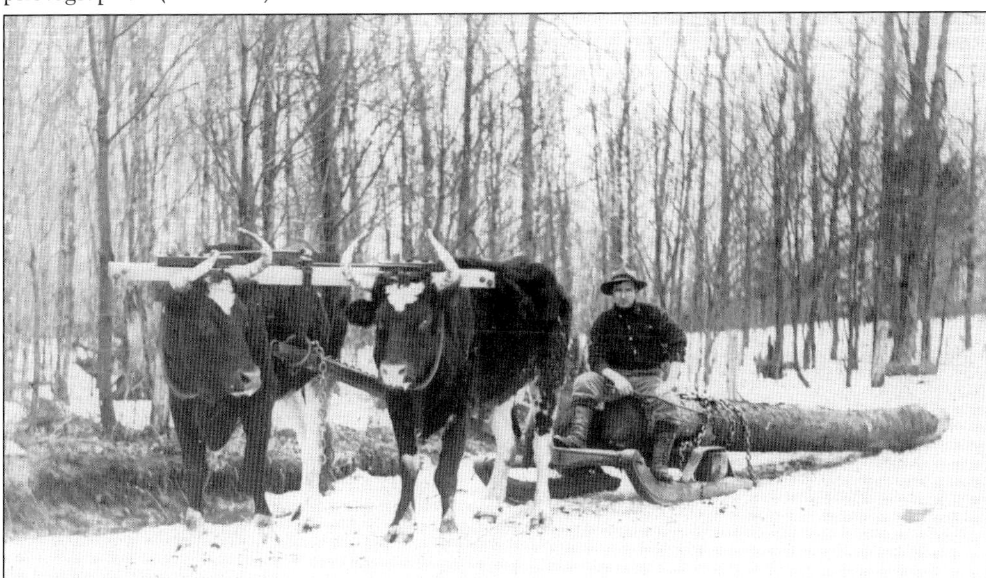

Winter in the Woods. When the ground is frozen and the brush is down, it is the time to cut and haul timber. Oxen tackle the job more easily than machinery, even today, as they can maneuver among trees and around obstacles. (SLCHA.)

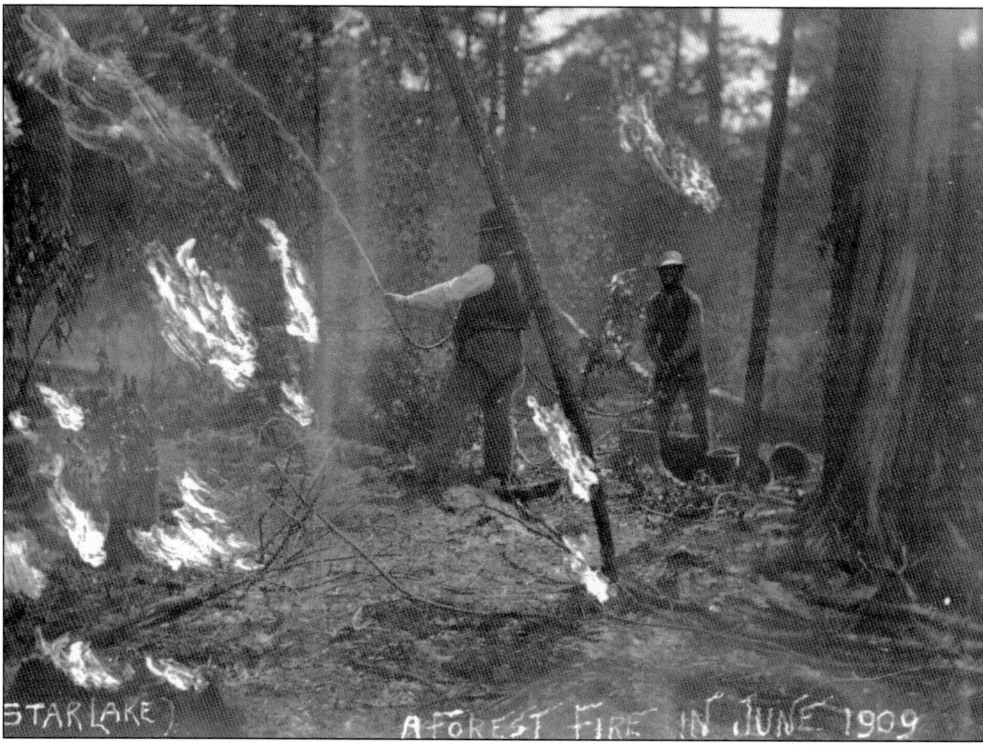

A FOREST FIRE NEAR THE STAR LAKE INN, JUNE 1909. Fires were fought with a primitive pumping system. (SLCHA.)

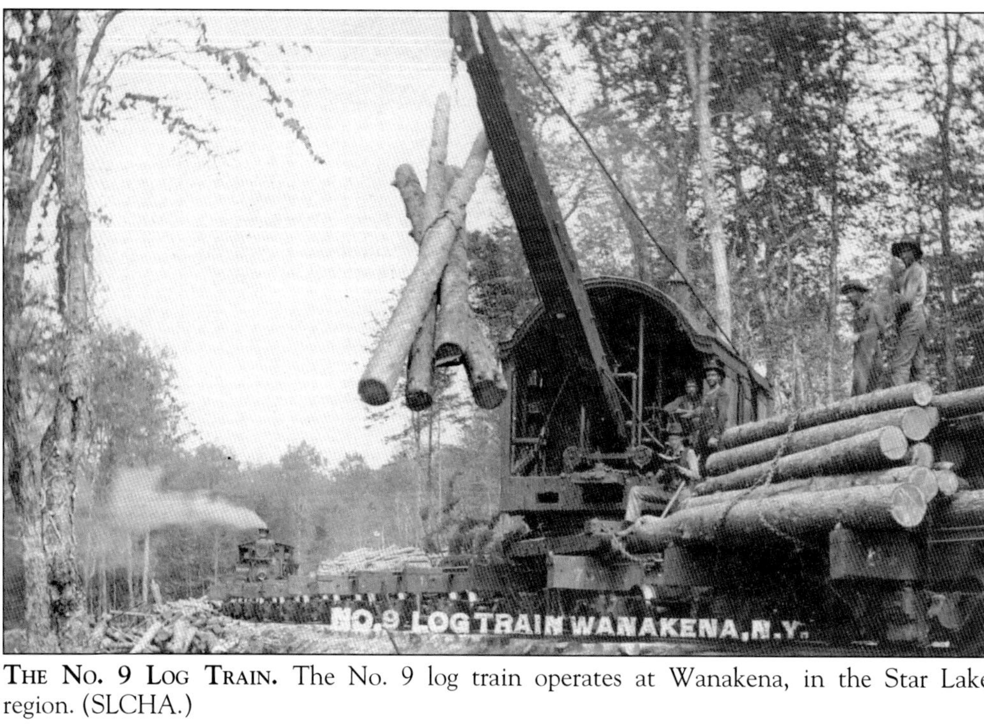

THE NO. 9 LOG TRAIN. The No. 9 log train operates at Wanakena, in the Star Lake region. (SLCHA.)

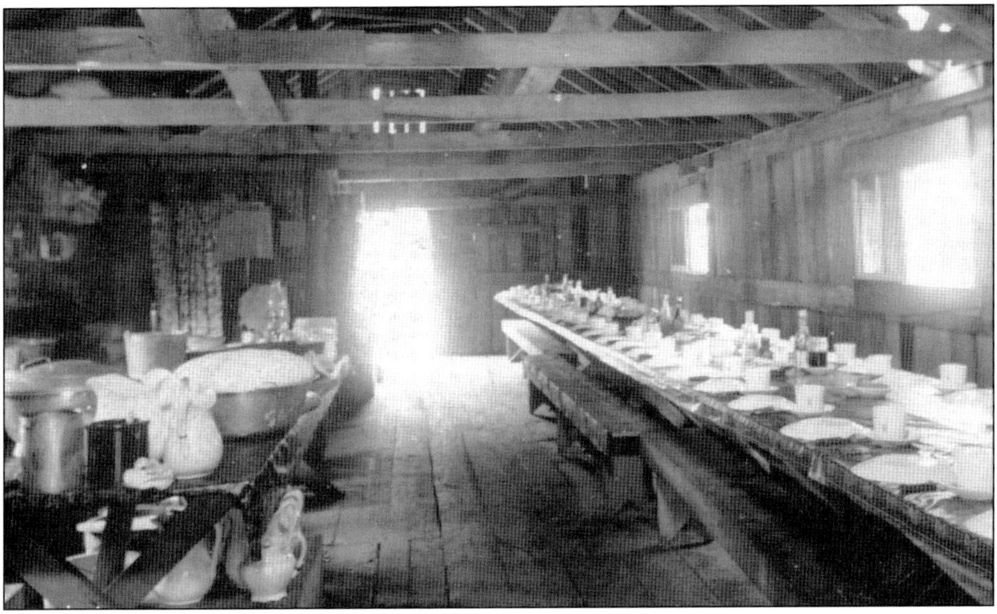

THE CAMP DINING ROOM. This photograph shows the dining room at the Newbridge Lumber Camp, on the south branch of the Grass River. (SLCHA.)

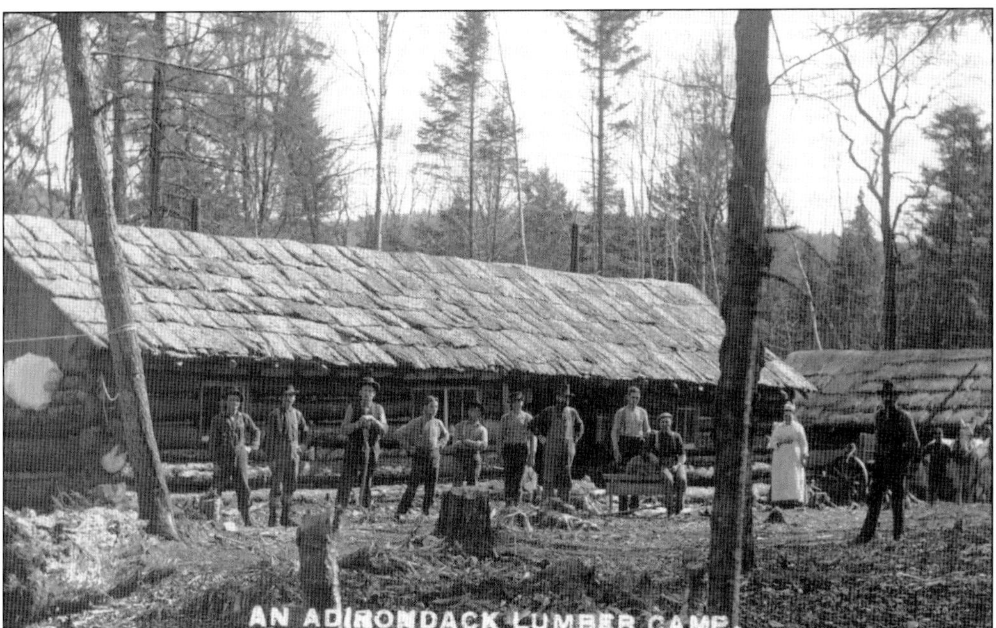

AN ADIRONDACK LUMBER CAMP. Note the bark roof. (SLCHA.)

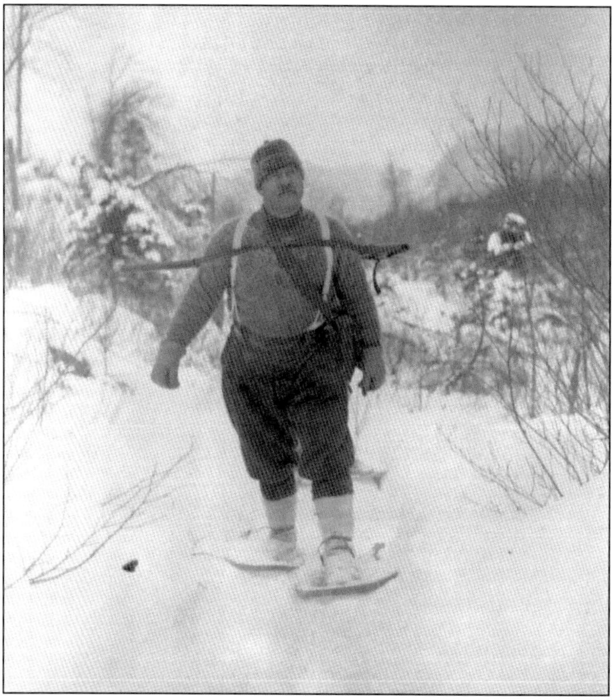

FREDERIC REMINGTON. The artist was in his element and dressed for a tough winter outing, his famous girth perhaps amplified by layered winter clothes. (Courtesy Frederic Remington Art Museum.)

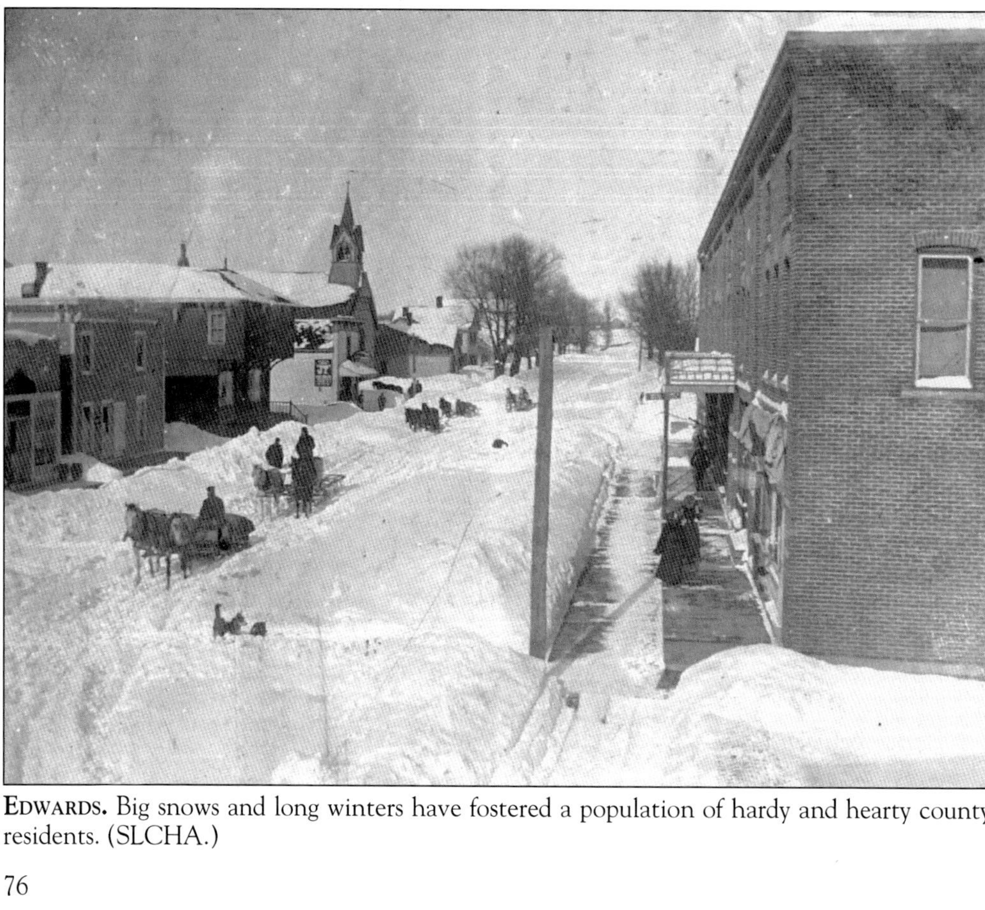

EDWARDS. Big snows and long winters have fostered a population of hardy and hearty county residents. (SLCHA.)

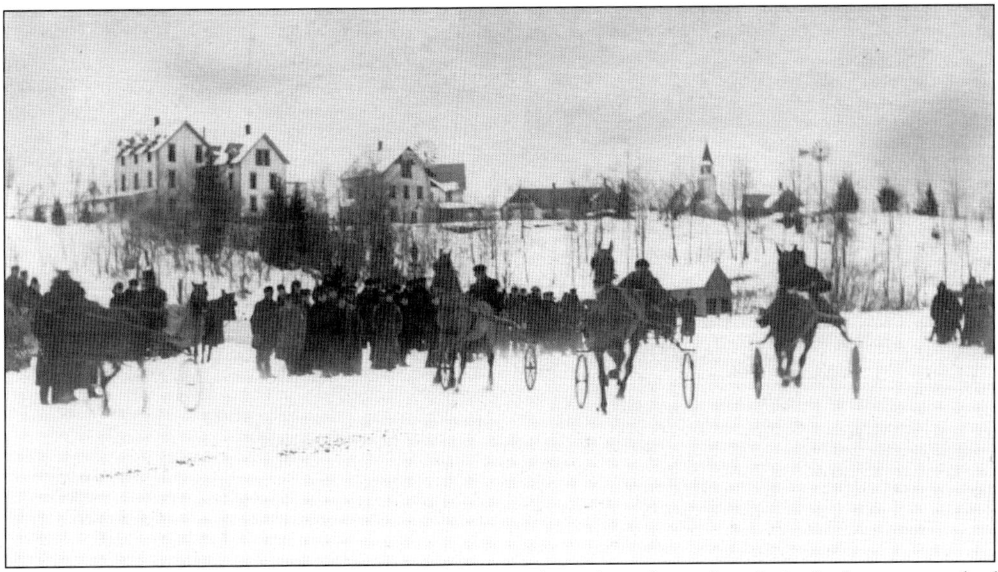

RACE DAY ON STAR LAKE. Sulkies compete on a cleared track on Star Lake before a crowd of spectators. (SLCHA.)

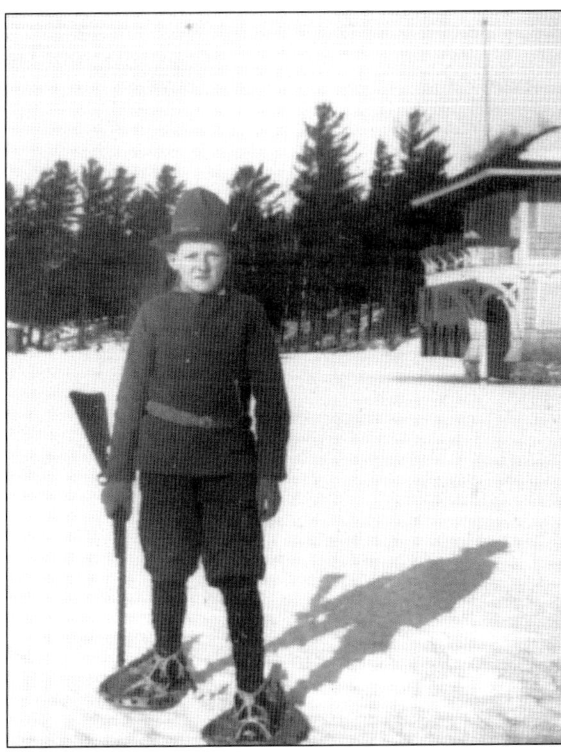

"SPIKE." This young fellow is ready for a day of winter hunting in 1913. Notice the straps holding his snowshoes. It was not uncommon to tie one's snowshoes on with candle wicking. (SLCHA.)

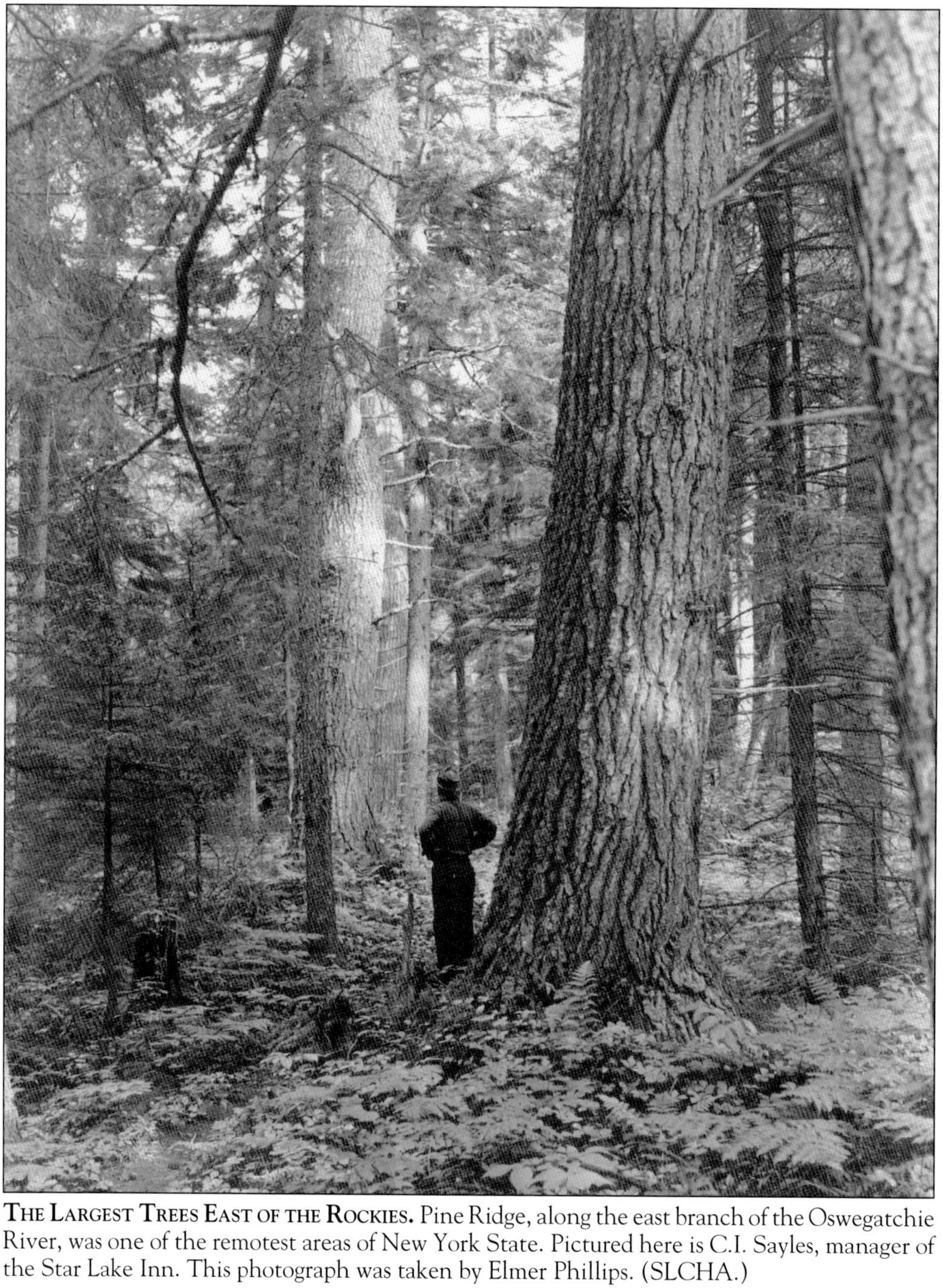

The Largest Trees East of the Rockies. Pine Ridge, along the east branch of the Oswegatchie River, was one of the remotest areas of New York State. Pictured here is C.I. Sayles, manager of the Star Lake Inn. This photograph was taken by Elmer Phillips. (SLCHA.)

Four

LIVING ON THE WATER

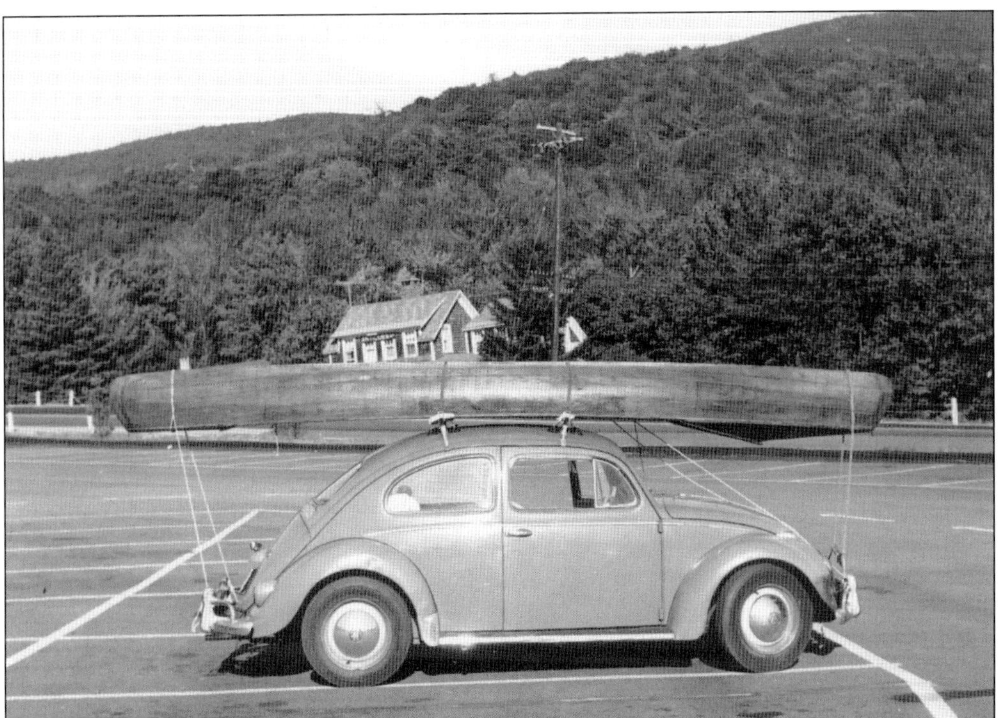

TWO CLASSICS. The owner travels in style whether on land or water. (SLCHA.)

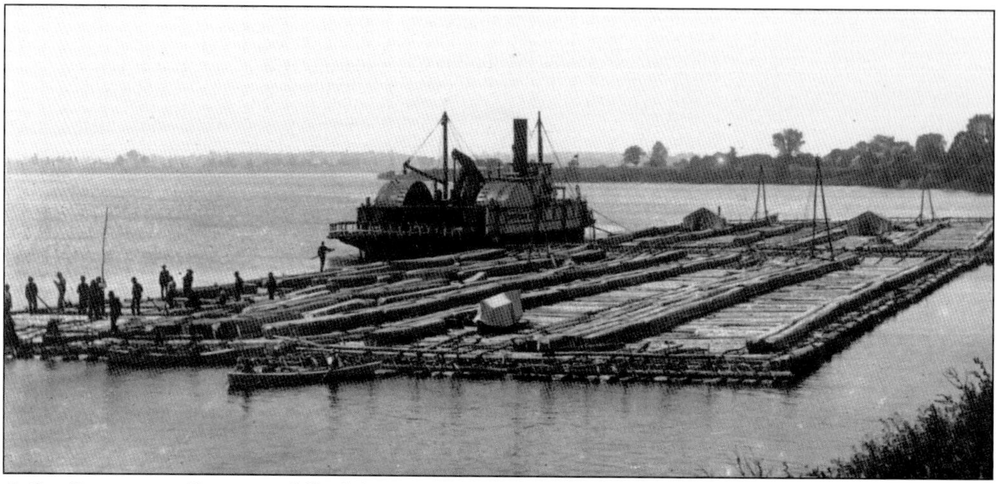

A ST. LAWRENCE LOGJAM. All of the county's rivers carried timber at one time or another, but perhaps the most impressive of these floating log piles were the giant timber rafts that traveled down the St. Lawrence. They originated in Jefferson County and Ontario. A steamer propelled the rafts because it drew little water and was easy to handle through the rapids. At first, the steamer left the raft after the rapids. Later, it accompanied the raft the entire way. (Courtesy the Antique Boat Museum.)

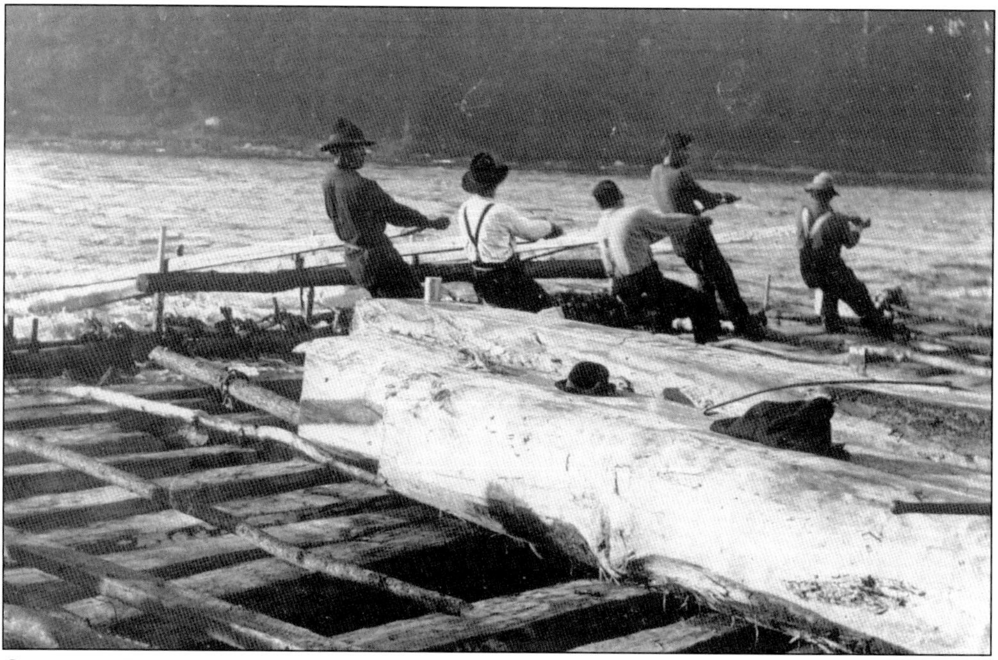

CRIBS AND DRAMS AND SWEEPS. Rafts had to "live" for about a month (later for only about a week) and were built of "cribs," consisting of an open framework 60 feet wide and 42 feet long. A succession of cribs formed a "dram," or unit of the raft. A dram was 60 feet wide and anywhere from 250 to 300 feet long. Oak had to be rafted with pine to give it more buoyancy. Pine and elm could be rafted three tiers deep because they were so buoyant. The rafts were maneuvered using "sweeps," long oars made from small pine trees. A crew on the raft consisted of one foreman, one cook, and two people for each dram of timber. To run the rapids, 200 additional people were required. (Courtesy the Antique Boat Museum.)

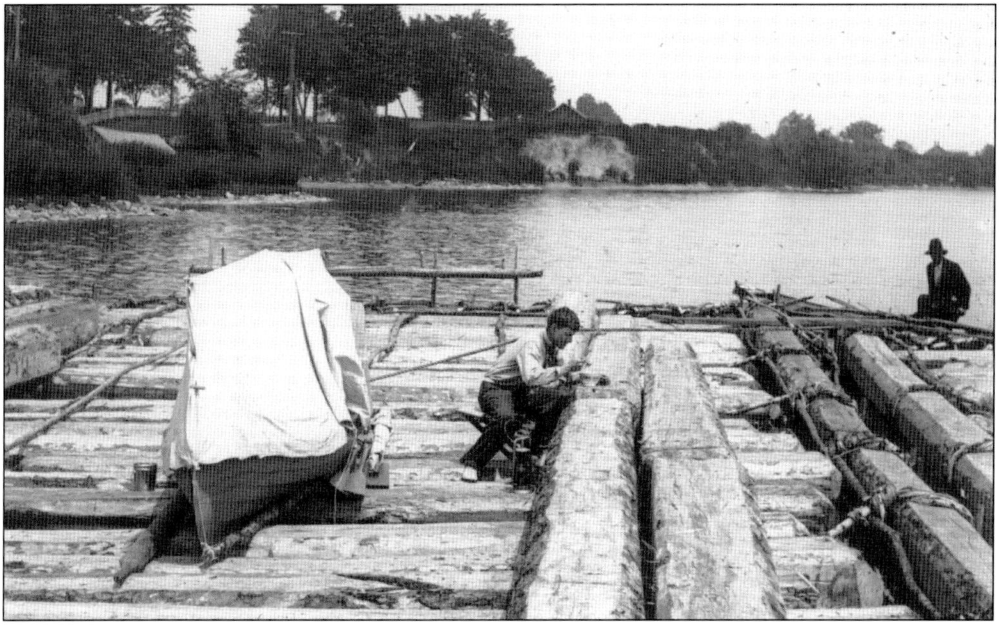

At Home on the River. Each dram had two cabins, one for the foreman and one for the cook and the rest of the crew. Cooking was done on an outdoor hearth made from a piece of sheet iron covered with earth and ashes. (Courtesy the Antique Boat Museum.)

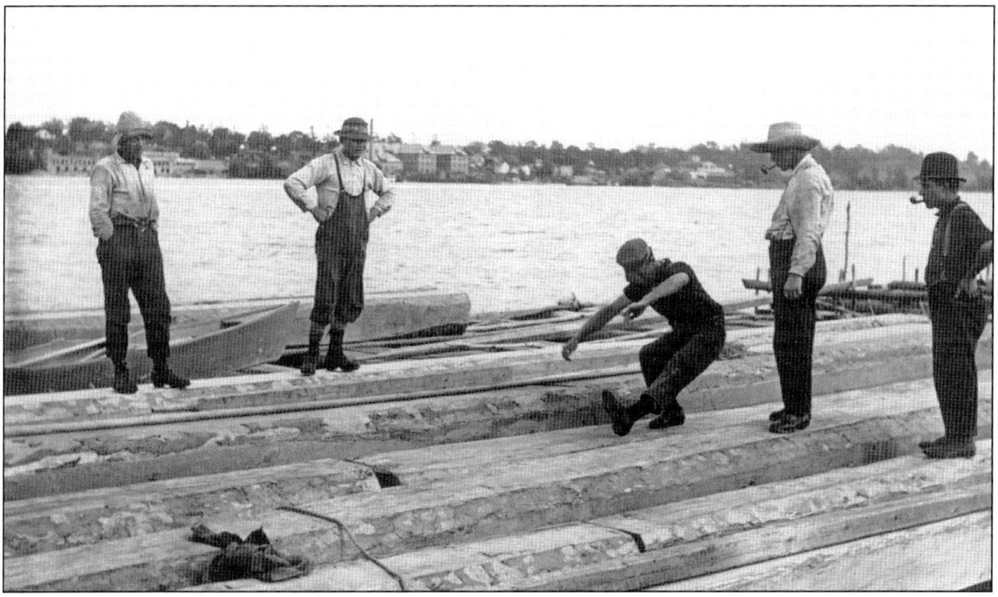

Making the Journey. The rafts left Garden Island off Kingston, Ontario, in the late afternoon. By evening two days later, they were at the top of the Long Sault Rapids, just below Prescott. There, crews were taken aboard there; the rafts were broken up into drams, which ran the rapids individually. The raft was then reassembled, the extra crew paid off, and the trip proceeded to the next set of rapids. The procedure was repeated, and the raft traveled across Lake St. Louis to the top of the Lachine Rapids. Again, the raft was dismantled and reassembled after the rapids. The crew wanted to get well below Montreal before stopping to avoid the temptations the city offered. (Courtesy the Antique Boat Museum.)

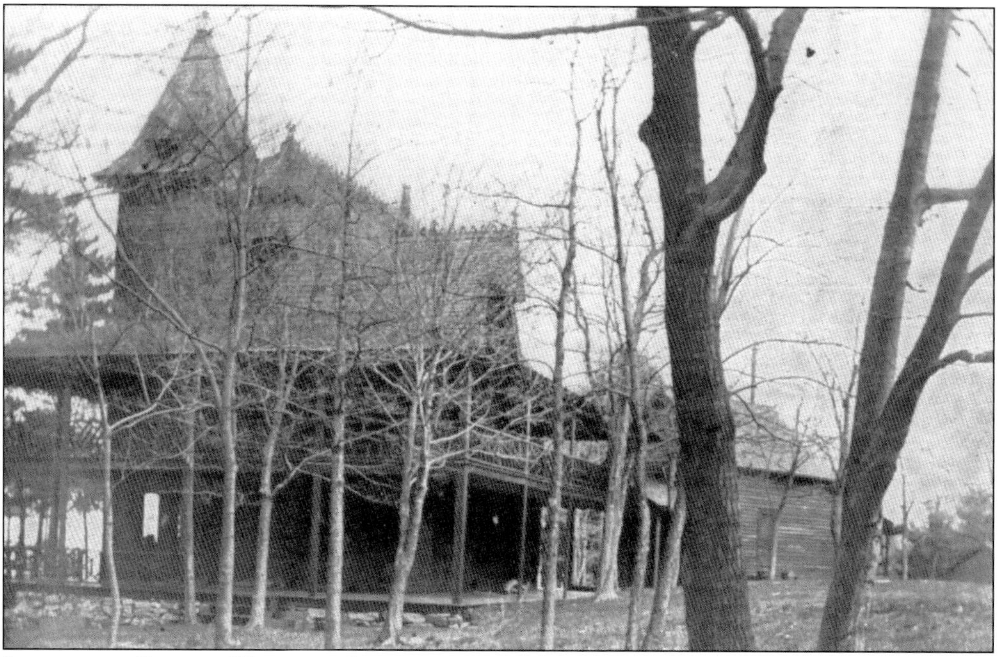

INGLENEUK, SUMMER HOME OF CANTON NATIVE SON FREDERIC REMINGTON. Although best known for his paintings of the American West, the artist featured the St. Lawrence River and other North Country scenes on many of his canvases. Frederic Remington sold Ingleneuk in 1909; the house burned in 1963. (SLCHA.)

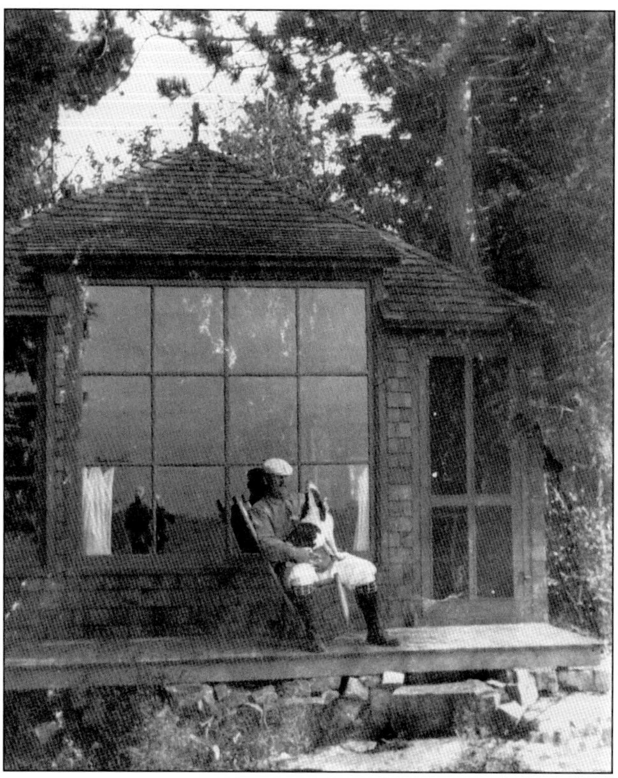

THE ARTIST RELAXING IN FRONT OF HIS STUDIO. Frederic Remington relaxes in front of his studio at Ingleneuk with one of his dogs. (Courtesy Frederic Remington Art Museum.)

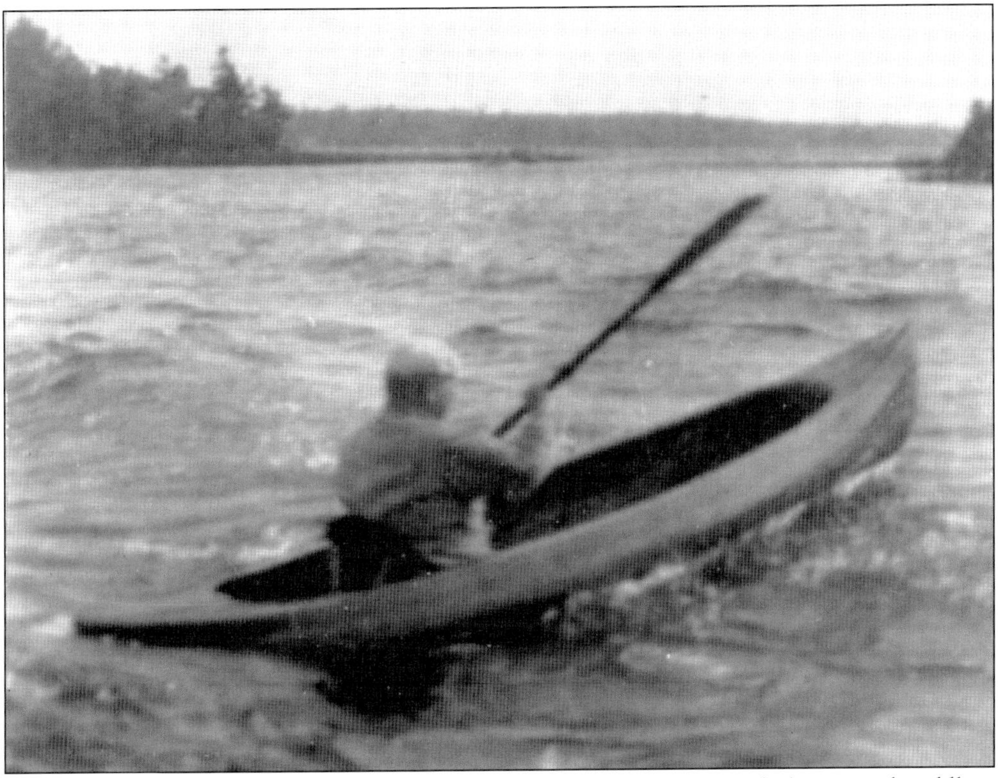

AN ACCOMPLISHED OUTDOORSMAN. Artist Frederic Remington particularly enjoyed paddling the canoes built by his friend and fellow Canton native J. Henry Rushton. (SLCHA.)

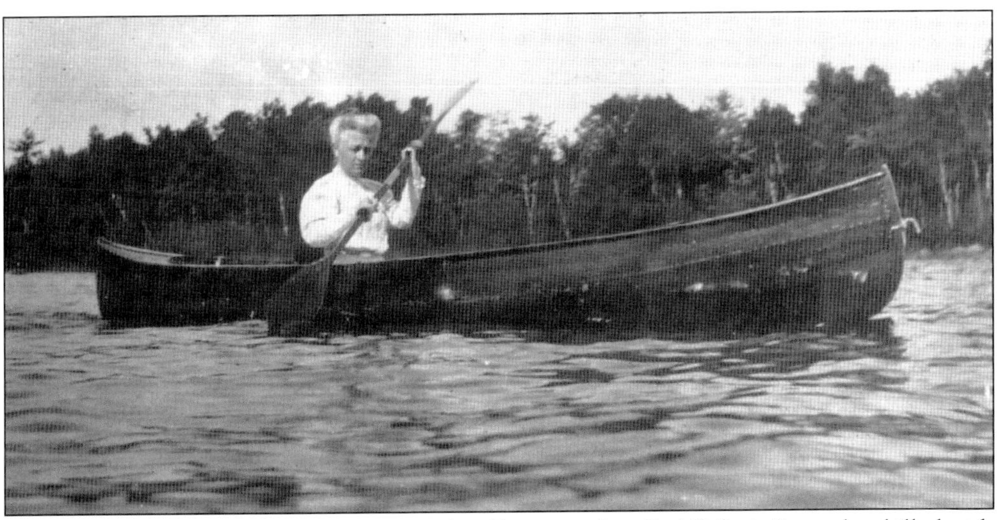

EVA REMINGTON. Frederic Remington's wife, affectionately called "Missie," was also skilled with the paddle. (SLCHA.)

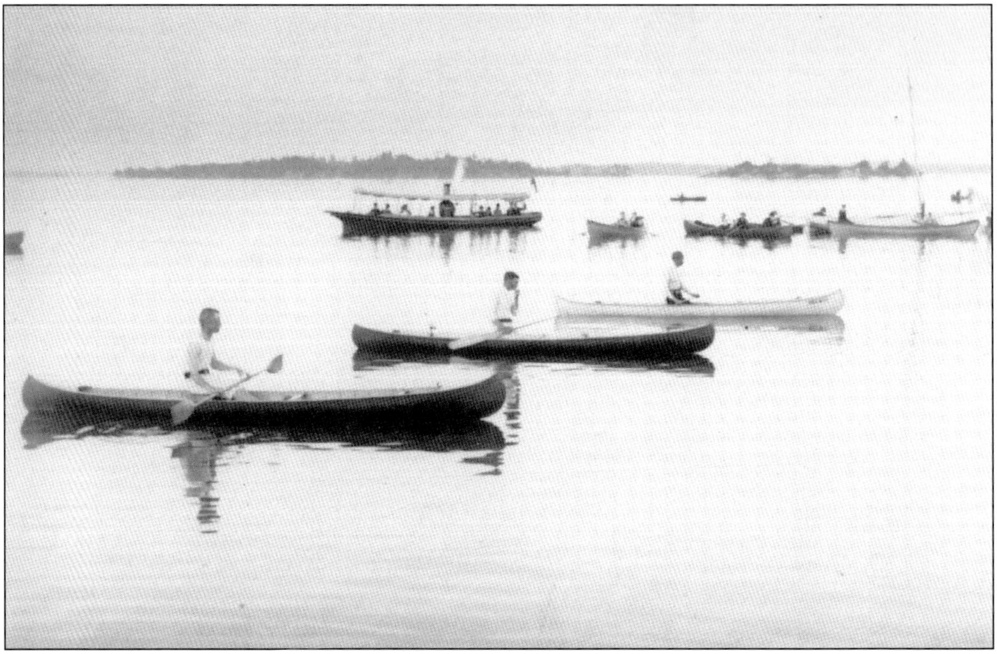

THE 1895 MEET OF THE AMERICAN CANOE ASSOCIATION. Rushton canoes were plentiful at the meets, which put both paddlers and craft to the test. (Seneca Ray Stoddard photograph, courtesy the Antique Boat Museum.)

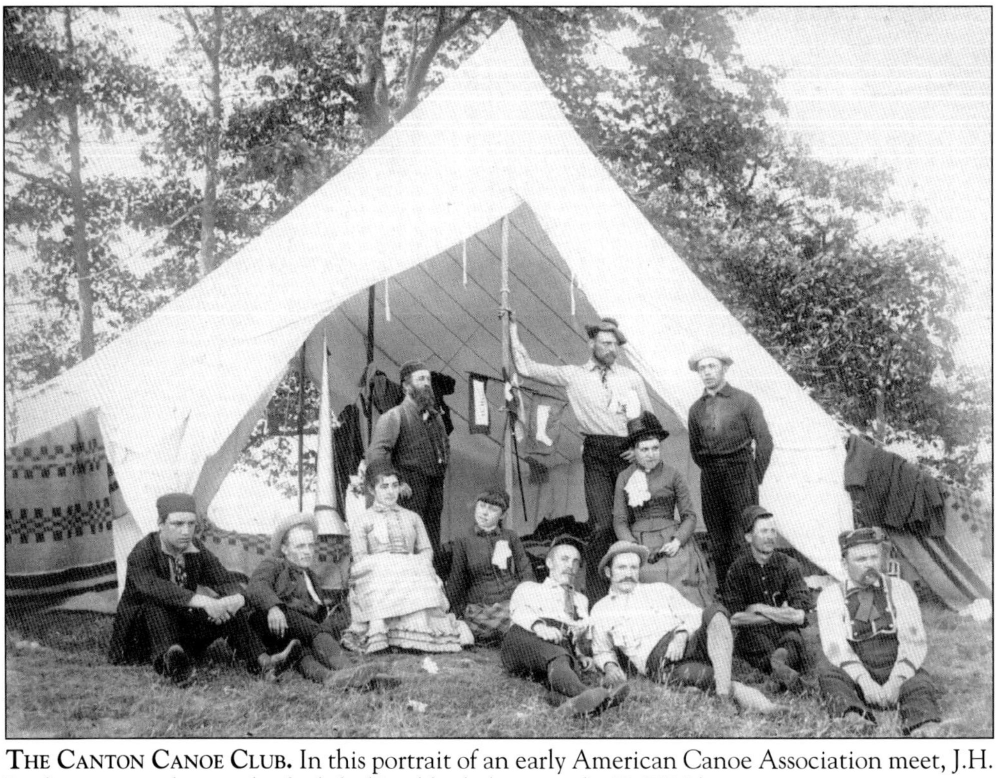

THE CANTON CANOE CLUB. In this portrait of an early American Canoe Association meet, J.H. Rushton is standing at the far left. (Stoddard photograph, SLCHA)

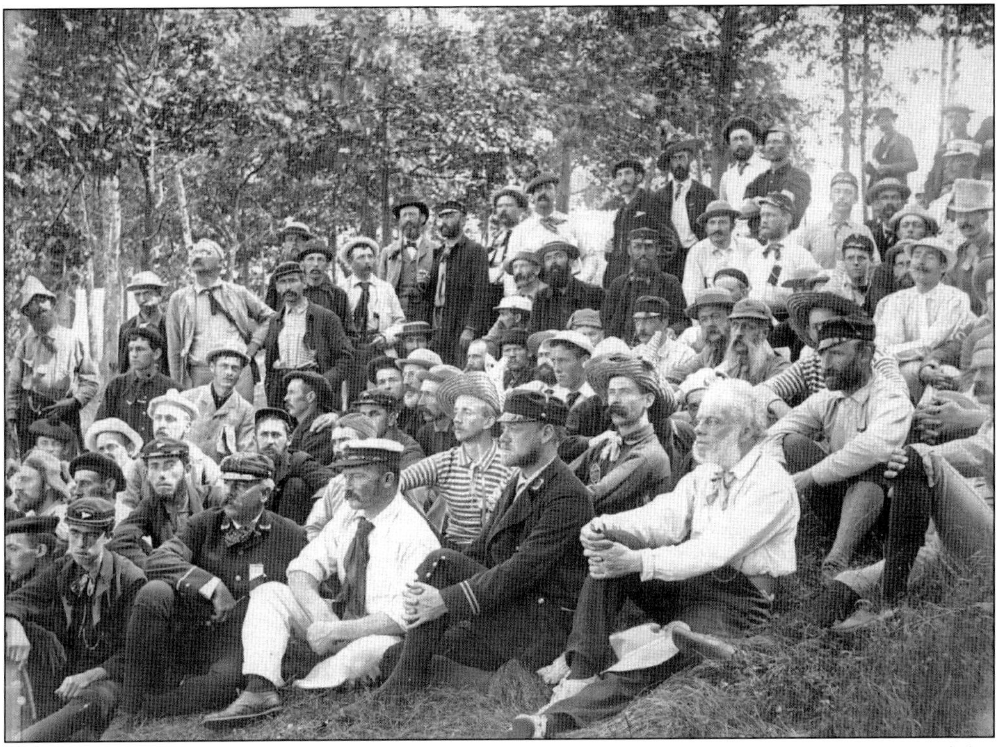

American Canoe Association Members. Sporting the uniforms of their various clubs, American Canoe Association participants pose for a group photograph. Notably absent from the portrait are the meet's female participants, who did not paddle or sail but encouraged the male competitors from a discreet distance. (SLCHA.)

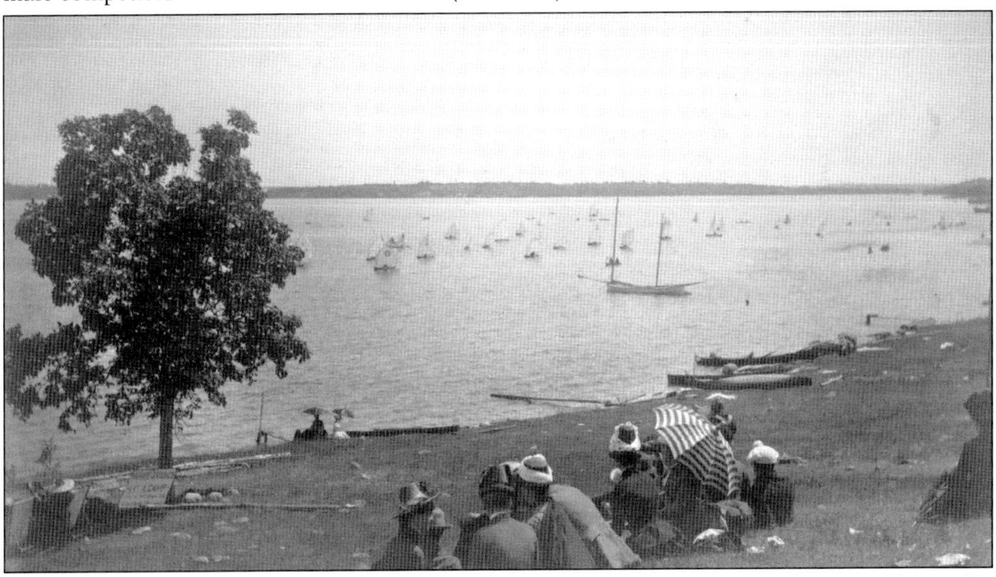

Watching the Impressive Fleet of Sailing Canoes. Women camped separately at the American Canoe Association meets; when men called on the female encampment, they lowered their sails so as not to reveal club affiliations as they paddled their ladyloves about. (Stoddard photograph, courtesy the Antique Boat Museum.)

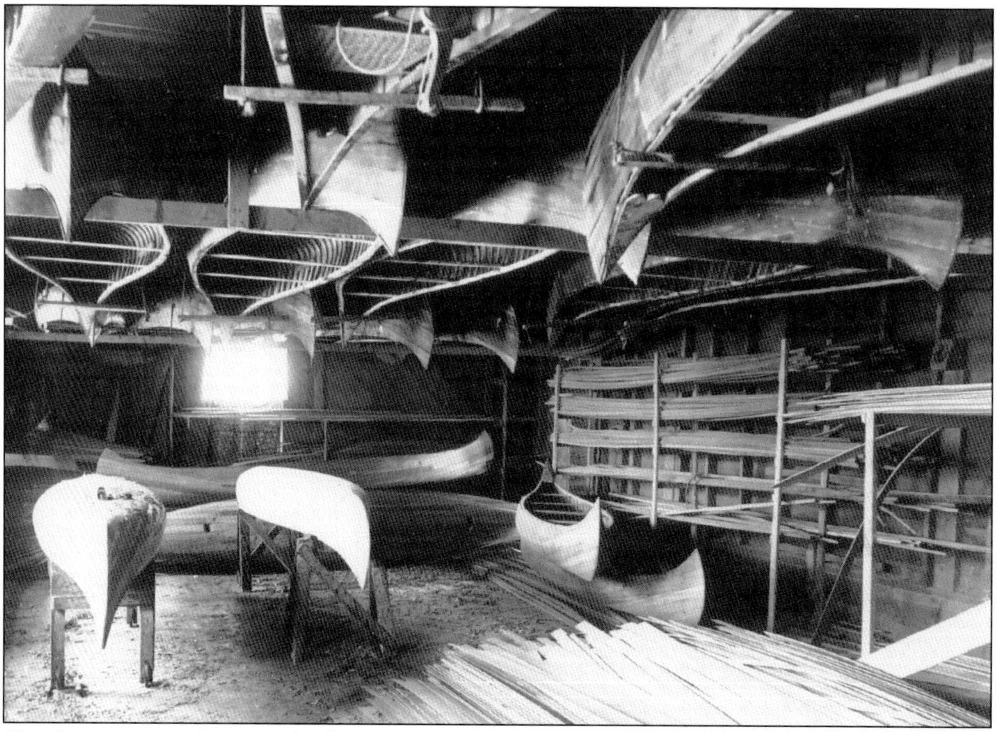

THE INTERIOR OF RUSHTON'S CANTON BOATSHOP. J. Henry Rushton's career as a boatbuilder got a boost in 1880, when outdoor writer George Washington Sears, better known by his pen name Nessmuk, commissioned Rushton to build him the 10.5-pound craft *Sairy Gamp*. Within five years, Rushton had a highly successful business and was the best-known canoe craftsman in the nation. His Canton shop closed in 1917, 11 years after his death. (SLCHA.)

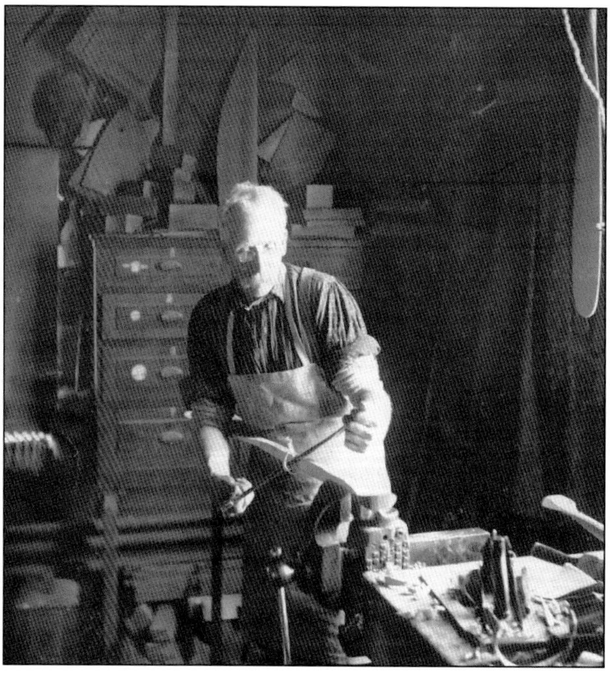

NELSON BROWN. Nelson Brown was J. Henry Rushton's shop foreman from 1878 until the close of the shop. (SLCHA.)

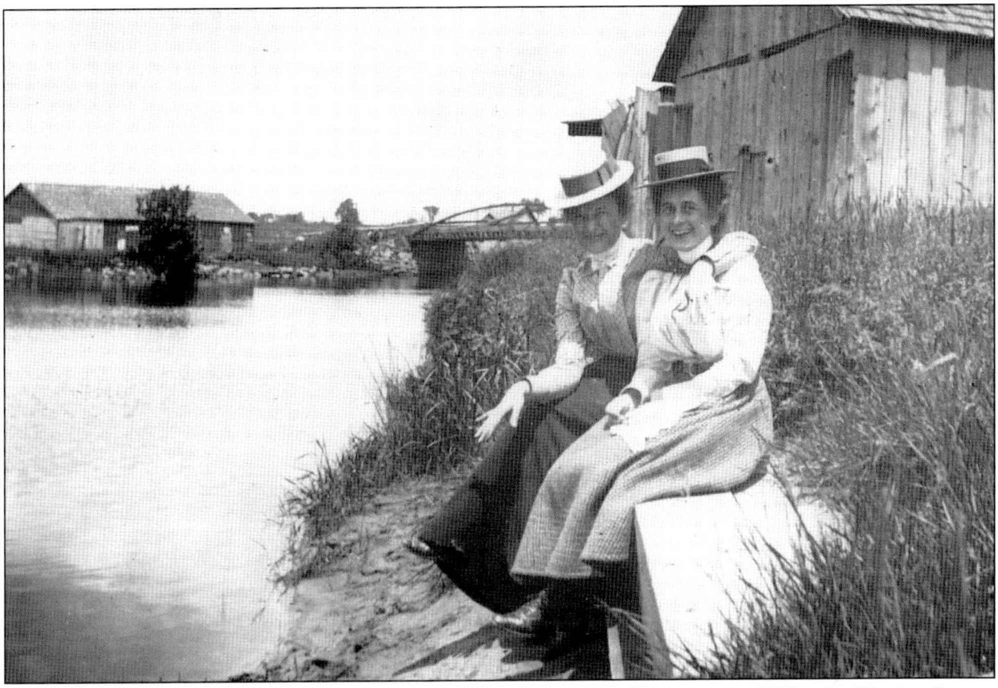

CANTON GRAMMAR SCHOOL TEACHERS. Harriett Ferry, who later married Charles D. Appleton, and Anna Jay perch near the Little River Bridge. Rushton's boathouse sits on the opposite shore. (SLCHA.)

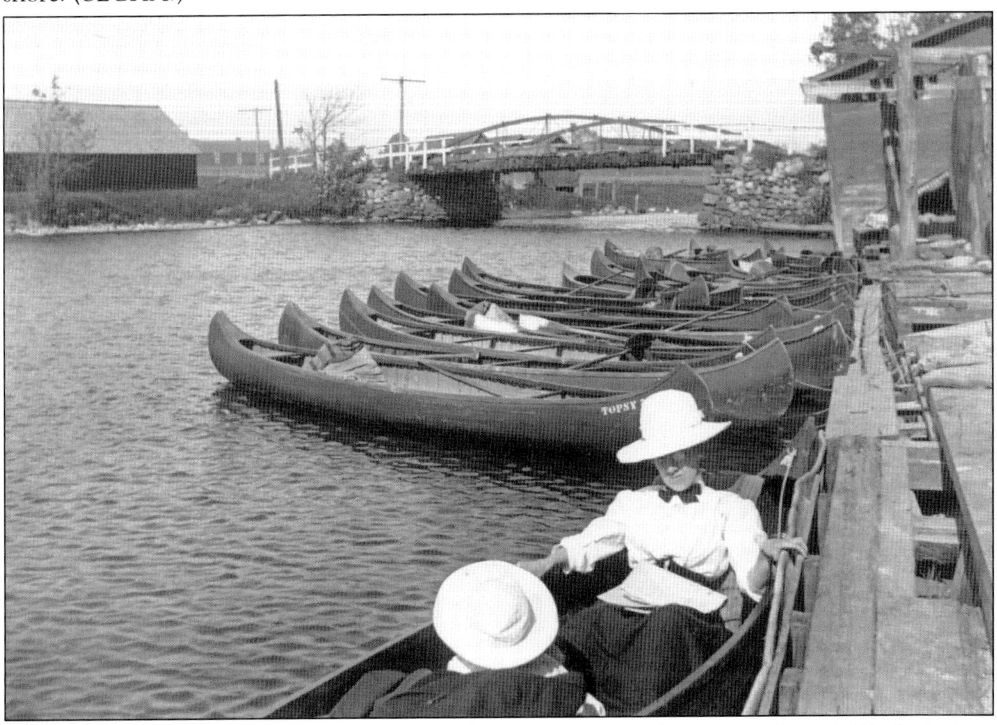

RUSHTON INDIAN GIRL CANOES, C. 1910. These canoes were for rent at Winnie Taylor's Boat Livery, at Little River Bridge. The Rushton boathouse is at the left. (SLCHA.)

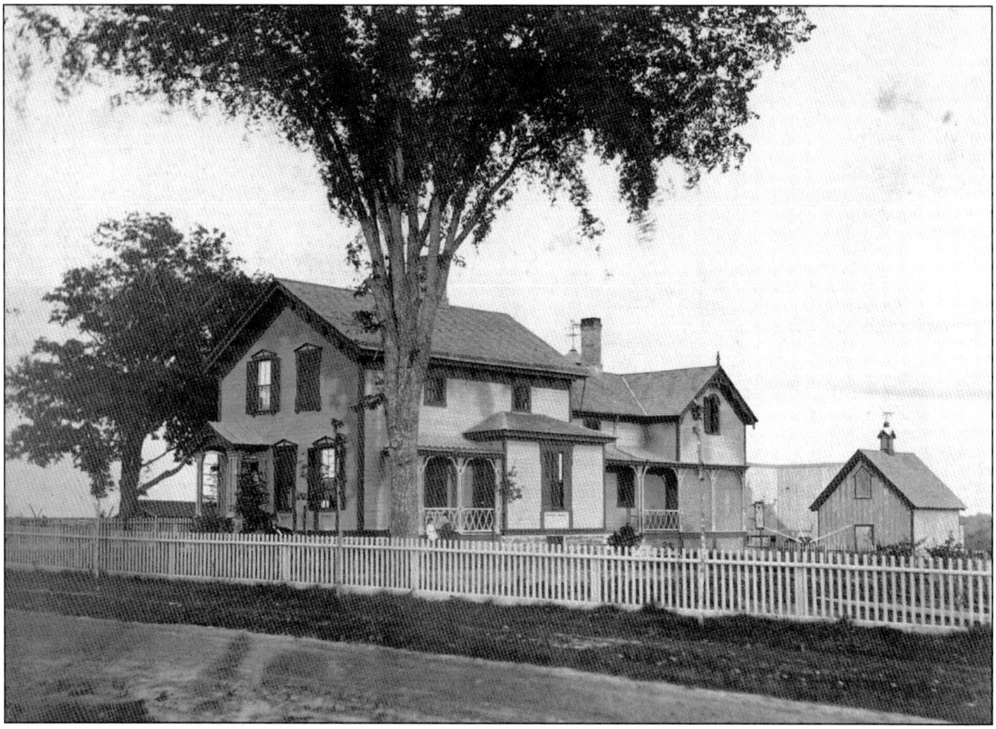

THE JUDSON HOME. The home is pictured under one of the once common American elm trees along Black Lake. The home still stands and is today known as the Lakeside Inn. (SLCHA.)

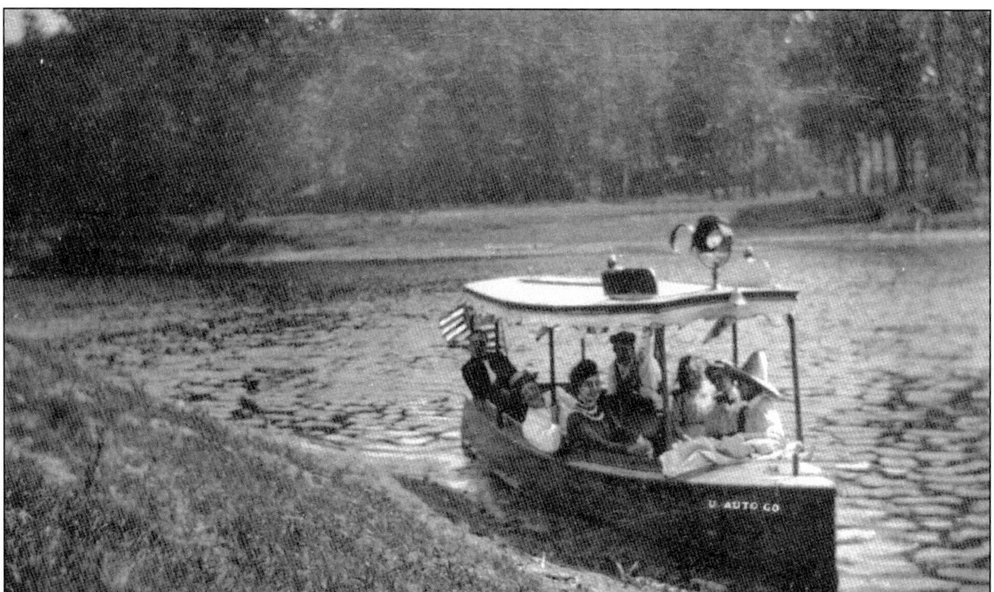

THE *U AUTO GO* NAVIGATING THE GRASS RIVER, CANTON. Throughout the county, liveries took paying customers out on the water. Even the most land-bound of urban dwellers could find themselves in the middle of a lake or drifting down a lazy river. (SLCHA.)

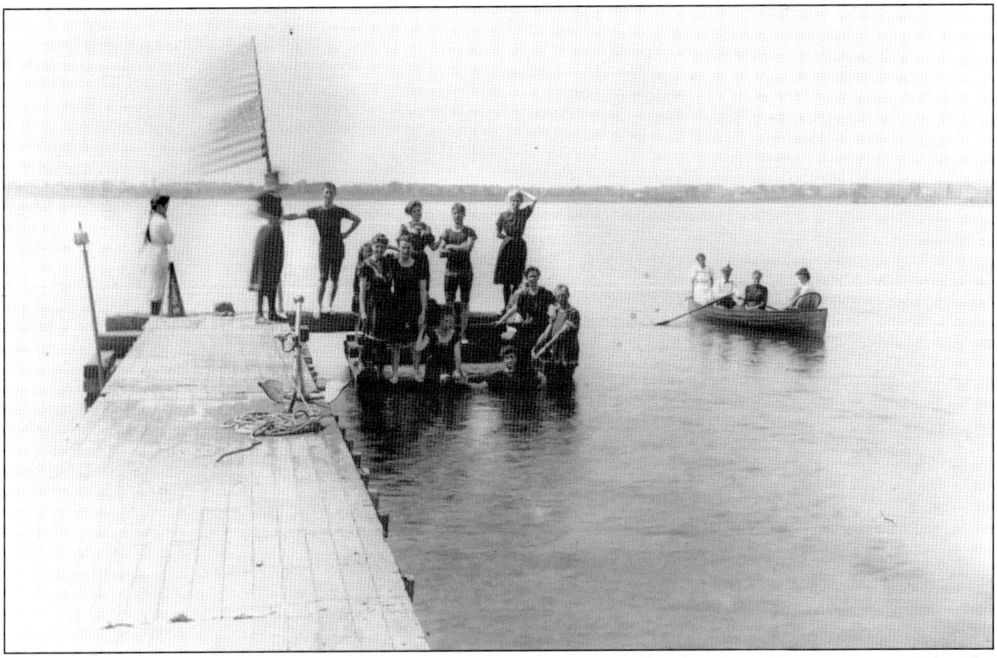

WHERE THERE IS WATER THERE IS WATER SPORT. Summer fun has long been a part of the St. Lawrence in Ogdensburg. Note the St. Lawrence skiff at the right, with its lapstrake construction, fixed oars, and wicker seat backs. (SLCHA.)

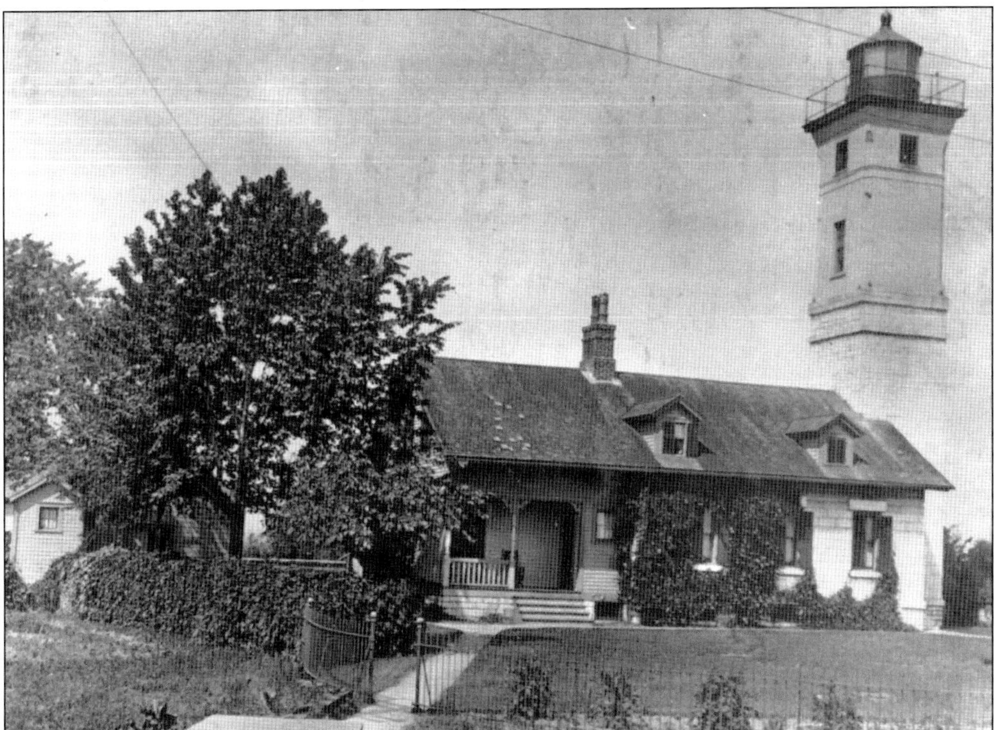

THE OGDENSBURG LIGHTHOUSE. The lighthouse was completed by the federal government in 1835 and was renovated in 1869–1870. (SLCHA.)

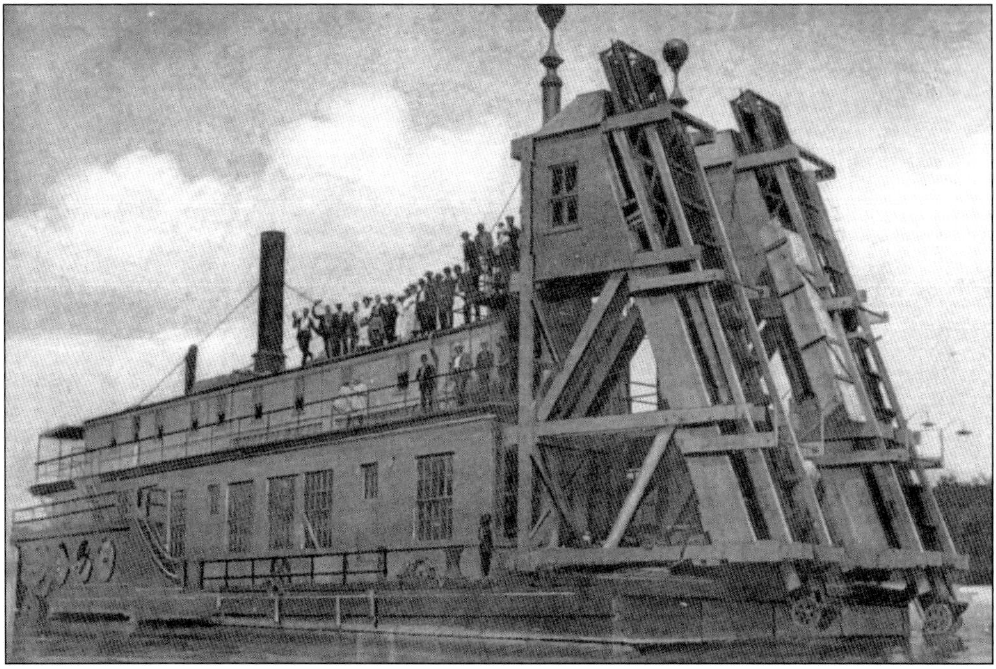

THE PEAT DREDGE, *HEUVELTON*. This dredge was built in the town of the same name in 1905 to harvest peat for fuel. The peat "scheme" included plans for a large smelting works that would need power fueled by the peat. The New York Central Railroad would reportedly lay a spur to the peat plant, and the North Country would boom. The dredge was finally taken down the Oswegatchie River to Black Lake in 1907, where it dredged a little peat. The process proved to be completely impractical and, in September 1908, the dredge burned. (Harold A. Storie manuscript, 1908, SLCHA.)

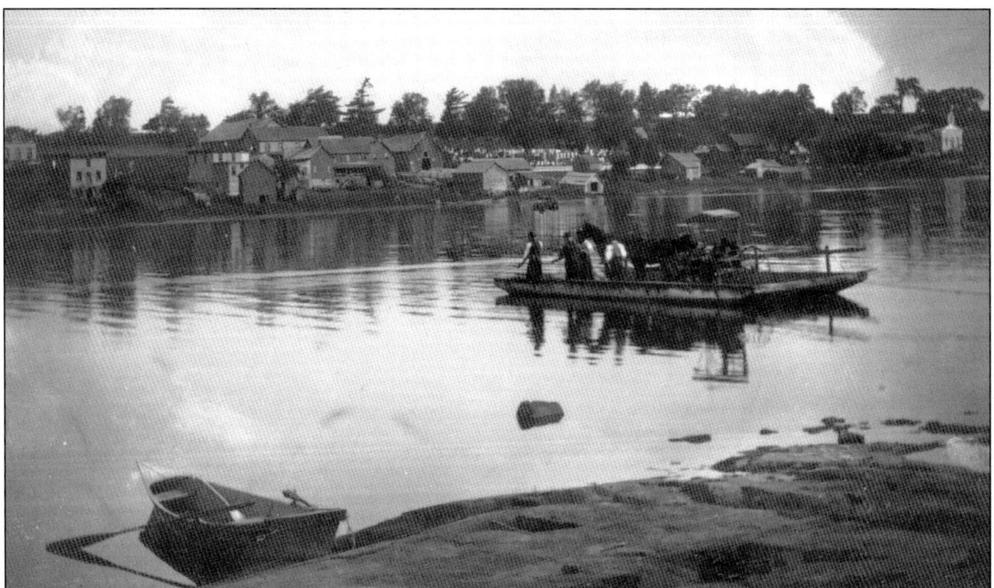

THE MORRISTOWN–EDWARDSVILLE FERRY BEING PULLED ACROSS BLACK LAKE. This was typical of many primitive ferries in use at the time. (SLCHA.)

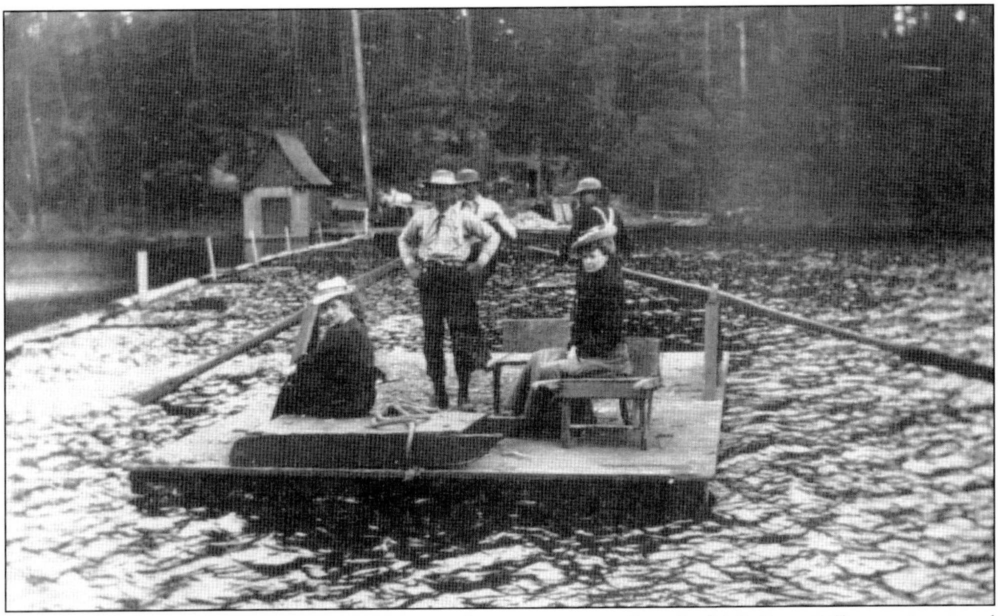

FERRY SERVICE ON CRANBERRY LAKE. Private businesses as well as the U.S. Post Office maintained service during the summer months. (SLCHA.)

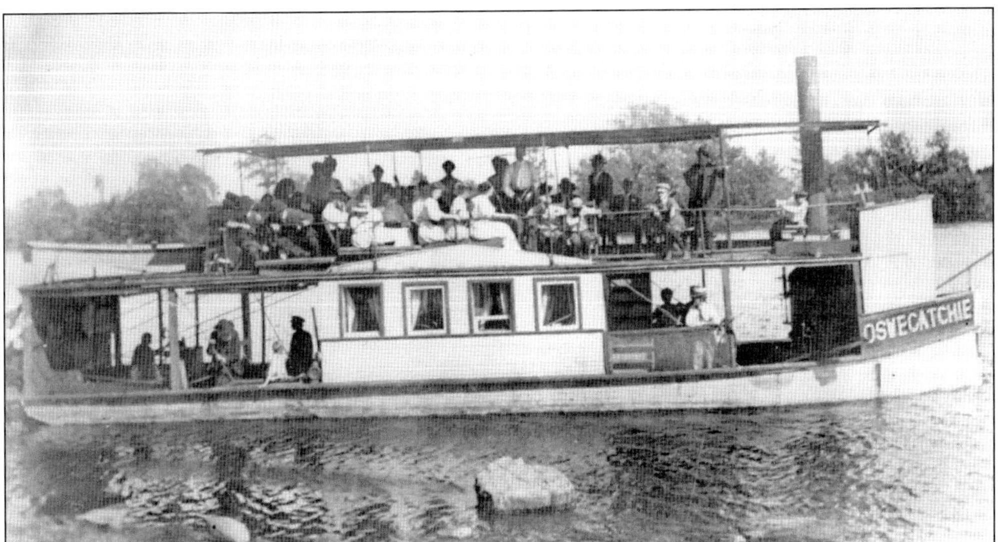

THE *OSWEGATCHIE*, THE LAST STEAMER TO RUN ON BLACK LAKE. This steamer ran from Rossie to Heuvelton, carrying freight and passengers. Monday was cheese day, when it stopped at all the factories around the lake. The steamer sank in a storm on August 8, 1908. An attempt to raise it a week later failed. The next step: "Two scows have been anchored on each side of the boat and a heavy timber strung between them and over the boat, which is chained to the timber. Jacks placed at each end of the timber will gradually raise the craft from the bottom and as fast as it is raised, the scows will be hauled into shallow water where it will be pumped out."—from an August 26, 1908 account in the *Gouverneur Free Press*. (SLCHA.)

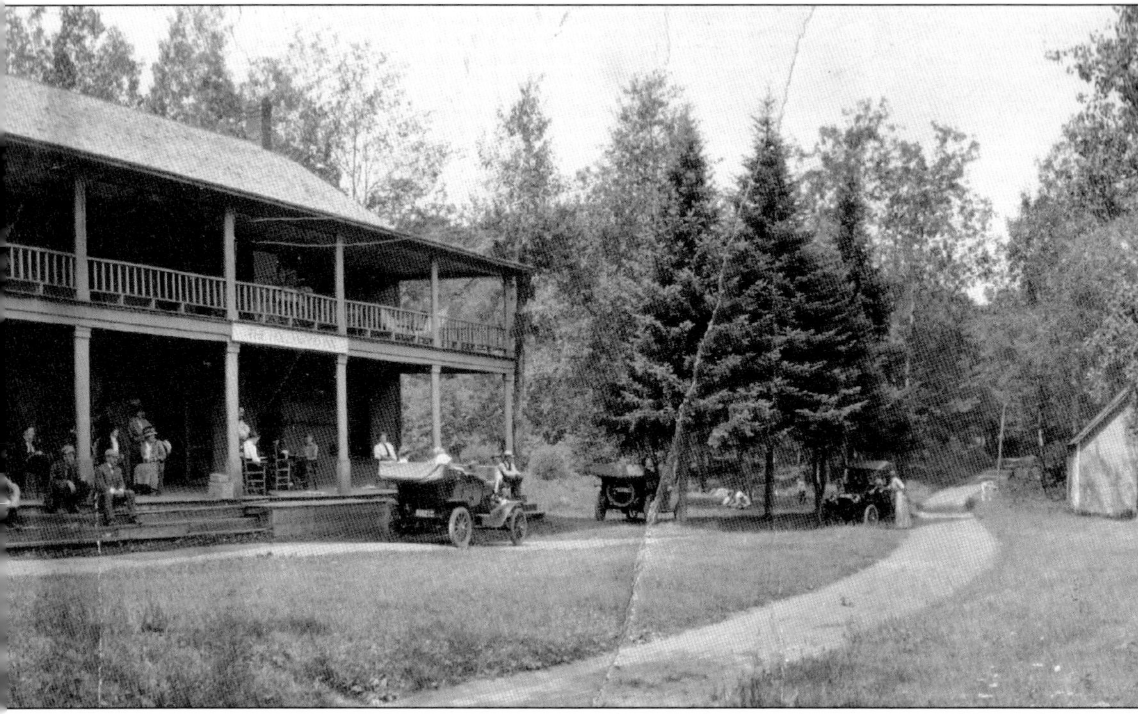

The Hollywood Inn, Stillwater. A member of the Kip family presumably took this

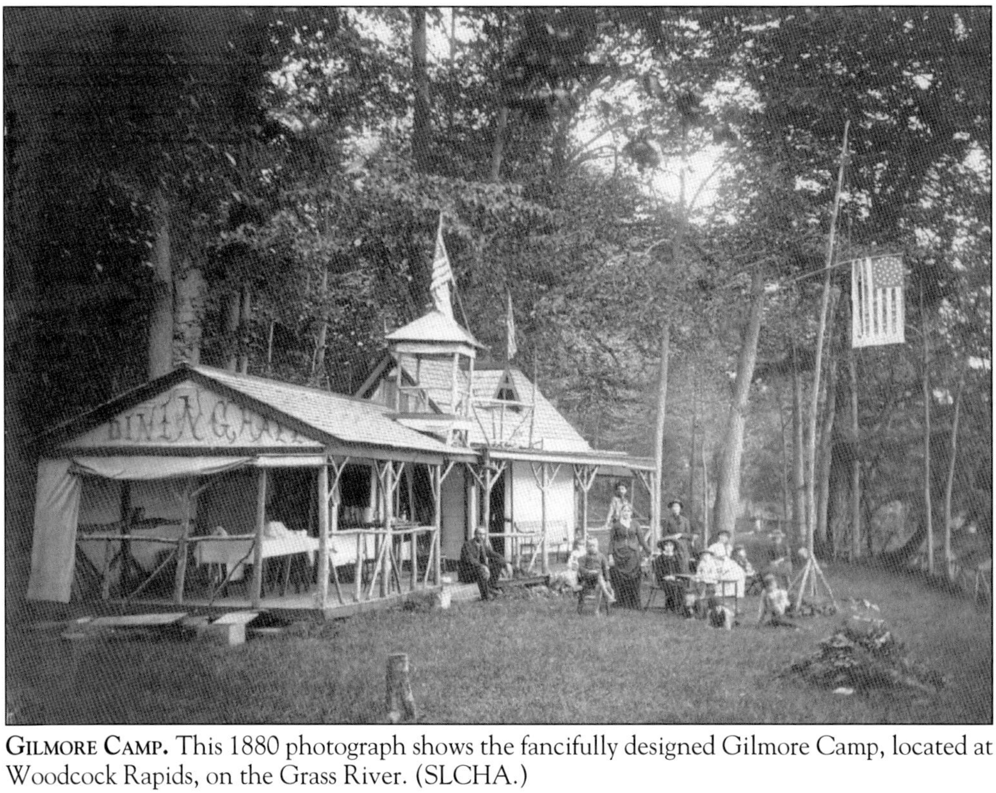

Gilmore Camp. This 1880 photograph shows the fancifully designed Gilmore Camp, located at Woodcock Rapids, on the Grass River. (SLCHA.)

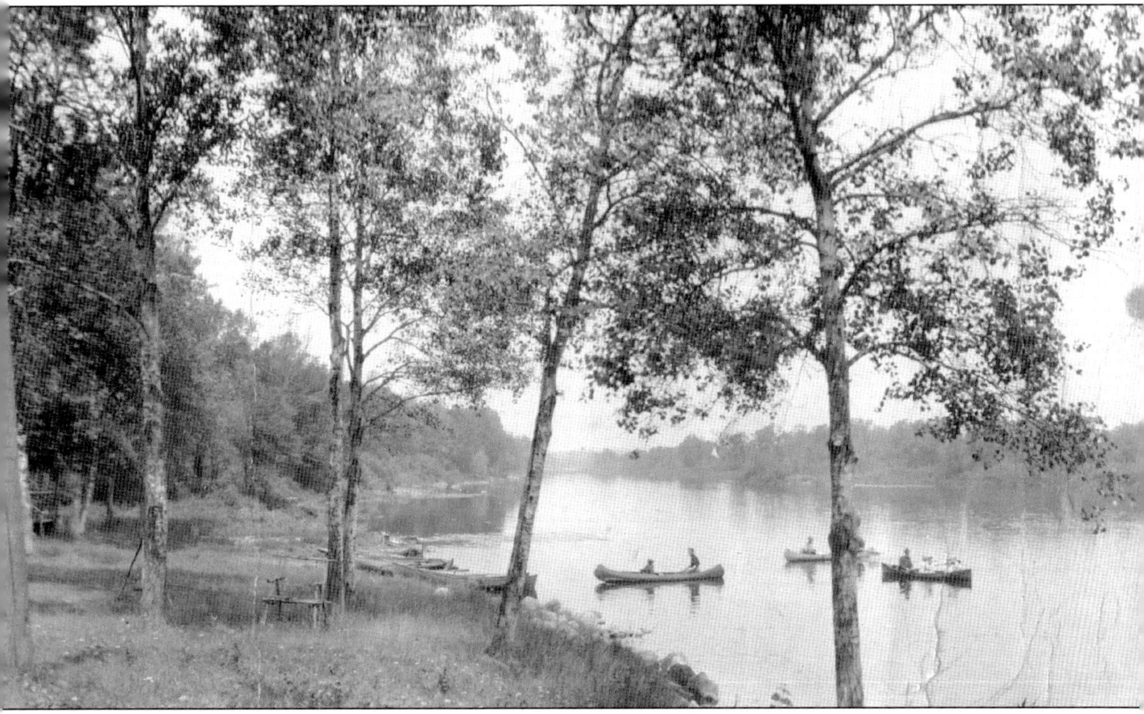

photograph. One of the automobiles is identified as a 1907 model. (SLCHA.)

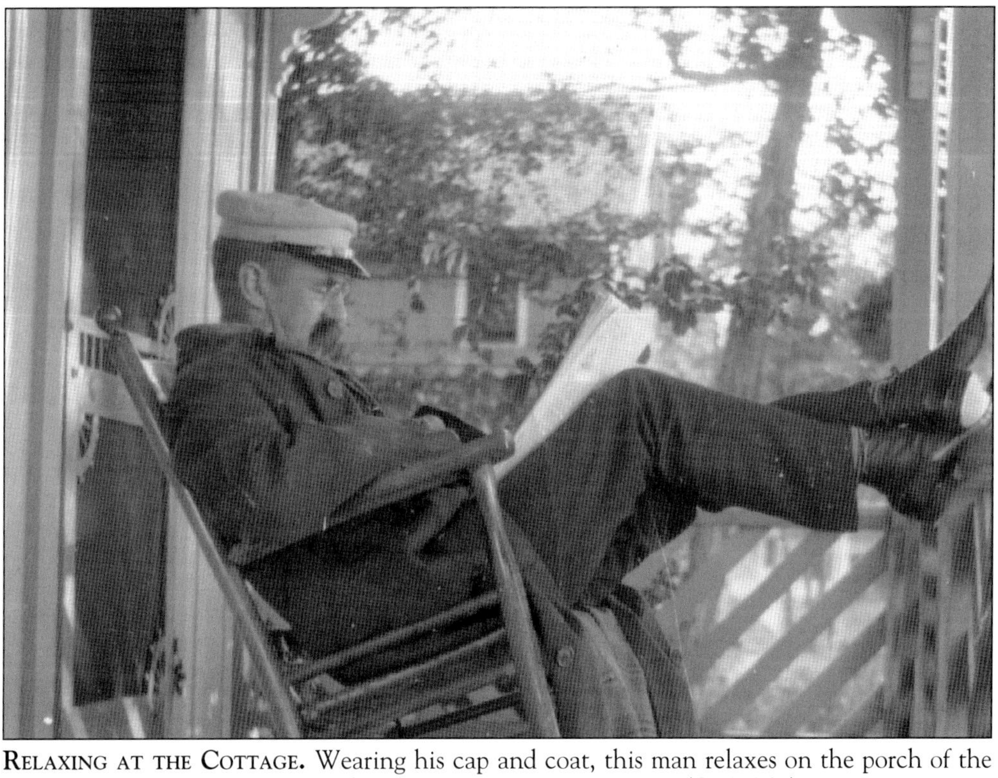

RELAXING AT THE COTTAGE. Wearing his cap and coat, this man relaxes on the porch of the Stevens Cottage, Edgewater, on the St. Lawrence River in 1901. (SLCHA.)

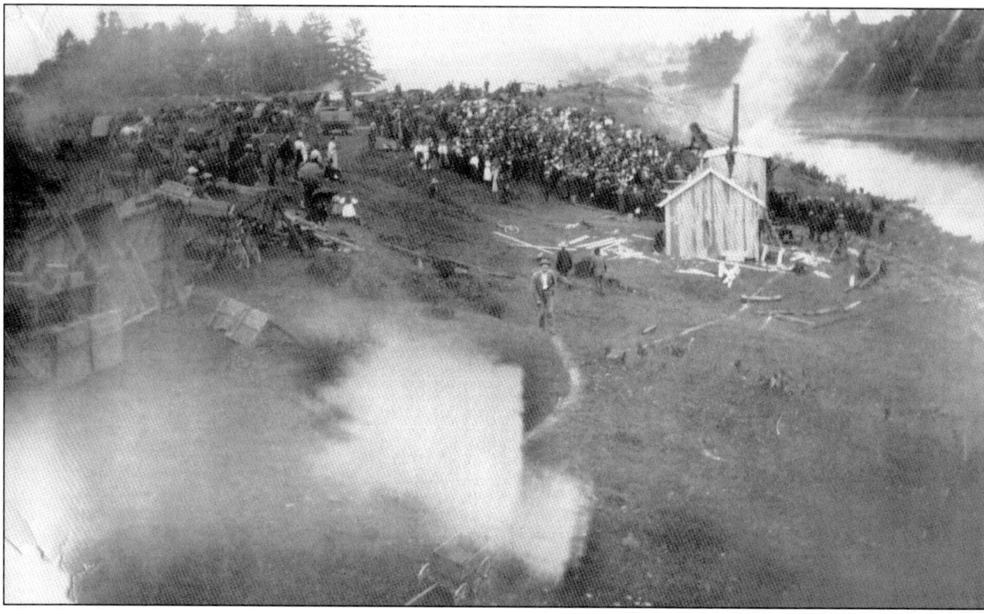

THE DEDICATION OF THE POWER CANAL AT MASSENA, AUGUST 11, 1897. Originally envisioned as a navigation route around the Long Sault Rapids on the St. Lawrence, the canal was constructed between the St. Lawrence and the Grass Rivers to capture hydropower and thereby attract industry to Massena. The canal was surveyed in 1897 and completed in 1902. (Courtesy Massena historian.)

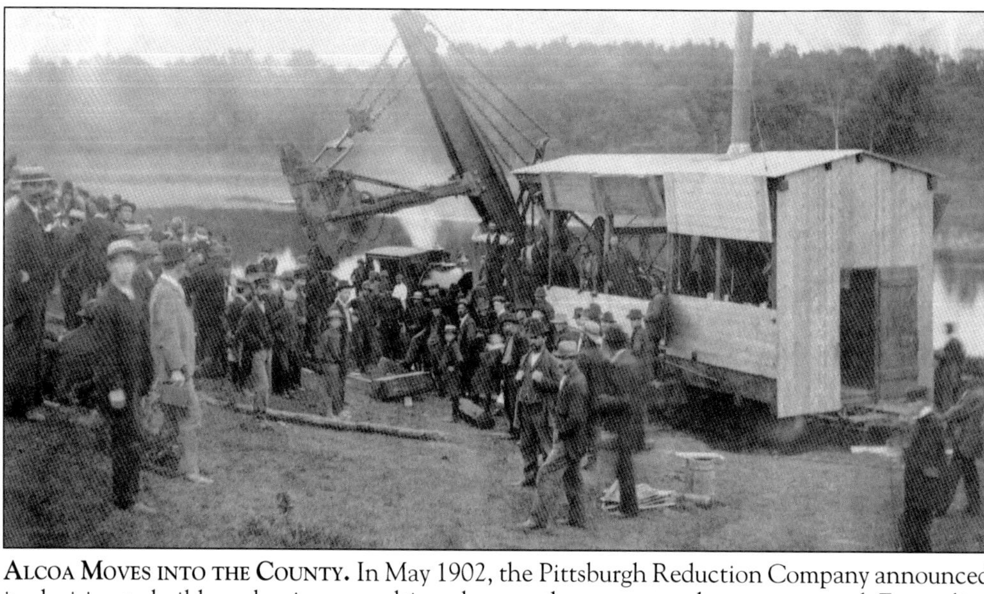

ALCOA MOVES INTO THE COUNTY. In May 1902, the Pittsburgh Reduction Company announced its decision to build an aluminum smelting plant on the near-complete power canal. Expanding on its existing plants at Niagara Falls and Shawinigan Falls, the company sought the cheap hydroelectric power promised at Massena. The company constructed five buildings on a 100-acre site at the terminus of the canal near the powerhouse and, in August 1903, began producing aluminum. The Pittsburgh Reduction Company became the Aluminum Company of America (ALCOA) in 1907 and subsequently acquired the canal from the St. Lawrence Power Company. (Courtesy Massena historian.)

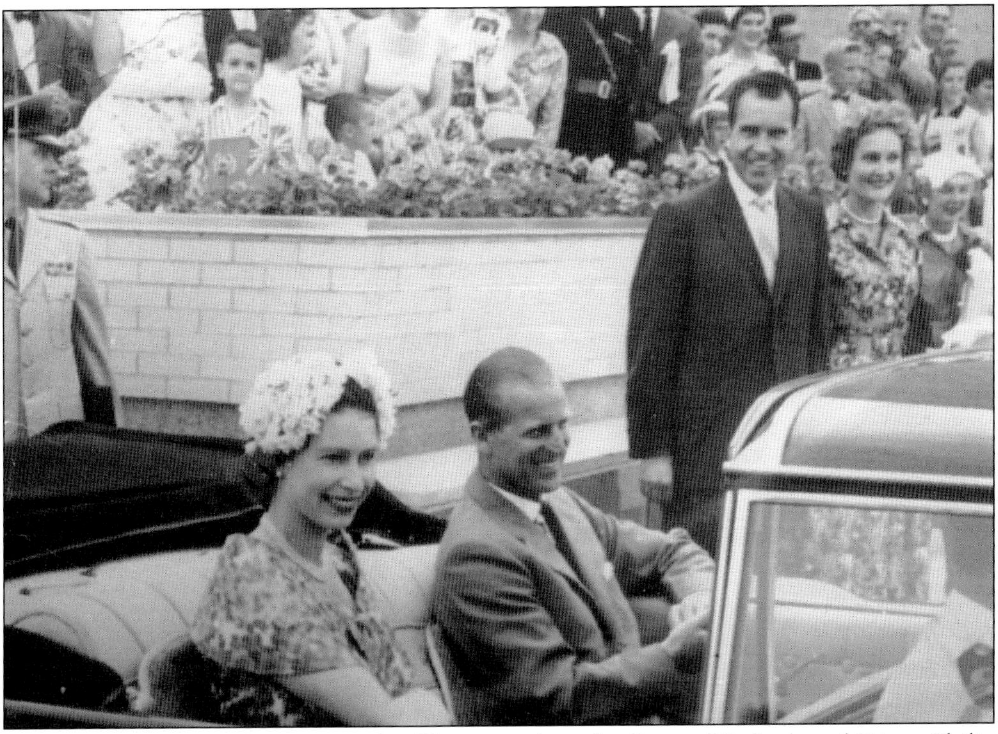

The Opening of the Seaway, 1959. This event brought Queen Elizabeth and Prince Philip to the shores of the St. Lawrence River, along with Vice Pres. Richard Nixon and Mrs. Nixon. (Courtesy the Antique Boat Museum.)

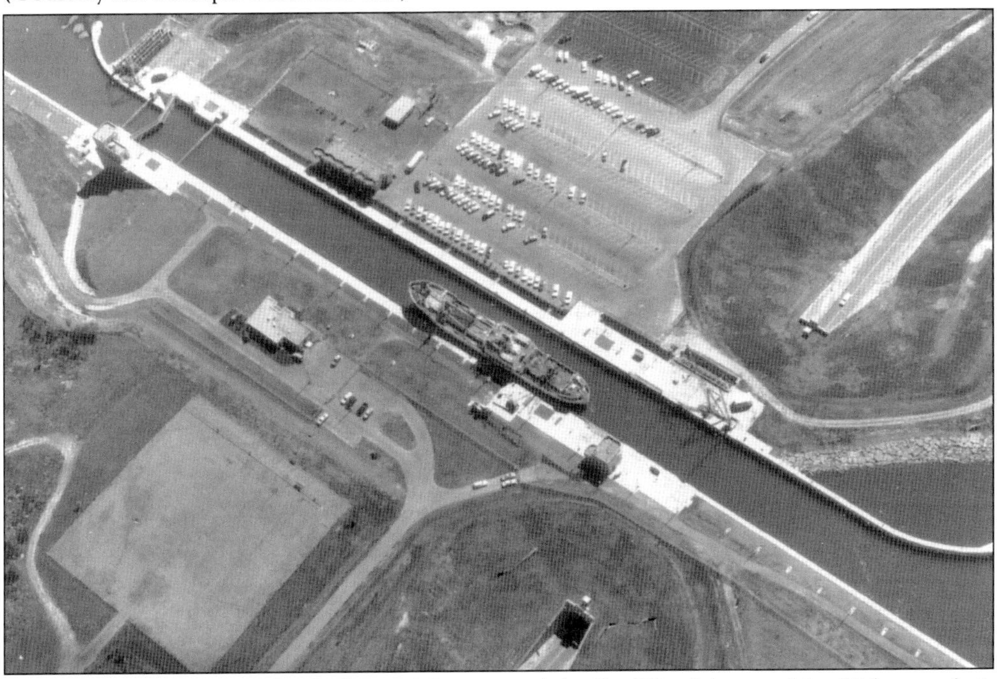

The Eisenhower Lock. This lock near Massena and the Snell Lock lowers ships 90 feet on their journey from the Great Lakes to the Atlantic. (Courtesy the Antique Boat Museum.)

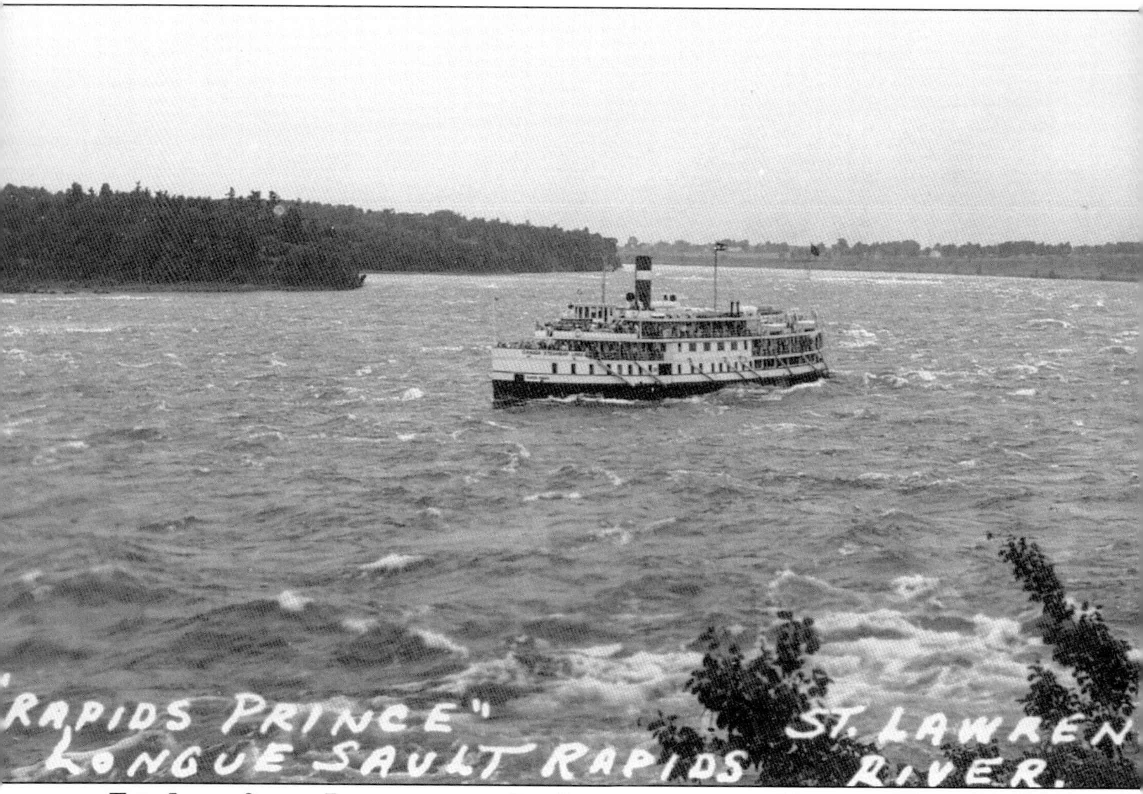

THE LONG SAULT RAPIDS IN THE ST. LAWRENCE, BELOW MASSENA. These rapids were bypassed by the construction of the St. Lawrence Seaway in the 1950s, allowing ships to make the journey from Duluth to Montreal without unloading. Before Seaway construction, cargo was unloaded at Ogdensburg and transported by rail or reloaded on ships below the rapids. Smaller boats, such as this passenger steamer, were able to run the rapids in relative safety. (SLCHA.)

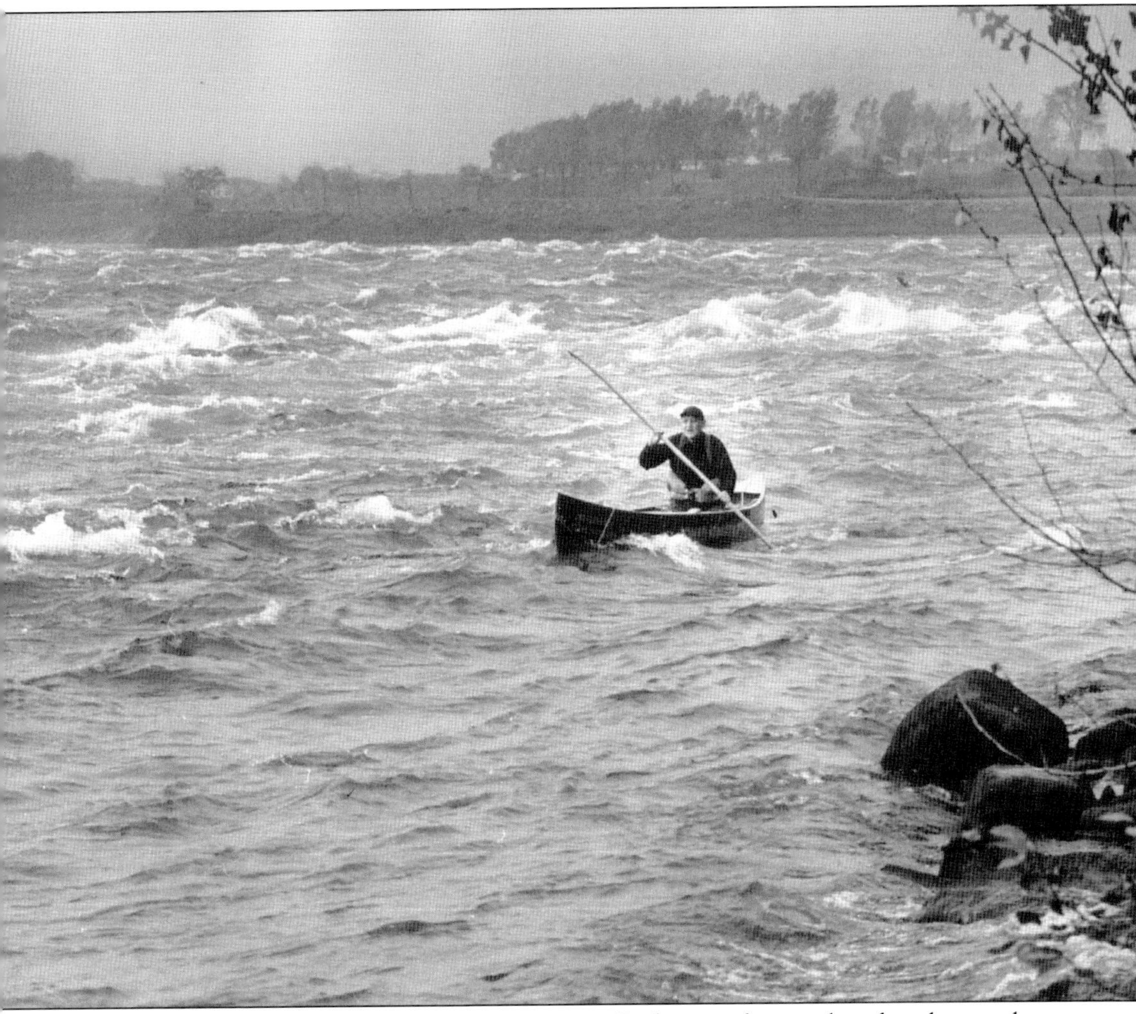

HOMER DODGE, A NATIVE OF OGDENSBURG. Homer Dodge was frequently referred to as the Dean of American canoeing. In 1958, after a career spanning nearly five decades, during which he was a physics professor, head of the physics department, and dean of the graduate school at the University of Oklahoma, and president of Norwich University, Dodge realized his longtime dream to take on the Long Sault Rapids in his canoe. The St. Lawrence Seaway project was going to calm those rapids; so, in October 1956, at the age of 69, Dodge ran the Long Sault in his red Grumman canoe. (Courtesy the Antique Boat Museum.)

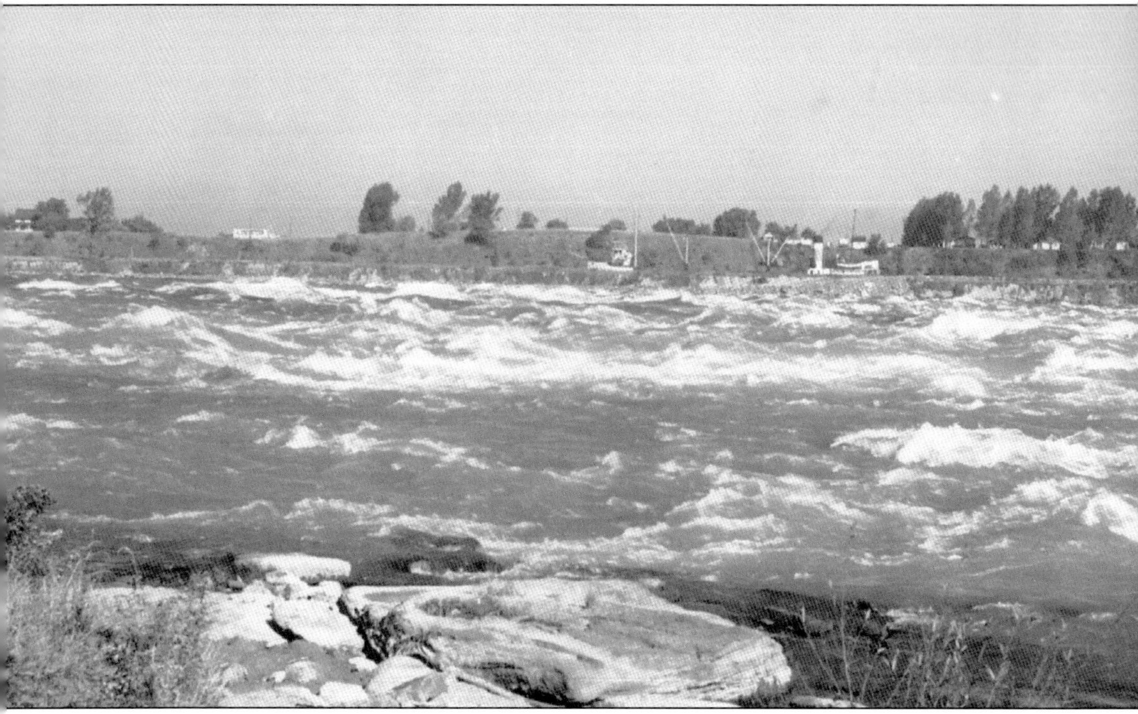

A Ship in the Cornwall Canal Bypassing the International Rapids. The rapids were soon to be pumped dry during stage II construction at Long Sault Rapids in 1956. (Power Authority of the State of New York photograph, courtesy the Antique Boat Museum.)

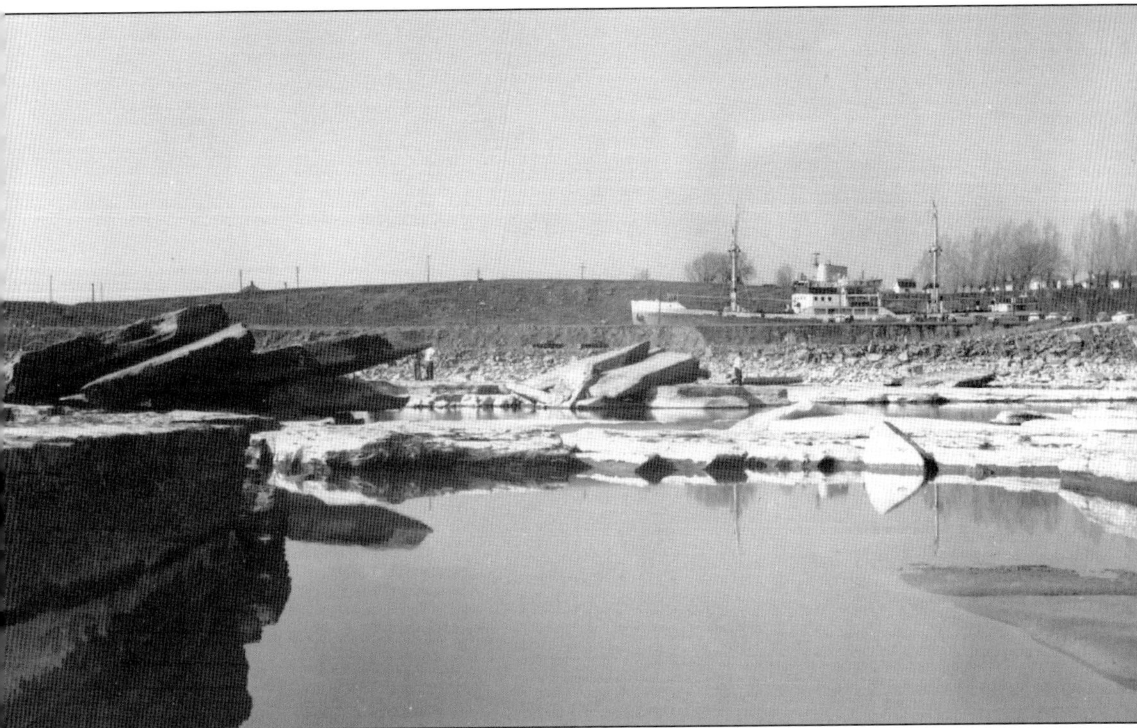

THE CORNWALL CANAL. A ship sails through beside what was formerly the most turbulent section of the Long Sault Rapids in 1957. (Power Authority of the State of New York photograph, courtesy the Antique Boat Museum.)

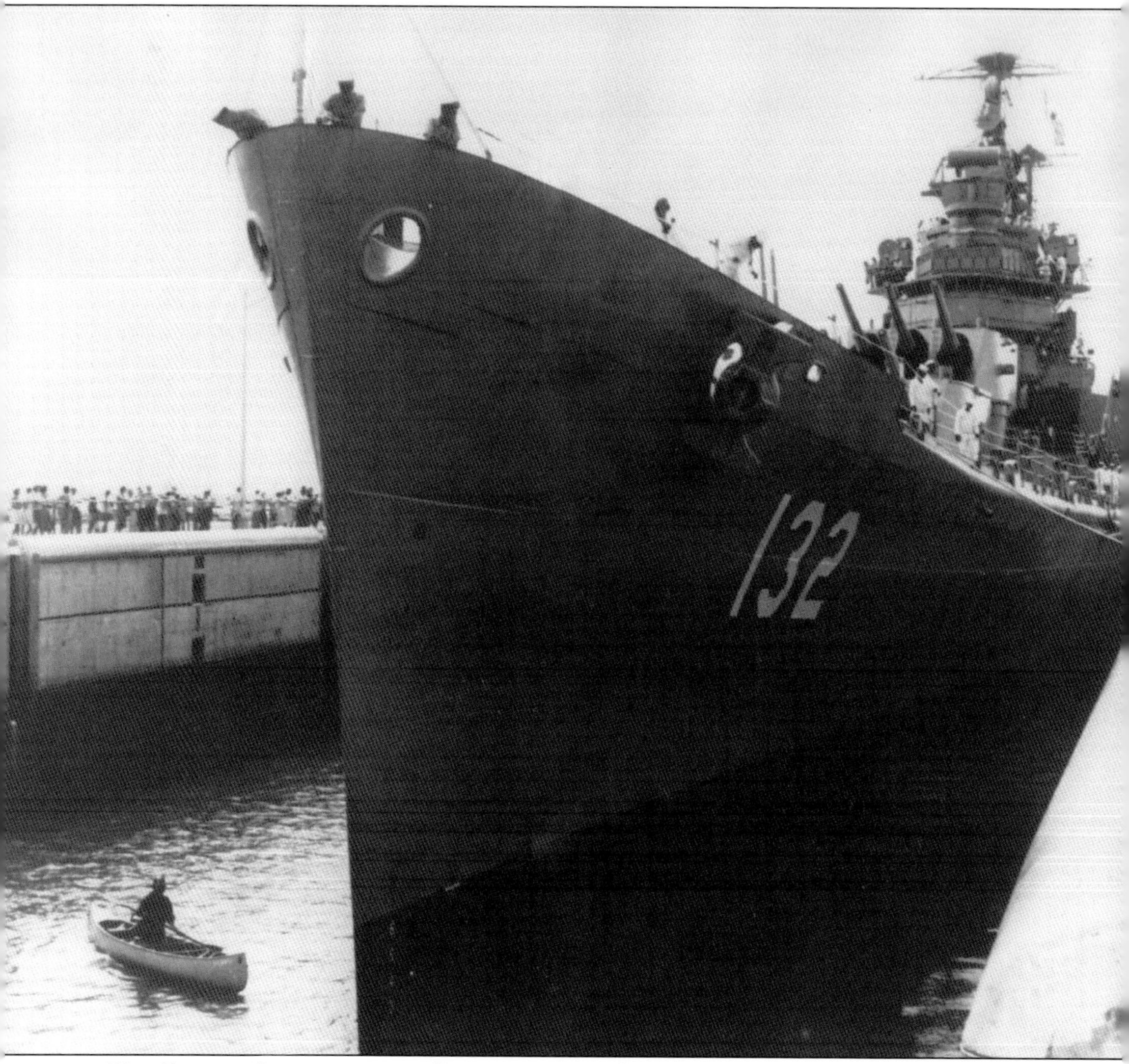

The Formal Opening of the Seaway, 1959. The U.S. Navy invited Homer Dodge aboard the heavy cruiser *Macon* as a spectator during the trip from Boston to Chicago through the new system. On its return, the 657-foot *Macon* was escorted through the lock by the 72-year-old Dodge in his 15-foot canoe. (Courtesy the Antique Boat Museum.)

Five

Partners on the Land

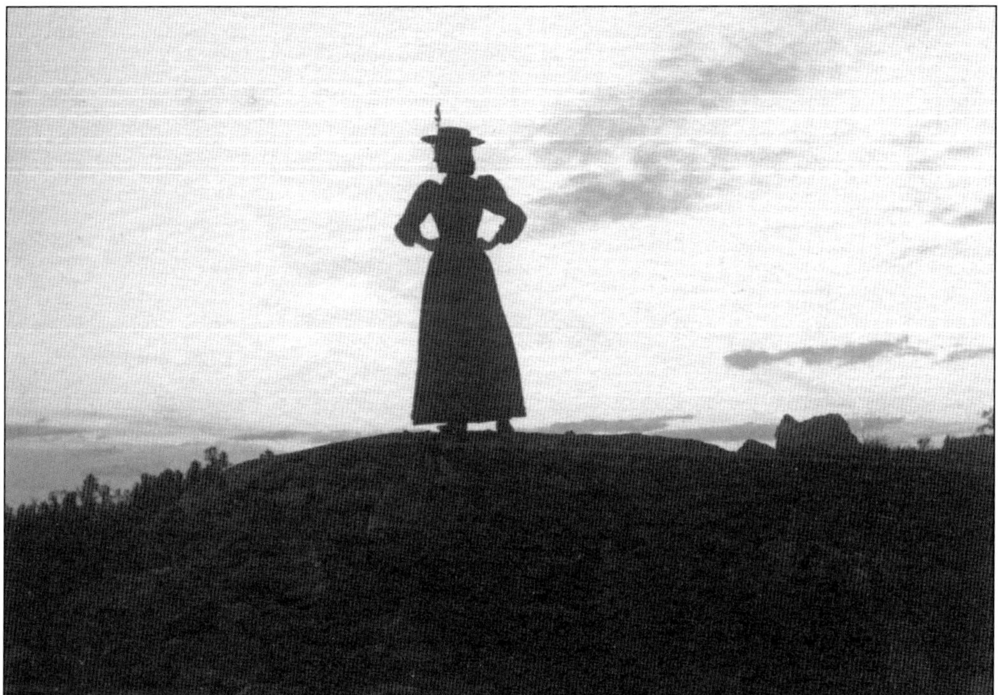

Partnership. Men and women each brought their own strengths, but it was their cooperation that enabled them to successfully tackle the wilderness and begin to build a new life in a new land. (SLCHA.)

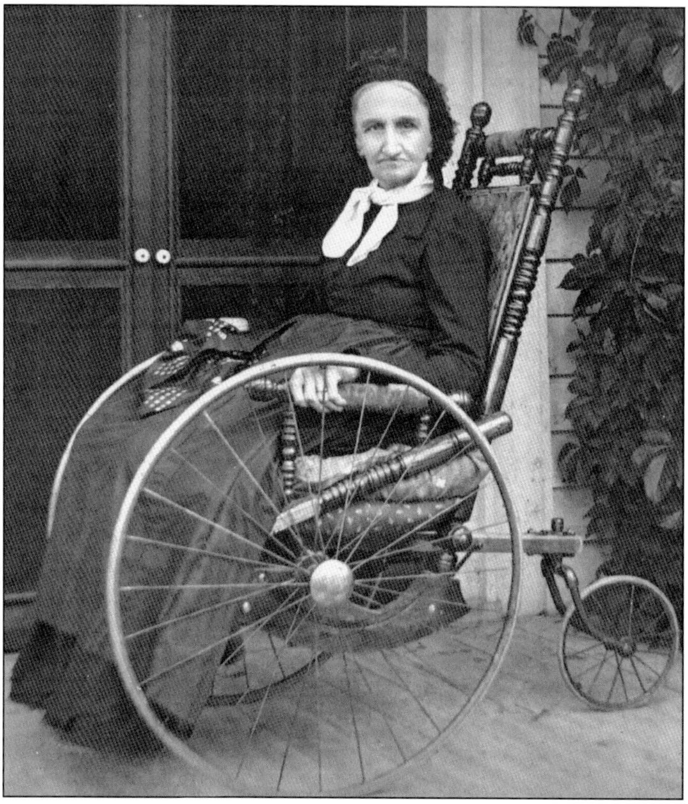

SALLY SNYDER SNYDER. The wife of John Samuel Snyder was not his blood relation, though her maiden name was Snyder. (SLCHA.)

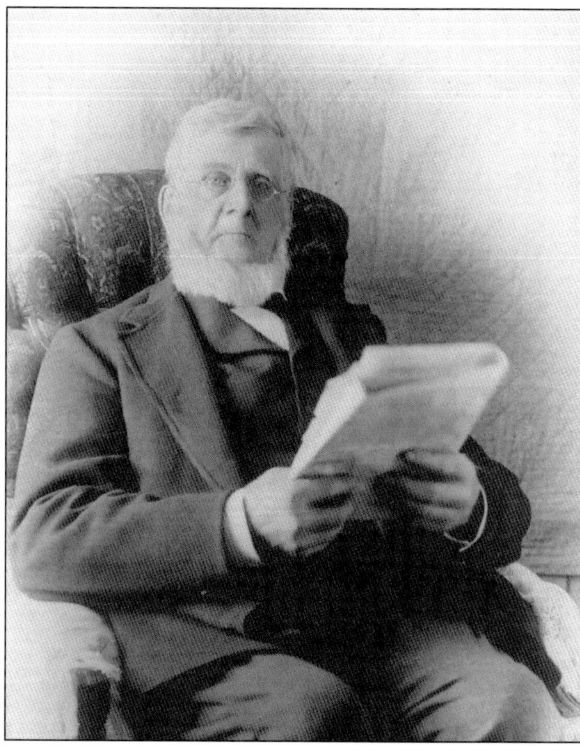

JOHN SAMUEL SNYDER. John Samuel Snyder was the husband of Sally Snyder. (SLCHA.)

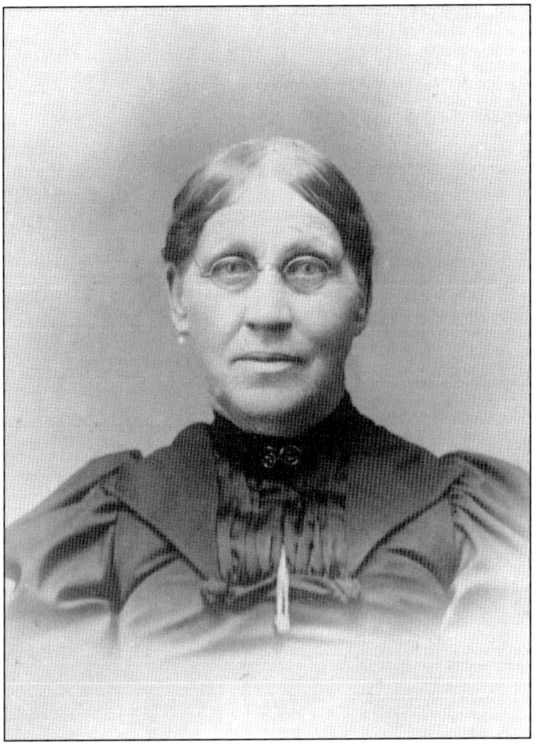

Sarah Billings, Wife of George Billings. "Mrs. Billings was highly esteemed by all who knew her. She was a model wife and mother, always looking to the wants of others, affectionate, self-sacrificing, kind-hearted, and true."—*from* the *St. Lawrence Plaindealer* obituary, August 9, 1893. (Courtesy Clare historian.)

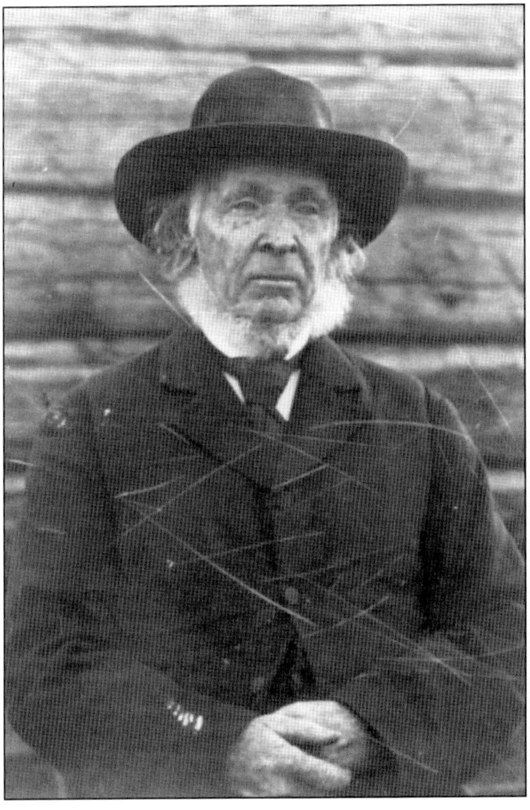

George Billings. George Billings was one of the oldest residents of DeGrasse when he died in 1903 at the age of 78. (Courtesy Clare historian.)

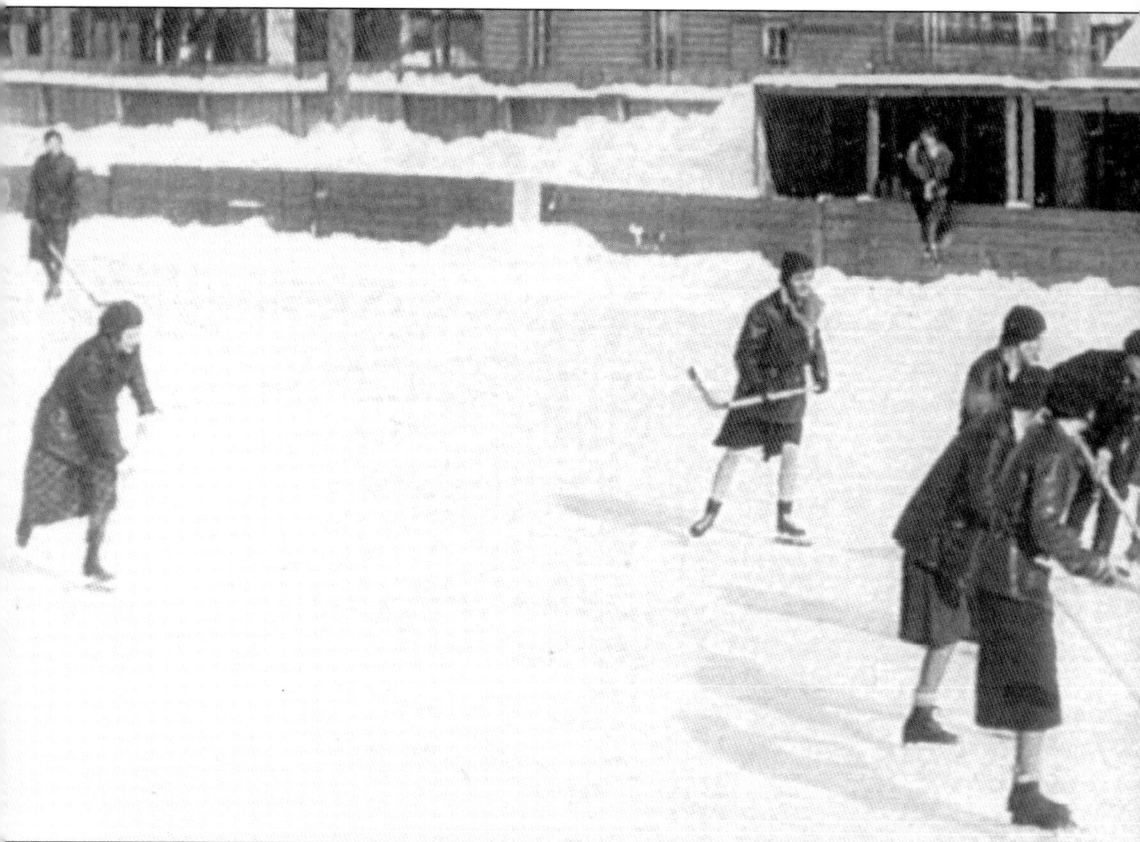

Hockey Practice. The State University of New York at Potsdam women's ice hockey team

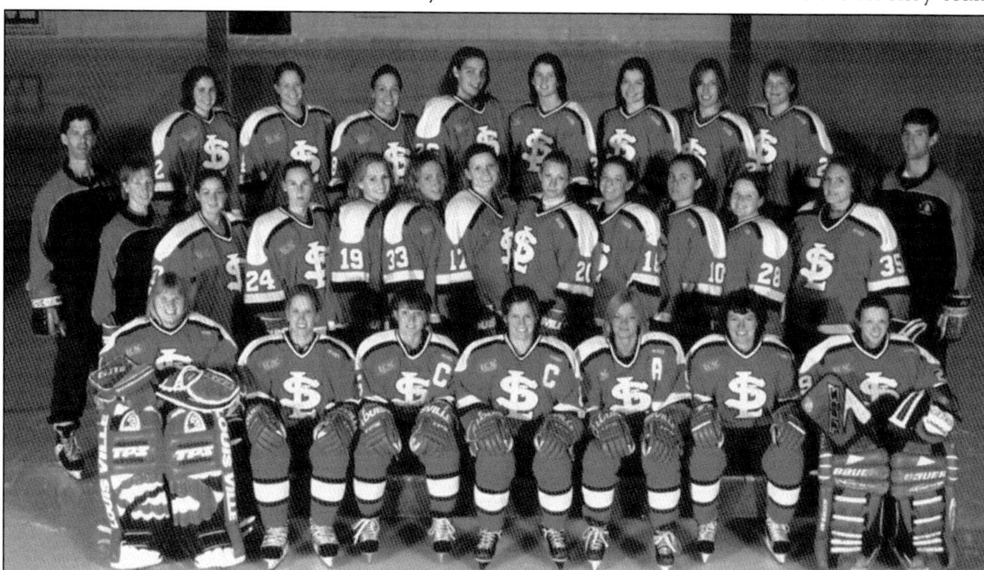

St. Lawrence University Women's Hockey Team, 2000–2001. This team went all the way to the national championship of the first "Frozen Four" women's playoffs in history, losing 4-2 to Minnesota-Duluth. (Courtesy St. Lawrence University.)

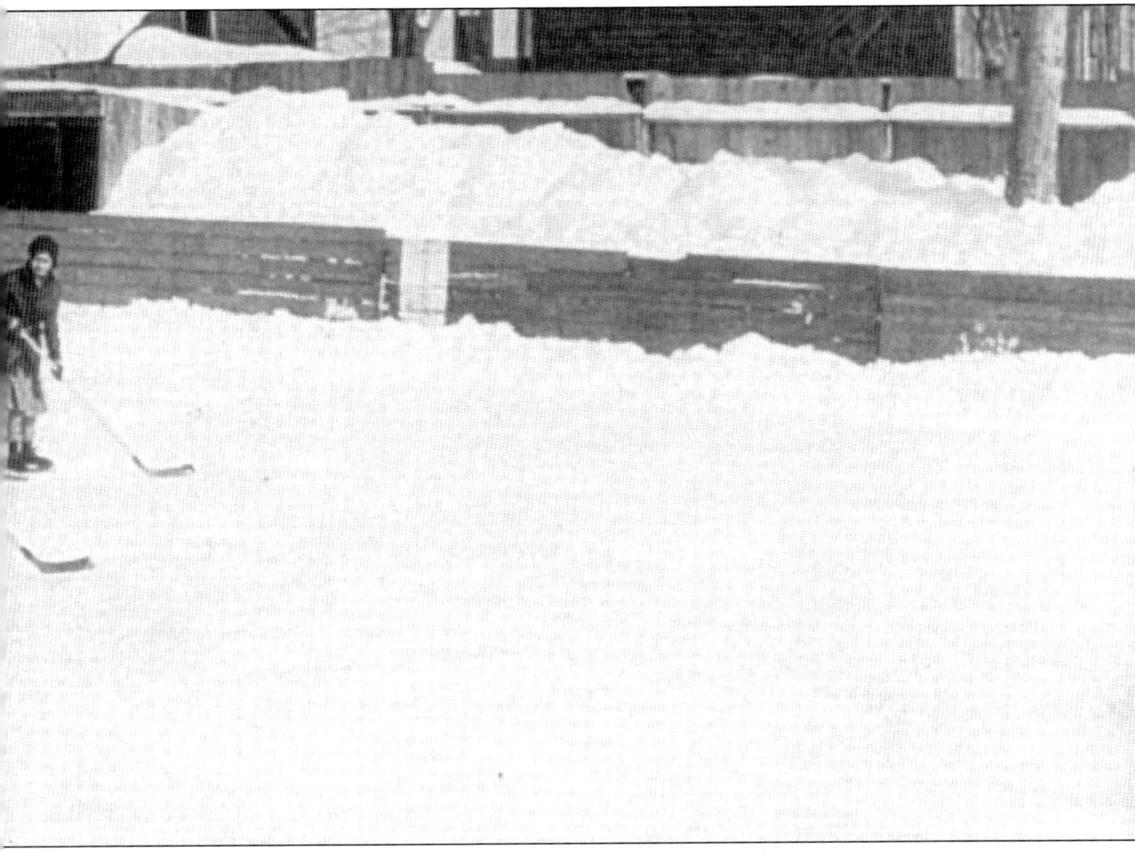

practices *c.* 1931. (Courtesy SUNY Potsdam.)

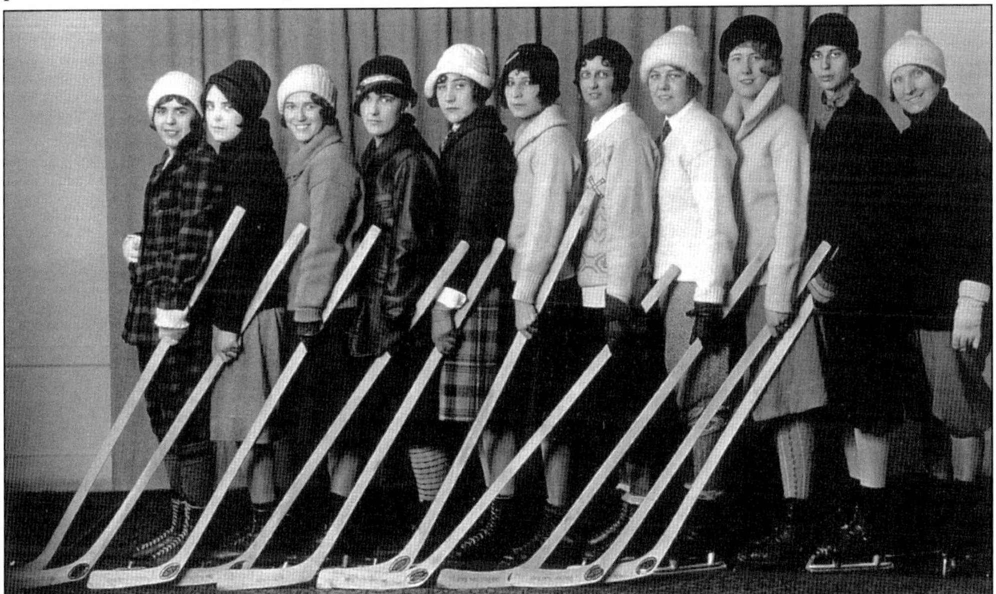

THE WOMEN'S ICE HOCKEY TEAM. The SUNY Potsdam team of 1927 lines up. (Courtesy SUNY Potsdam.)

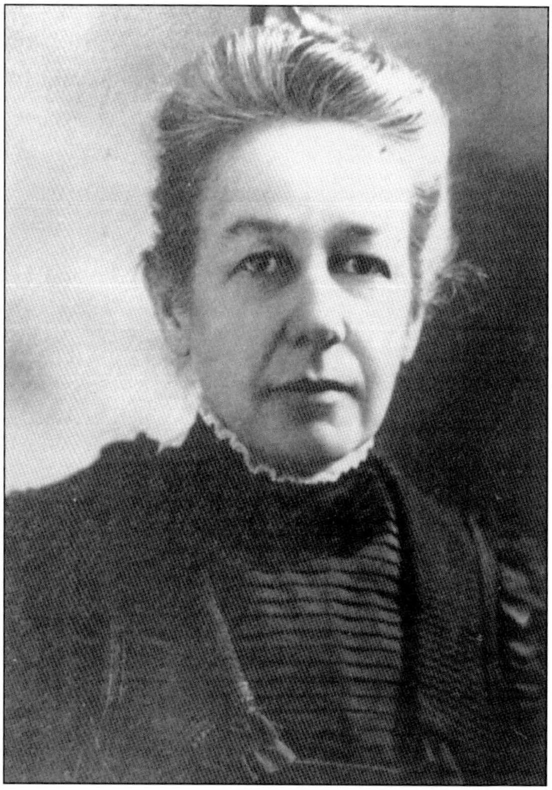

Dr. Lucia Heaton (1856–1944). Lucia Heaton was a Canton physician and the first woman physician in St. Lawrence County. (Courtesy Canton historian, SLCHA.)

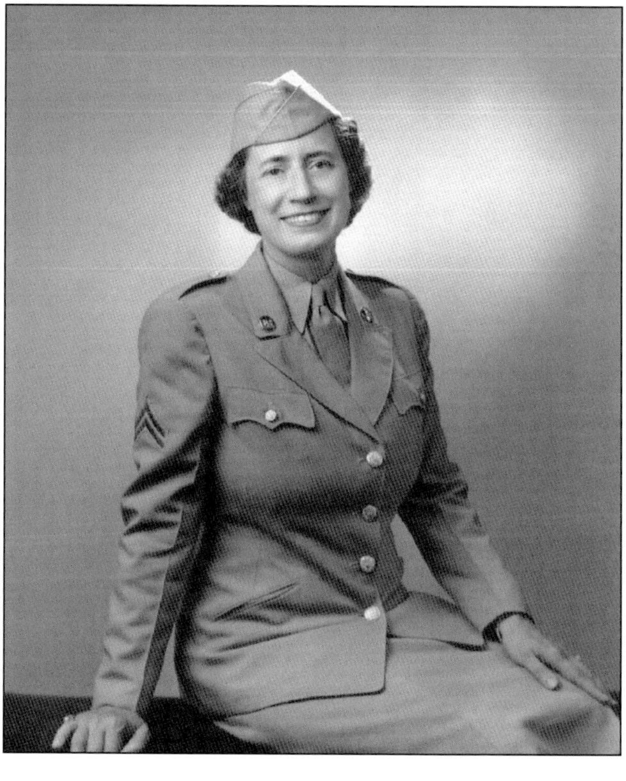

Helen Houston, Women's Army Corps Recruiter, Custom House, Ogdensburg, 1944. Helen Houston was later promoted to sergeant. (SLCHA.)

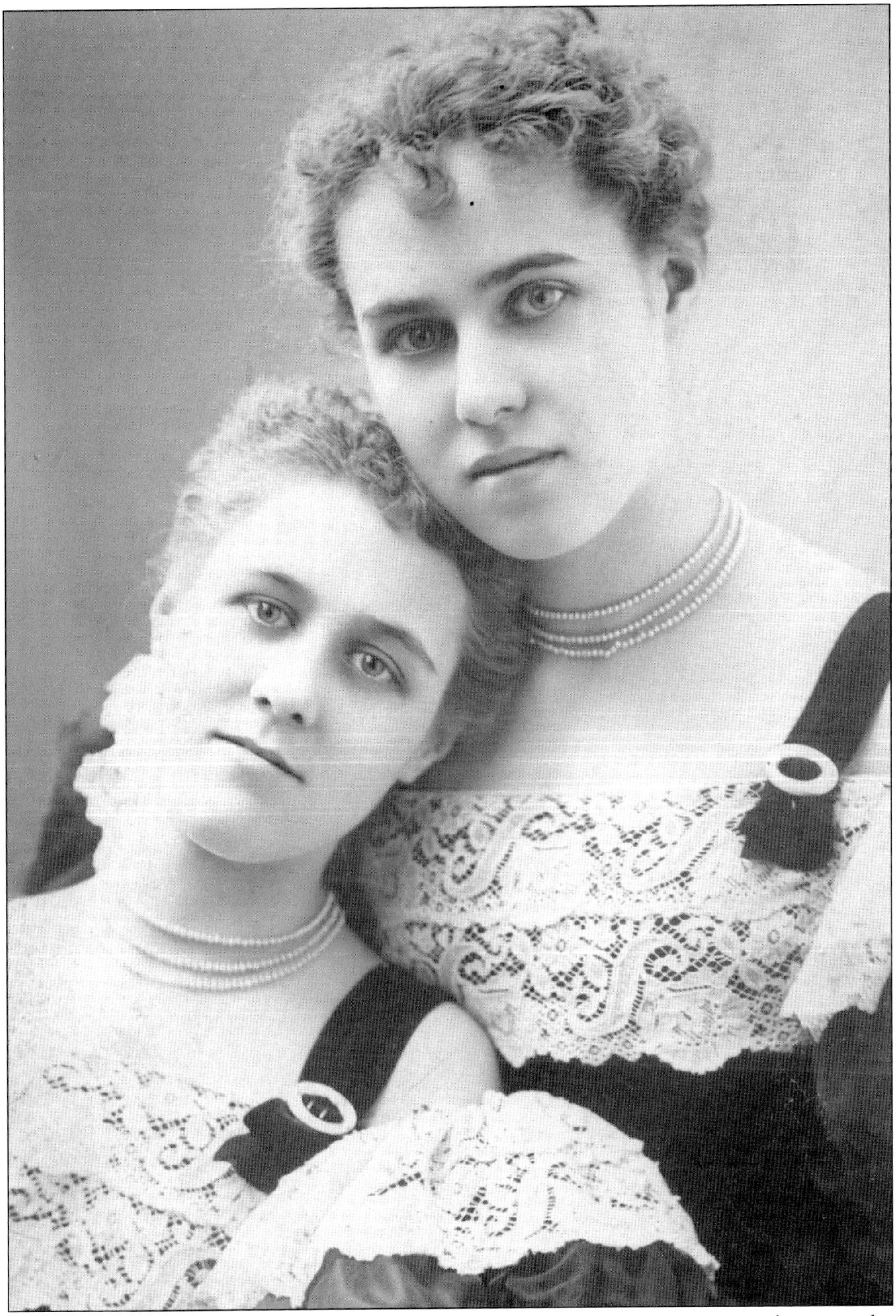

Bessie and Jessie Pickens, Twin Sisters and Heuvelton Singers. Bessie Pickens, on the right, went on to become an opera star. Born in 1878, the twins performed at Windsor Castle for King Edward VII and Queen Alexandra. (SLCHA.)

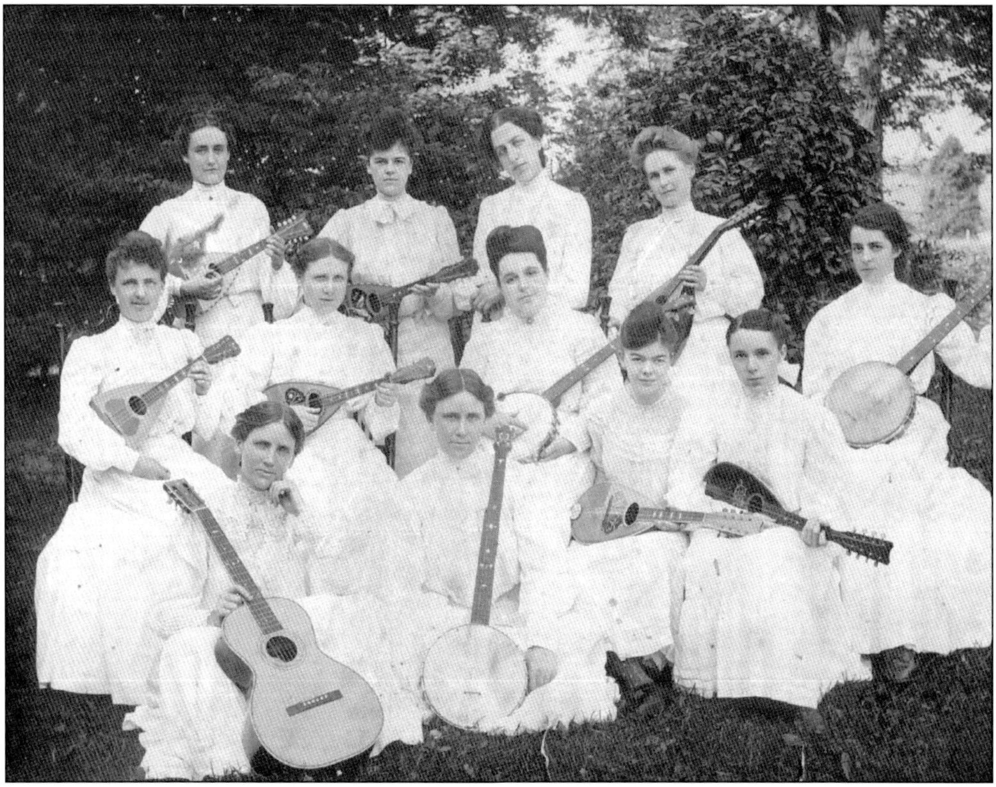

A String Ensemble, c. 1909. This women's musical group performed with a variety of stringed instruments. (SLCHA.)

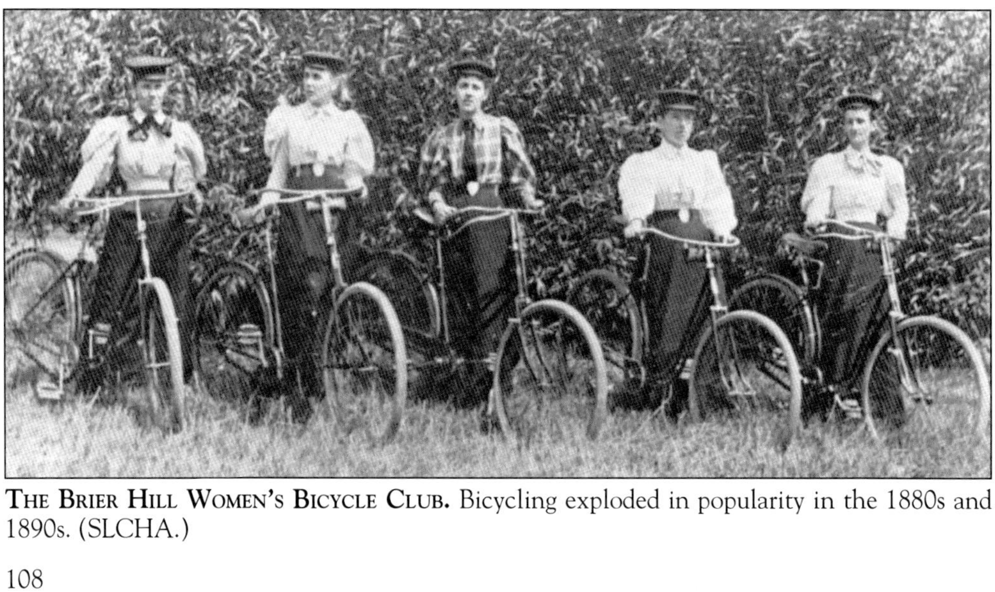

The Brier Hill Women's Bicycle Club. Bicycling exploded in popularity in the 1880s and 1890s. (SLCHA.)

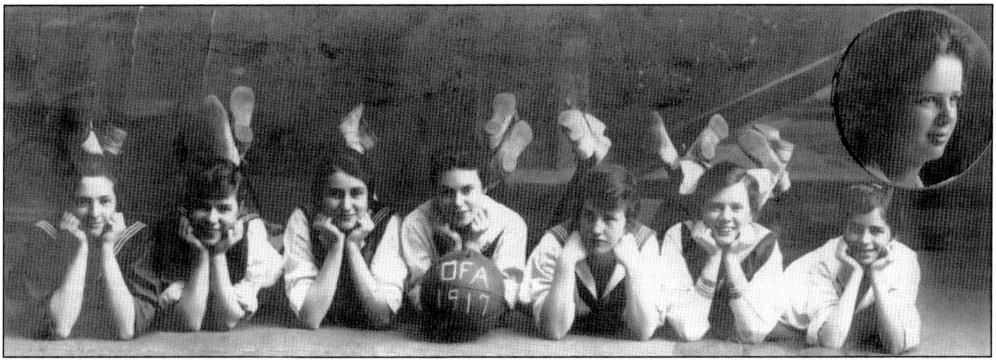

THE OGDENSBURG FREE ACADEMY WOMEN'S BASKETBALL TEAM, 1917. Ogdensburg Free Academy began as the Ogdensburg Academy in 1831, "an international private boarding school for young gentlemen and ladies." Among courses taught at its founding were orthography, reading, mental arithmetic, geography, penmanship, bookkeeping, moral philosophy, ornamental needlework, Latin, Greek, and French. (SLCHA.)

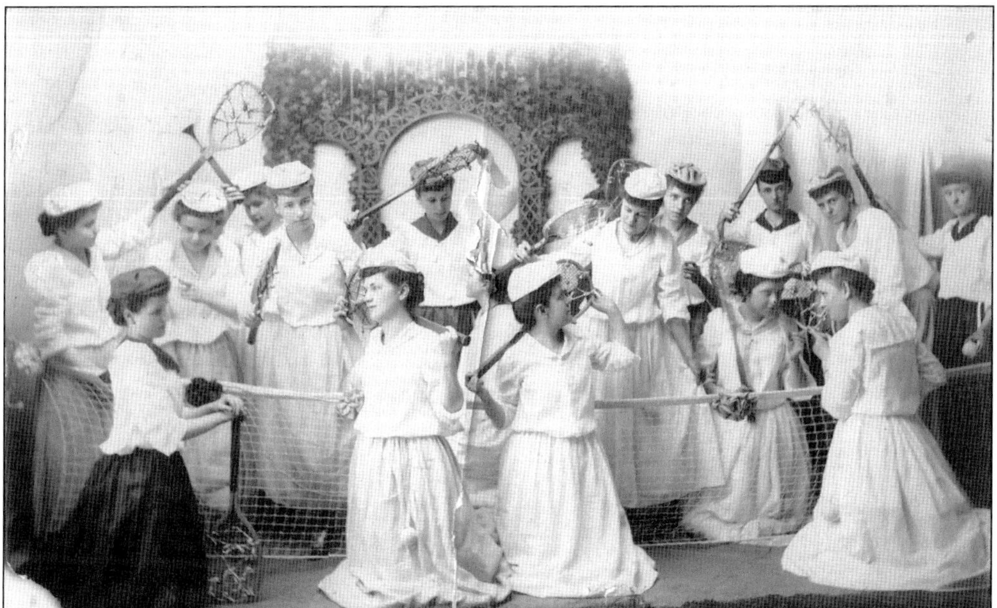

A TENNIS "DUEL" AT MINER HALL, CANTON, 1892. Note how meticulously this photograph is posed. (SLCHA.)

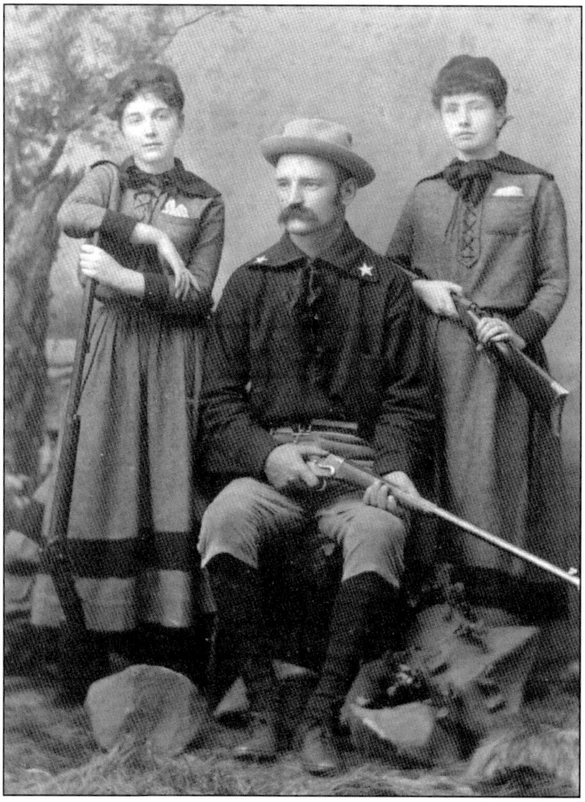

Gun Practice. Learning the use of firearms was important for girls and boys in the days when the family larder depended on the sharpness of one's eye. Anna Stockton and Jessie Judd Mead are photographed here by J. Hitchcock, a woman photographer from Canton, in 1886. (J. Hitchcock photograph, SLCHA.)

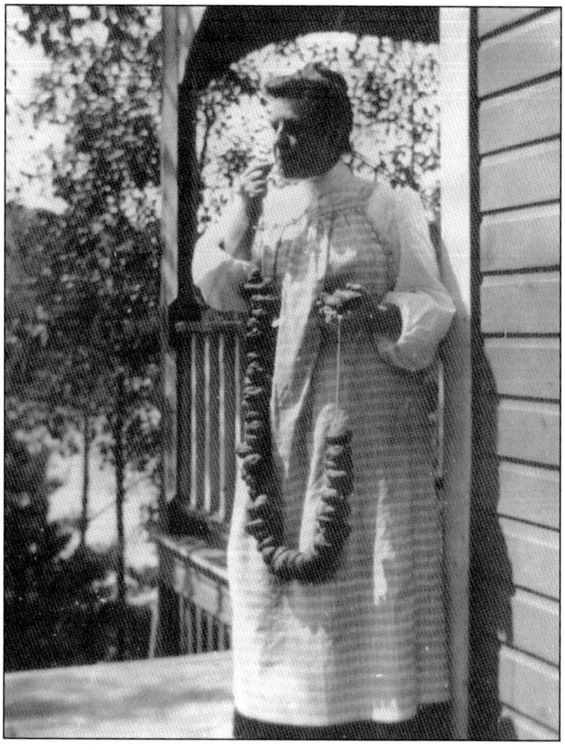

Star Lake, 1905. Perhaps one of the cooks at the Star Lake Inn is holding a string of dried apples or homemade donuts. (SLCHA.)

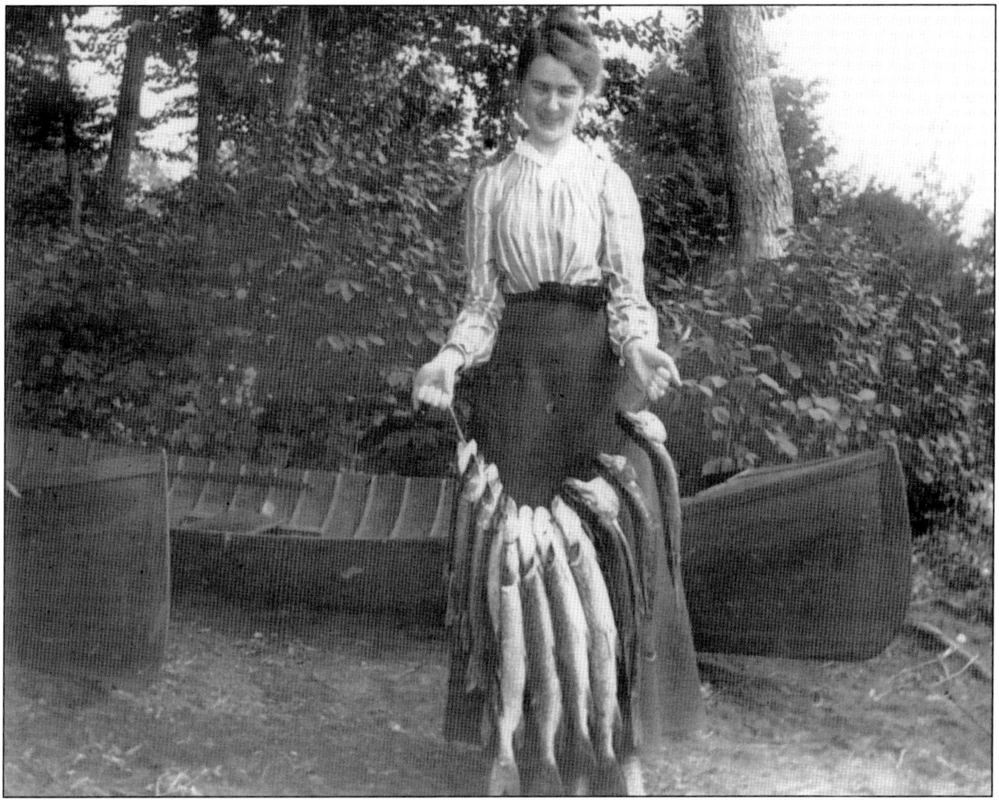

Showing off Her Day's Catch. This was an impressive string for anyone on the Grass River. (SLCHA.)

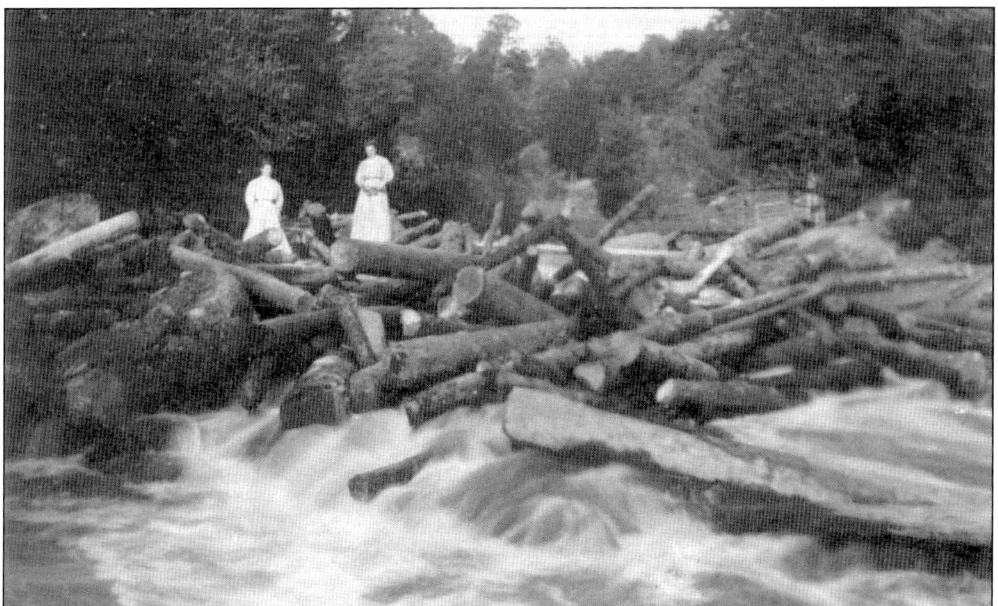

Posing Precariously. Two unidentified women, possibly of the Paro family, take their chances on a logjam for the privilege of having their photographs taken. (SLCHA.)

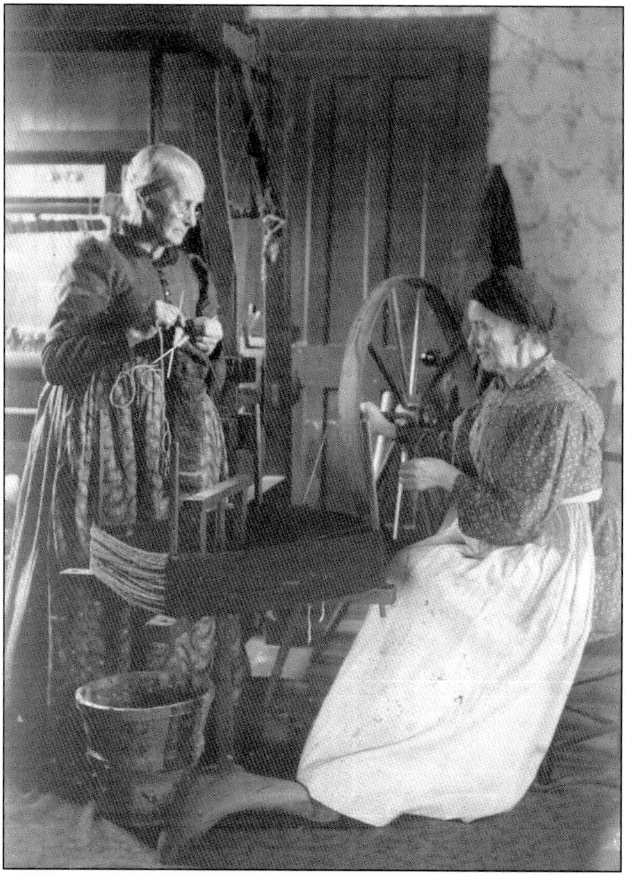

IANTHA HOGEBOOM AND SISTER, SPINNERS. Subsistence living required nearly everything to be provided through the labors of the family. (SLCHA.)

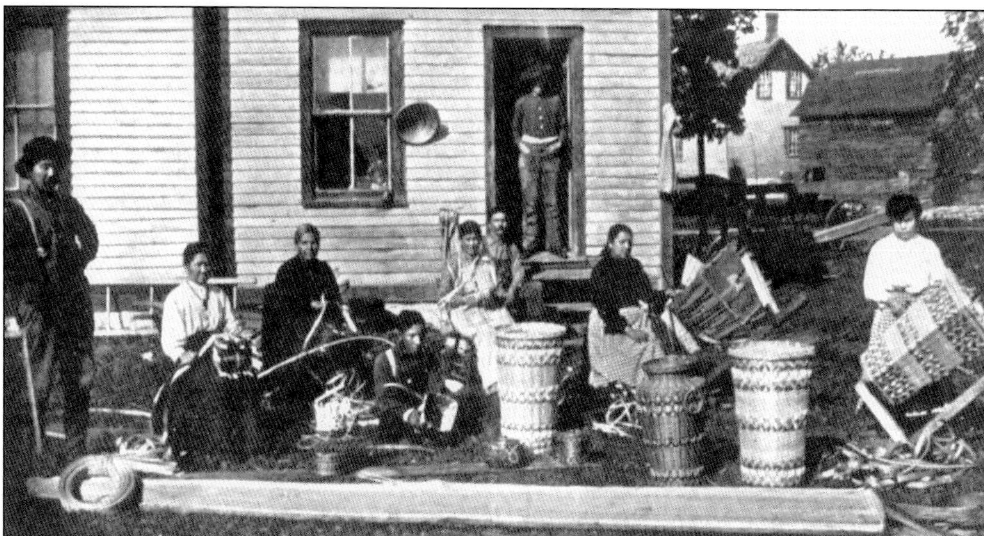

ST. REGIS INDIANS WEAVING ASH SPLINT BASKETS, HOGANSBURG, C. 1905. The Mohawk territory of Akwesasne-St. Regis borders St. Lawrence County to the east. The Mohawk, one of the Five Nations of the Iroquois Confederacy, have lived in the North Country for thousands of years. (SLCHA.)

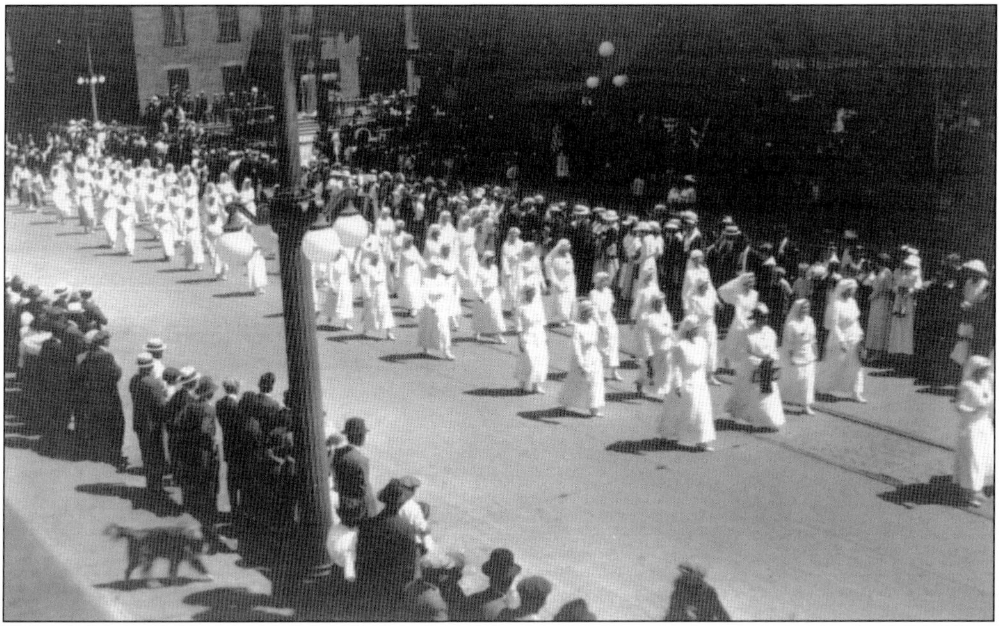

RED CROSS WOMEN MARCHING. When soldiers left Ogdensburg for World War I, the Red Cross women marched. (SLCHA.)

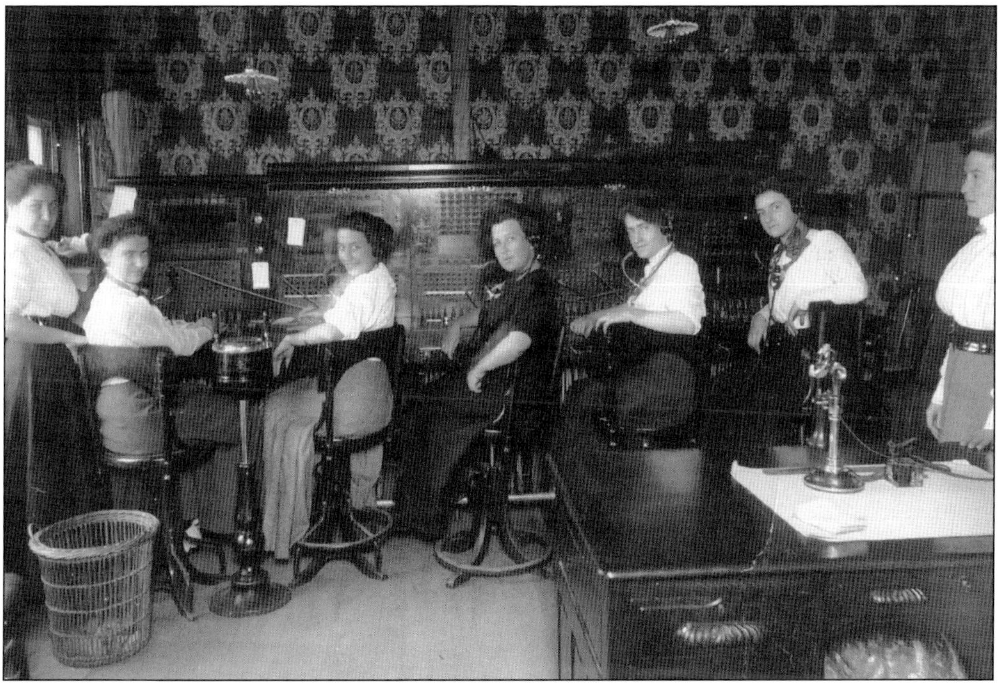

MOUNTAIN HOME TELEPHONE, CENTRAL BLOCK, MAIN STREET, GOUVERNEUR. Photographed, from left to right, are Francis Smith, Rose Plunket, Ina Bauck, Mabel Sheen, Elizabeth Garvin, Ruth Nevins, and Leta Morehouse. (SLCHA.)

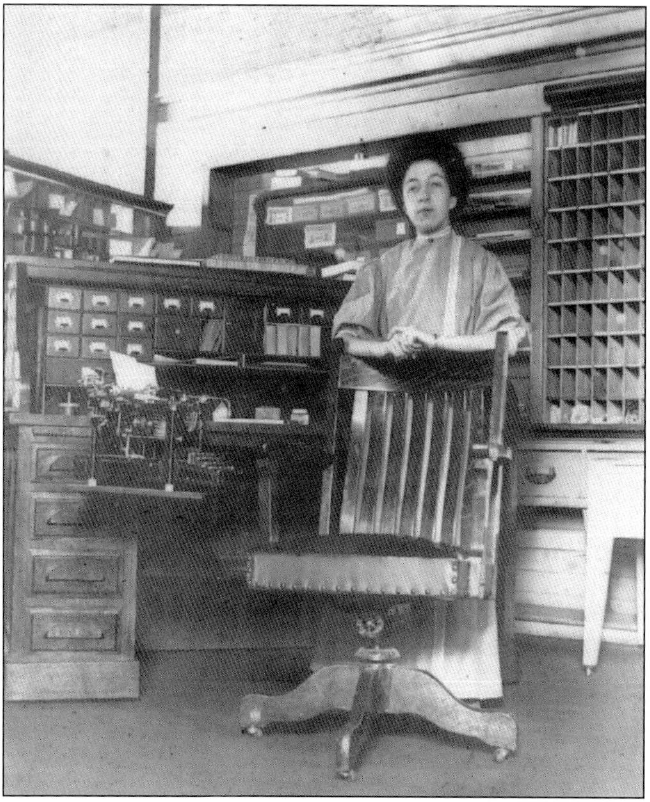

MYRTLE PENNY, ASSISTANT POSTMASTER, DEKALB, c. 1910. About this time, women were not allowed to be officially listed as postmasters; thus, many used their husband's name. (Courtesy DeKalb historian.)

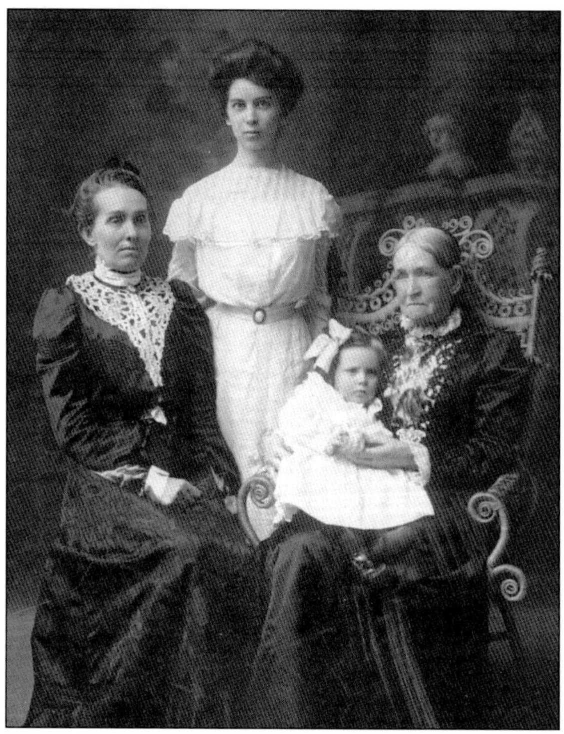

HIGH FINERY. Four generations of women pose in high finery of the period *c.* 1900. (SLCHA.)

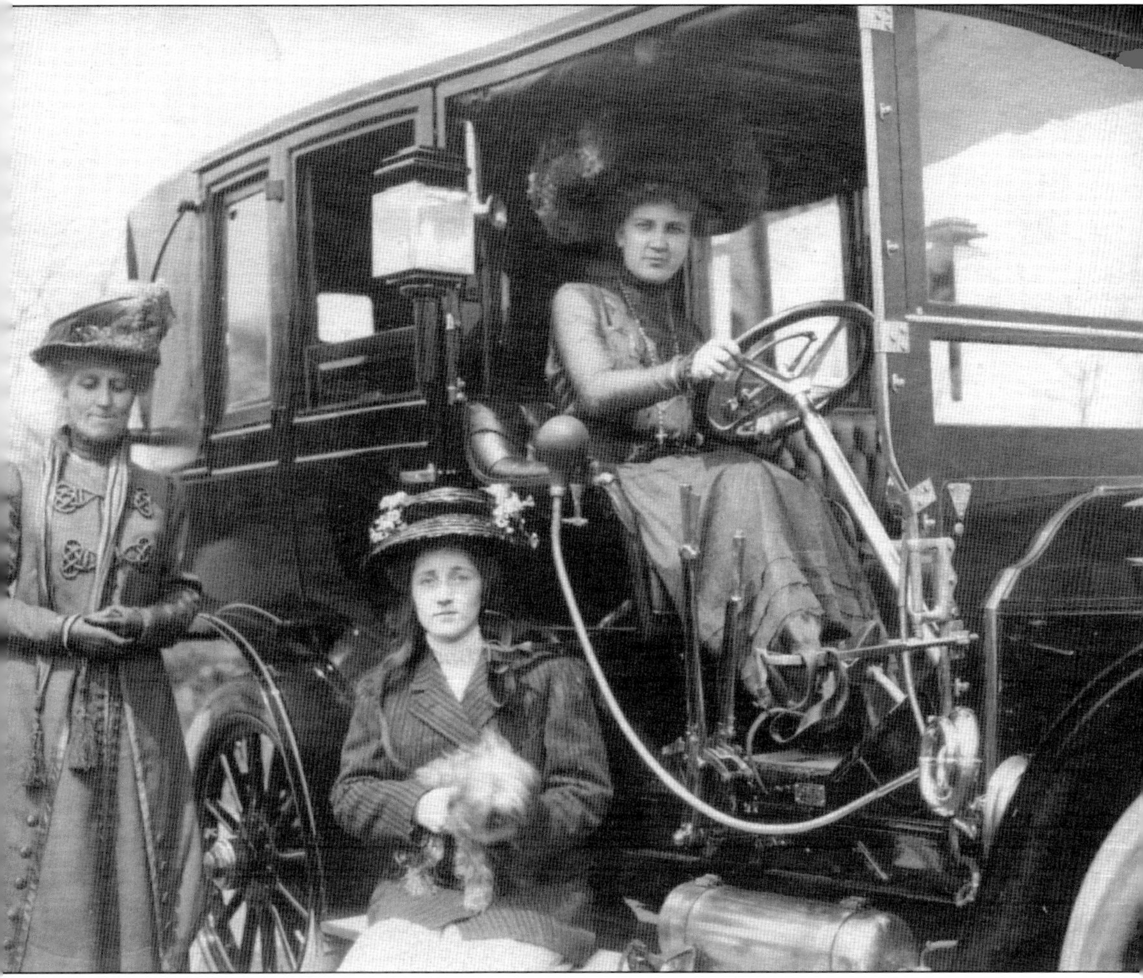

MRS. A. BARTON HEPBURN AND DAUGHTERS CORDELIA AND BEULAH, WITH THE FAMILY'S NEW LIMOUSINE, IN CONNECTICUT. A. Barton Hepburn, a native of Colton, was a businessman, politician, public servant, and philanthropist. The first boy in Colton to go to college, he valued education and endowed seven public libraries in the county, in addition to supporting hospitals, colleges, and universities around the world. He owned timber interests in the town of Clare and was a New York State legislator. He became national bank examiner for New York City and Brooklyn, and was later appointed comptroller of currency by Pres. Benjamin Harrison. He left public life to join Chase National Bank, serving over the years as vice president, president, and chairman of the board. He died in 1922. (SLCHA.)

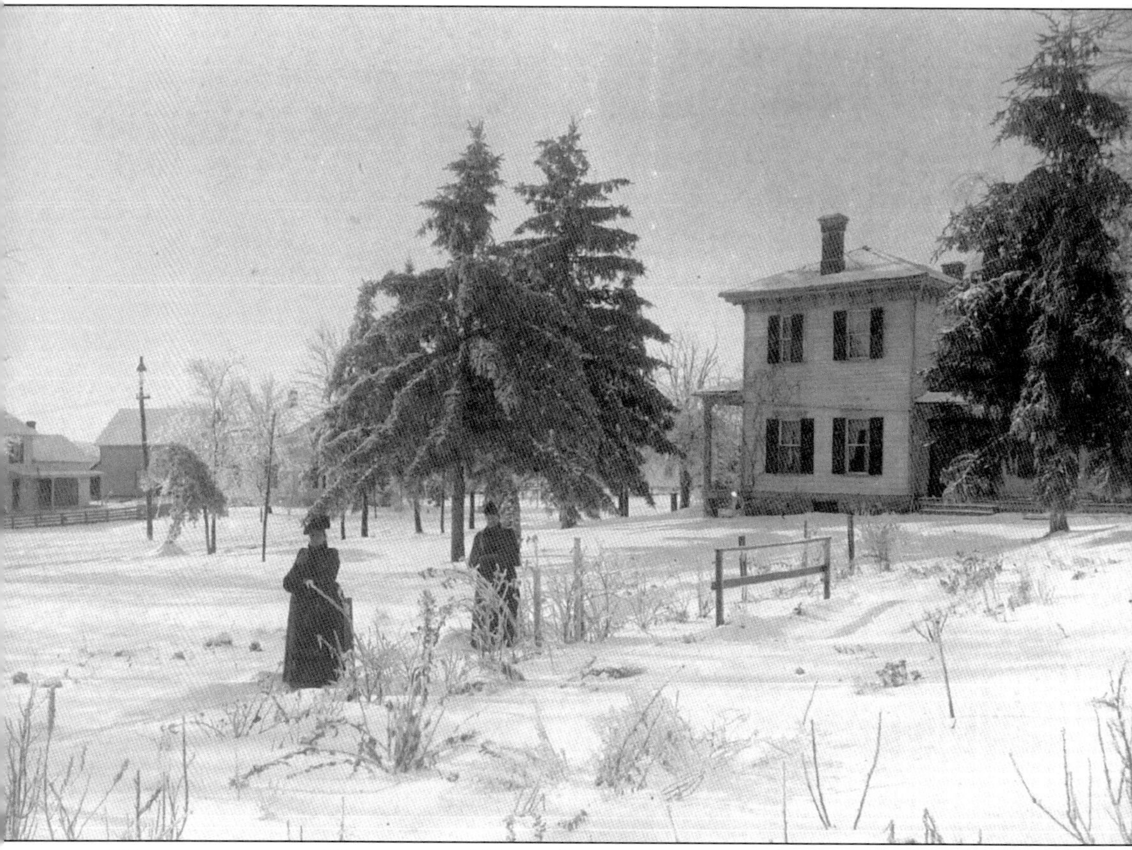

WALKING FROM THE WOODWORTH HOUSE, BARNEY STREET, GOUVERNEUR, EARLY 1900S. Mrs. W.F. Sudds and Mrs. A.C. Woodworth walk from Mrs. Woodworth's house, on Barney Street in Gouverneur, in the early 1900s. (Courtesy Gouverneur Museum.)

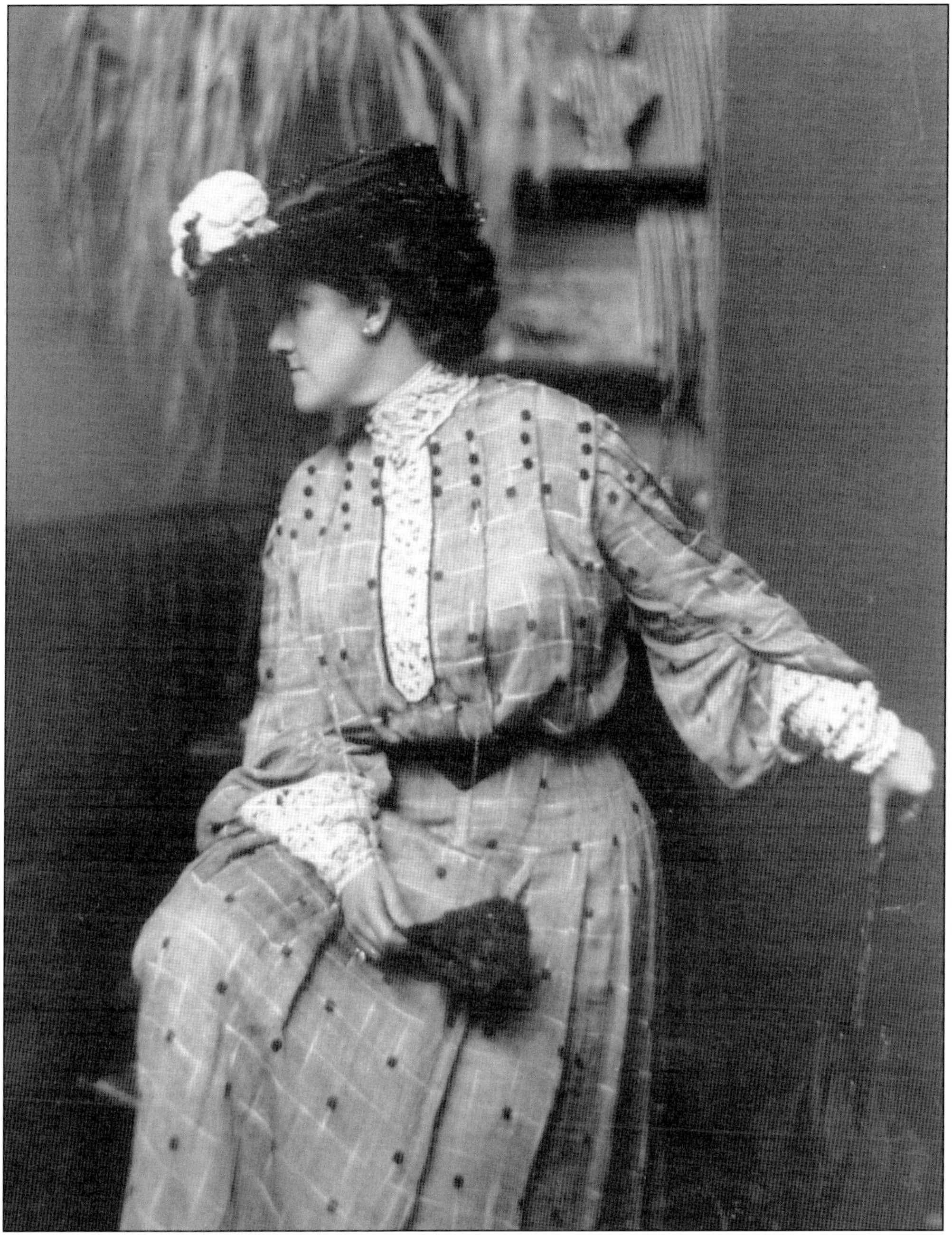

SALLY JAMES FARNHAM, OGDENSBURG NATIVE AND NOTED SCULPTRESS. Frederic Remington was her friend and mentor. Sally James Farnham was 32 when she decided to try her hand at sculpture, and she went on to a distinguished career. (Courtesy Frederic Remington Art Museum.)

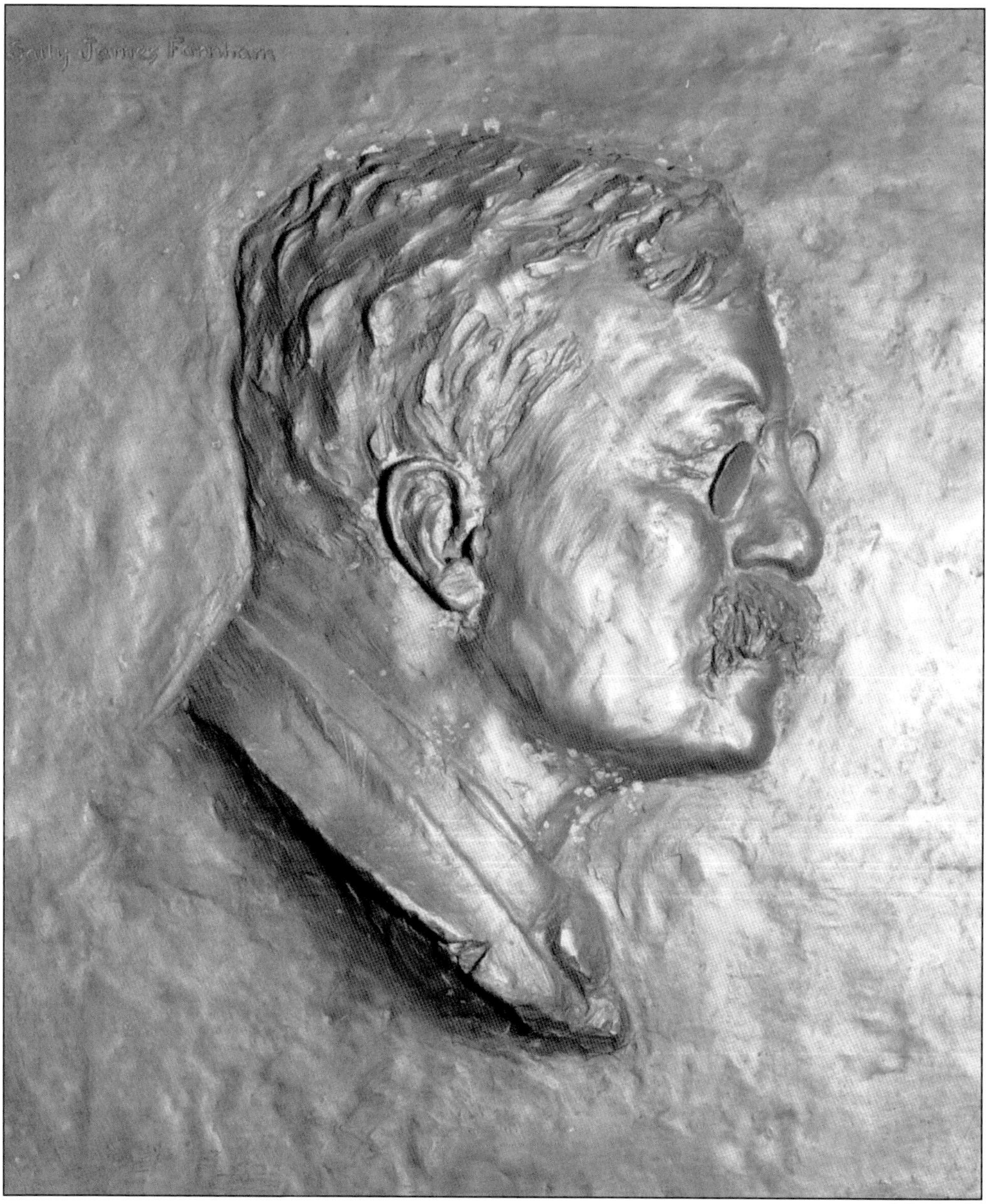

Sally James Farnham's Bas-relief of Pres. Theodore Roosevelt, 1906. She made the model for this piece during a single brief meeting of the president and his cabinet. (Courtesy Frederic Remington Art Museum.)

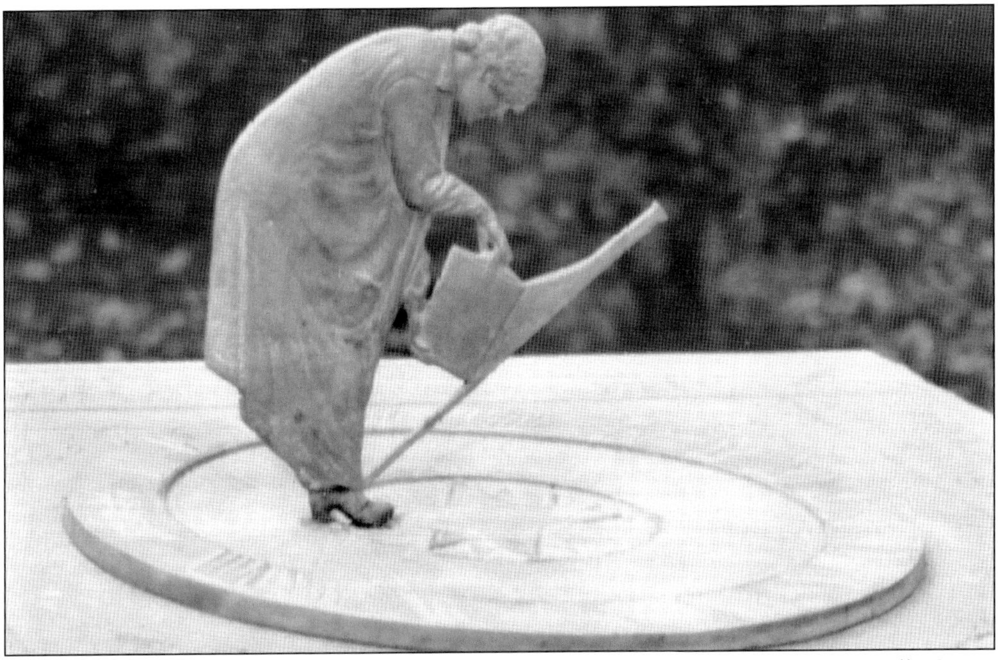

Bronze Sundial, by Sally James Farnham. This unique sundial represents Sally James Farnham's sister, Lucia James Madill, watering flowers in the garden of her home, on Caroline Street in Ogdensburg. (SLCHA.)

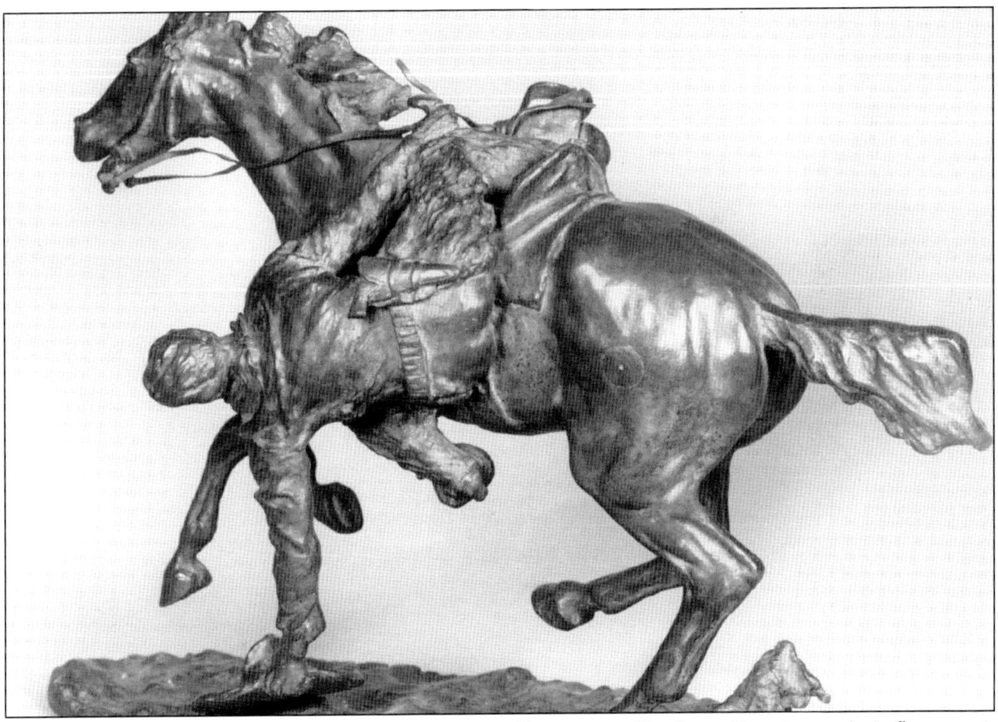

Horse and Rider, c. 1902, by Sally James Farnham. Frederic Remington's influence is evident both in subject and technique. (Courtesy Frederic Remington Art Museum.)

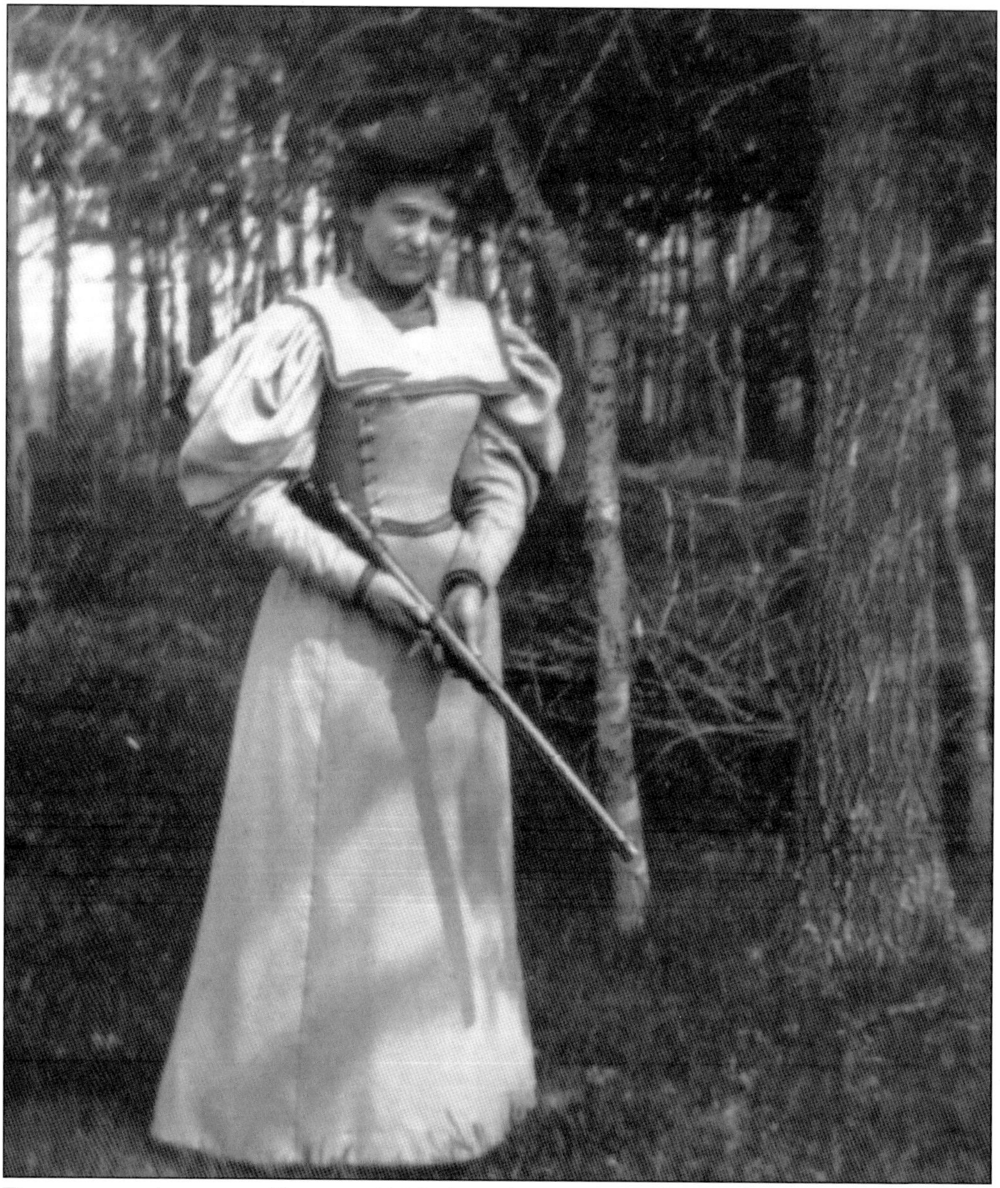

Dressed and Armed for Bear, c. 1900. A markswoman stands armed and ready. (SLCHA.)

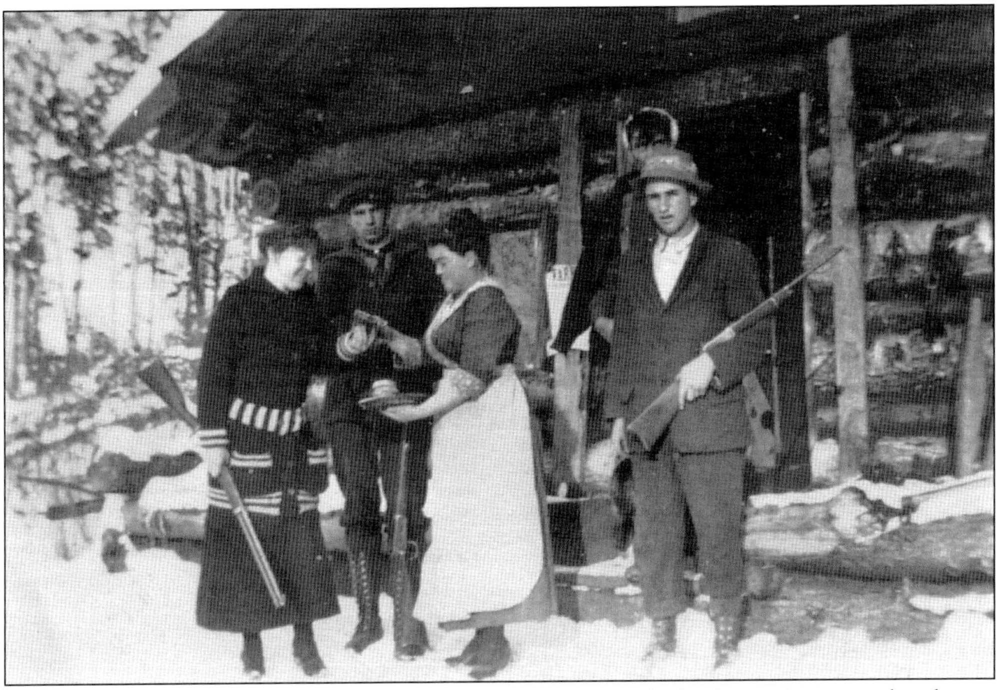

HUNTER'S CAMP IN PARISHVILLE, NOVEMBER 1916. Photographed at hunter's camp at lunchtime are, from left to right, Katie Coulon, unidentified, Effie Wilson, and Leonard Bisnett. (Courtesy Parishville historian.)

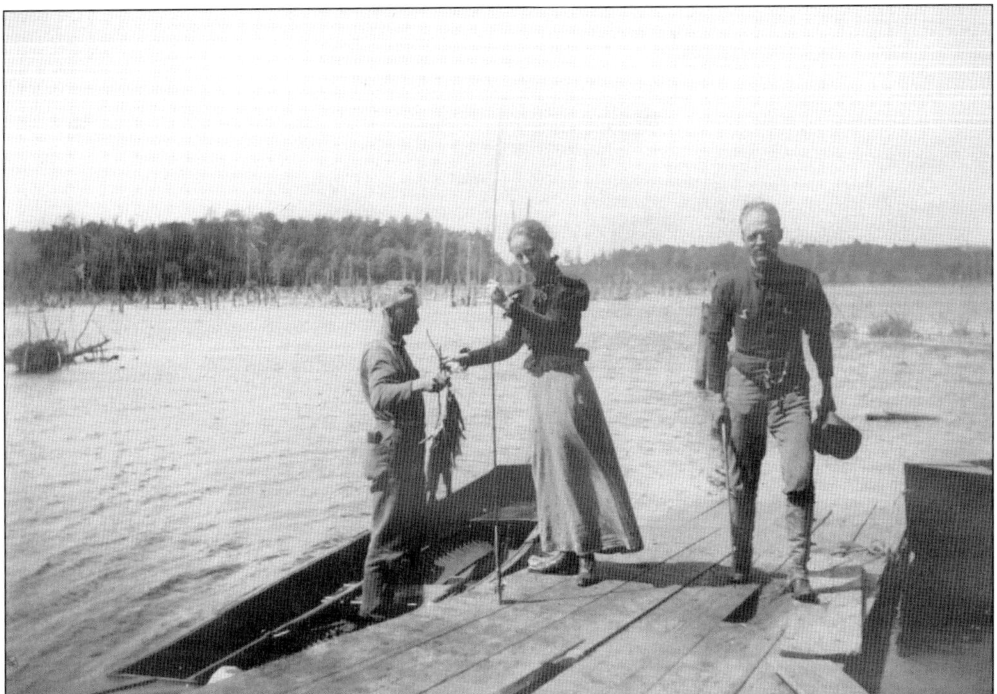

PARTNERS ON THE WATER. They are sharing fishing adventures on Cranberry Lake, though probably with the assistance of a guide. (SLCHA.)

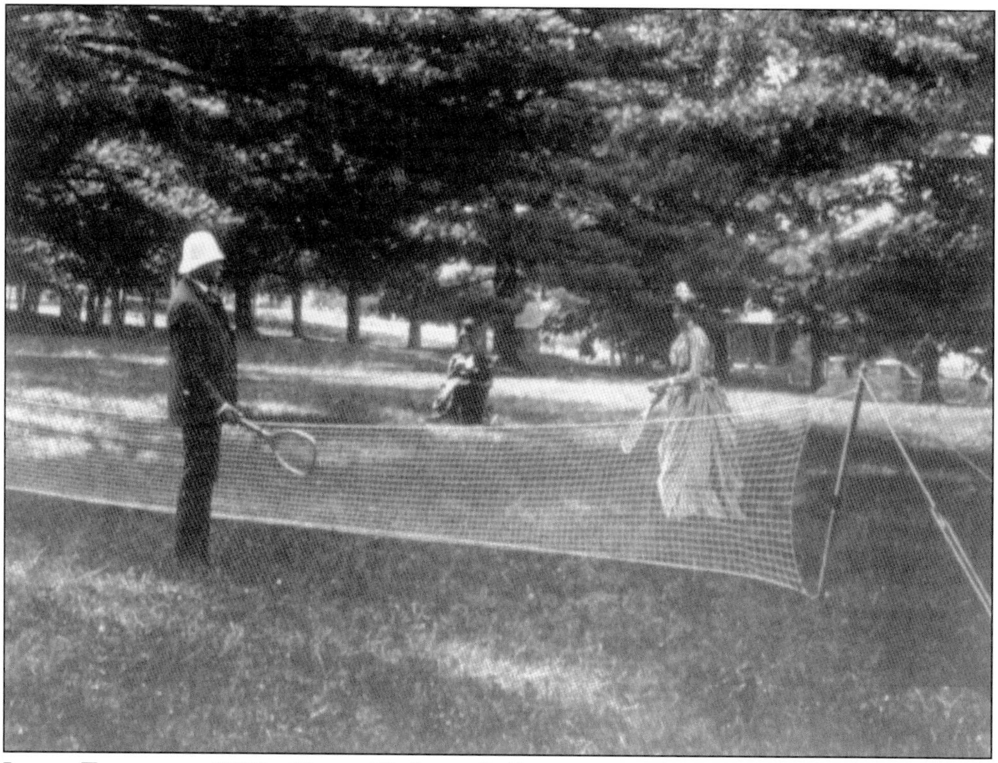

Lawn Tennis, c. 1900. These Clarkson College tennis players appear to be somewhat overdressed for the sport. (SLCHA.)

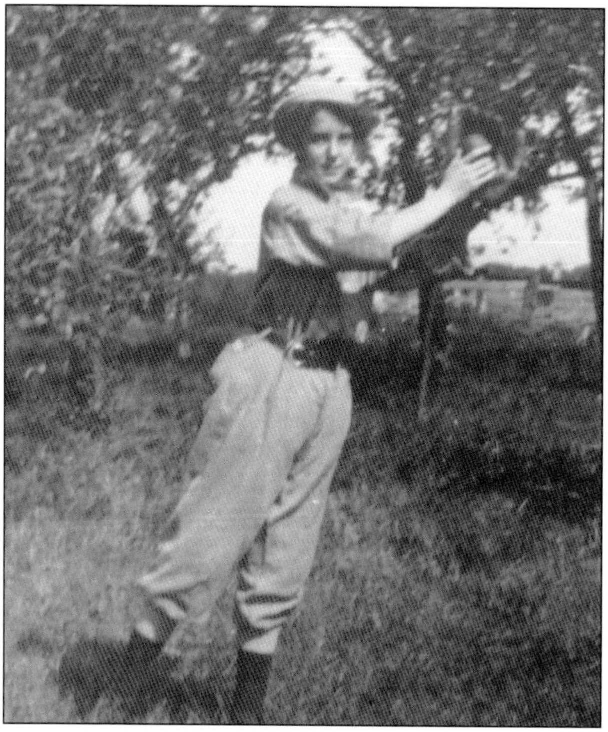

Playing Baseball, 1915. More suitably attired is Hazel Burnham Corey, playing baseball. (SLCHA.)

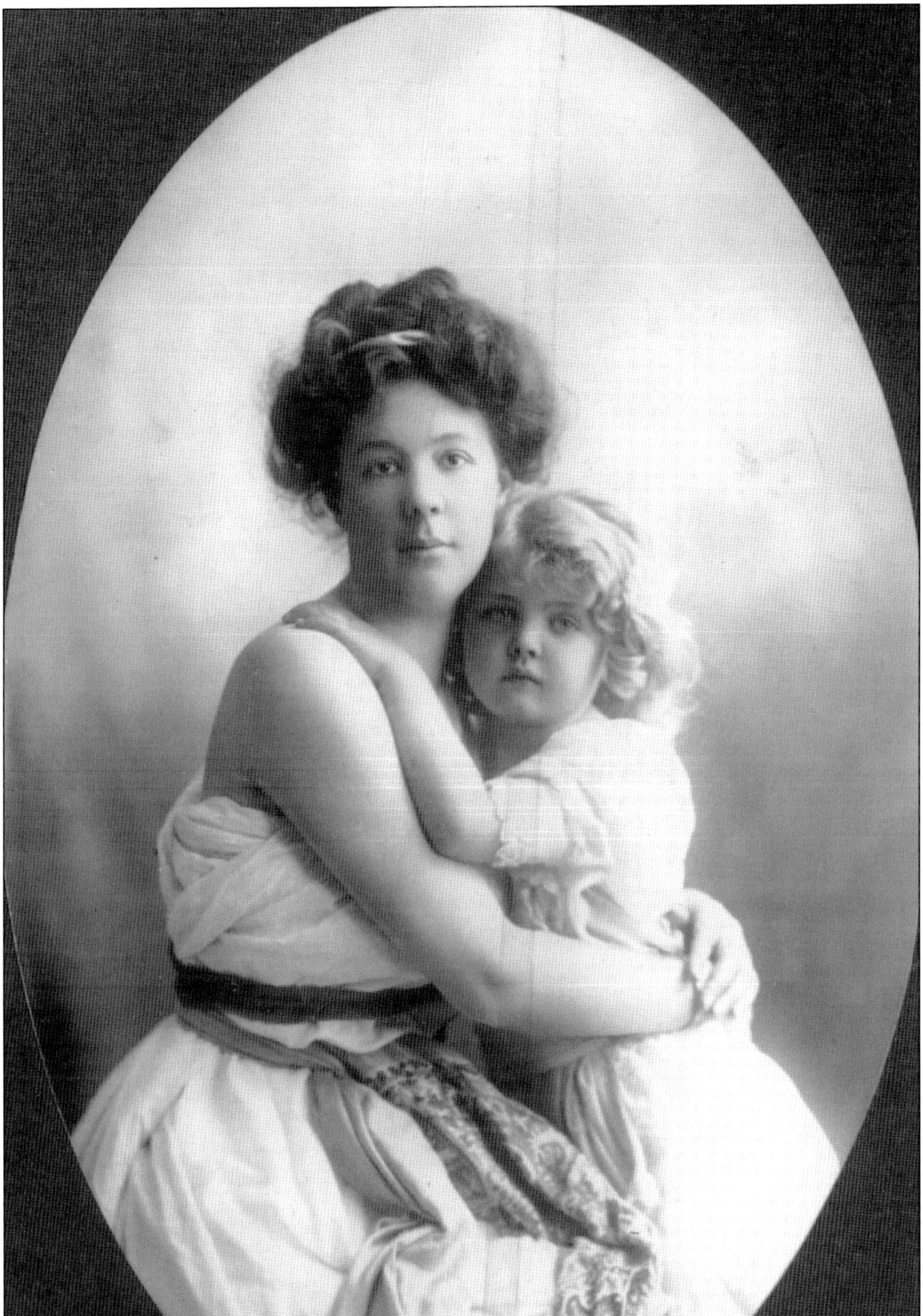

SALLY JAMES FARNHAM AS A YOUNG MOTHER. Sally James Farnham was married to George Paulding Farnham, a vice-president at Tiffany & Company, Fifth Avenue, New York City. Her husband was also one of the finest designers of jewelry and objets d'art in the United States. (Courtesy Frederic Remington Art Museum.)

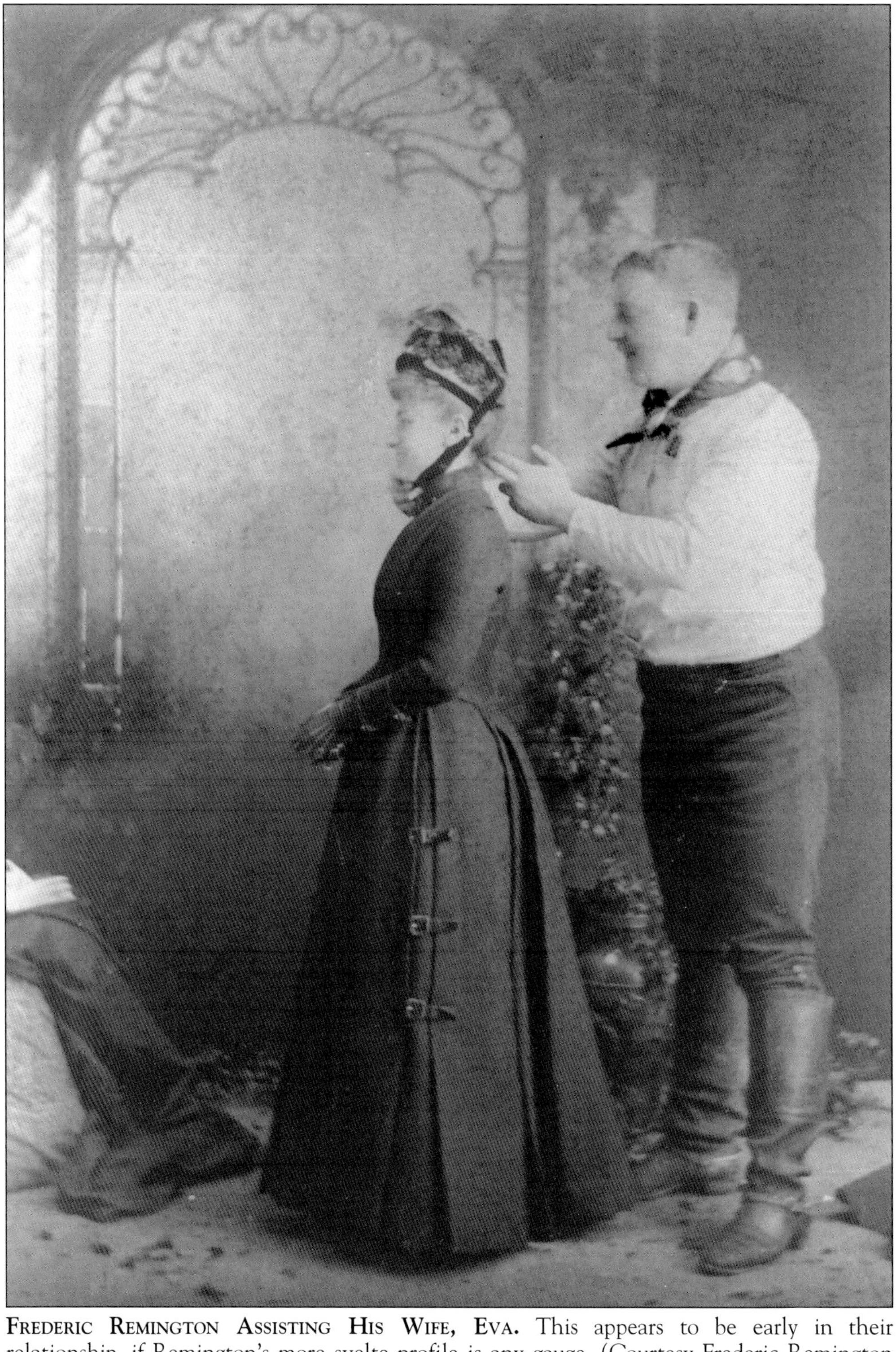

FREDERIC REMINGTON ASSISTING HIS WIFE, EVA. This appears to be early in their relationship, if Remington's more svelte profile is any gauge. (Courtesy Frederic Remington Art Museum.)

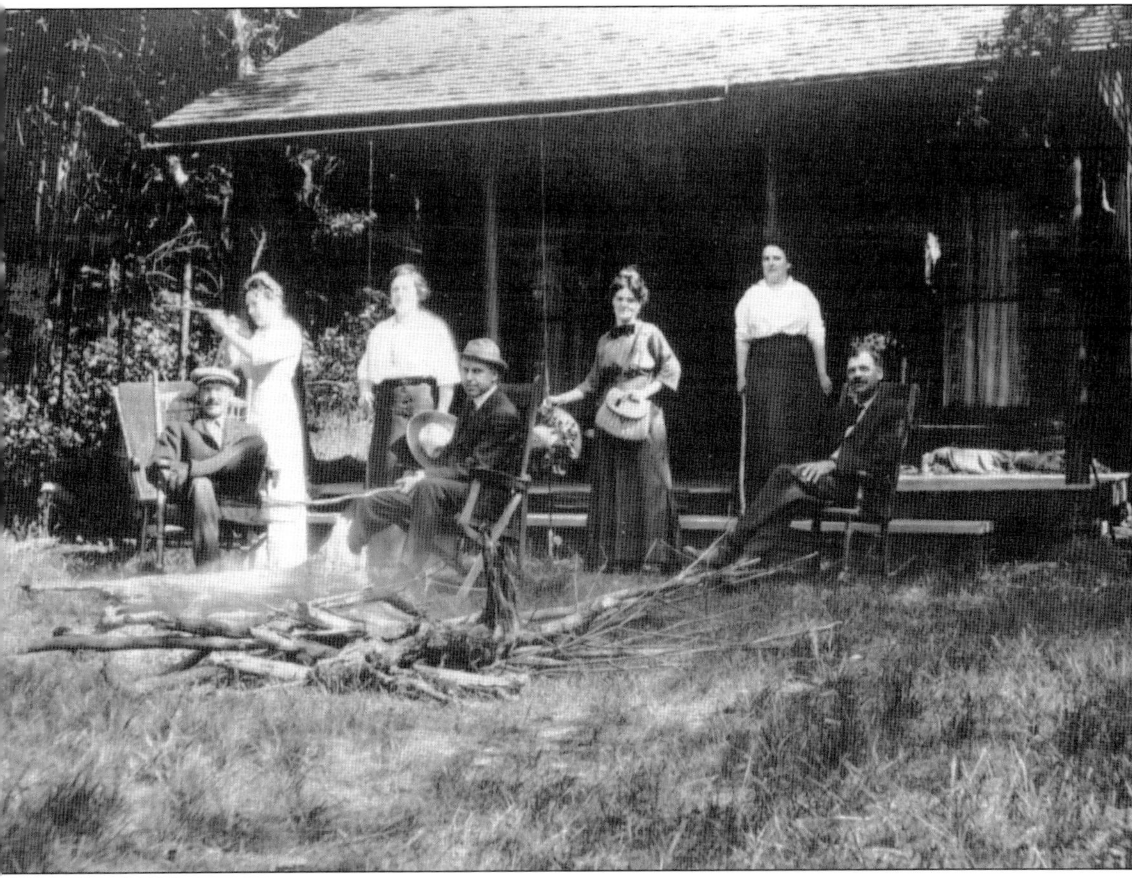

Hollywood Camp, 1914. The picture portrays "a good time with Professor and Mrs. Storrs at their Hollywood Camp, 1914." (SLCHA.)

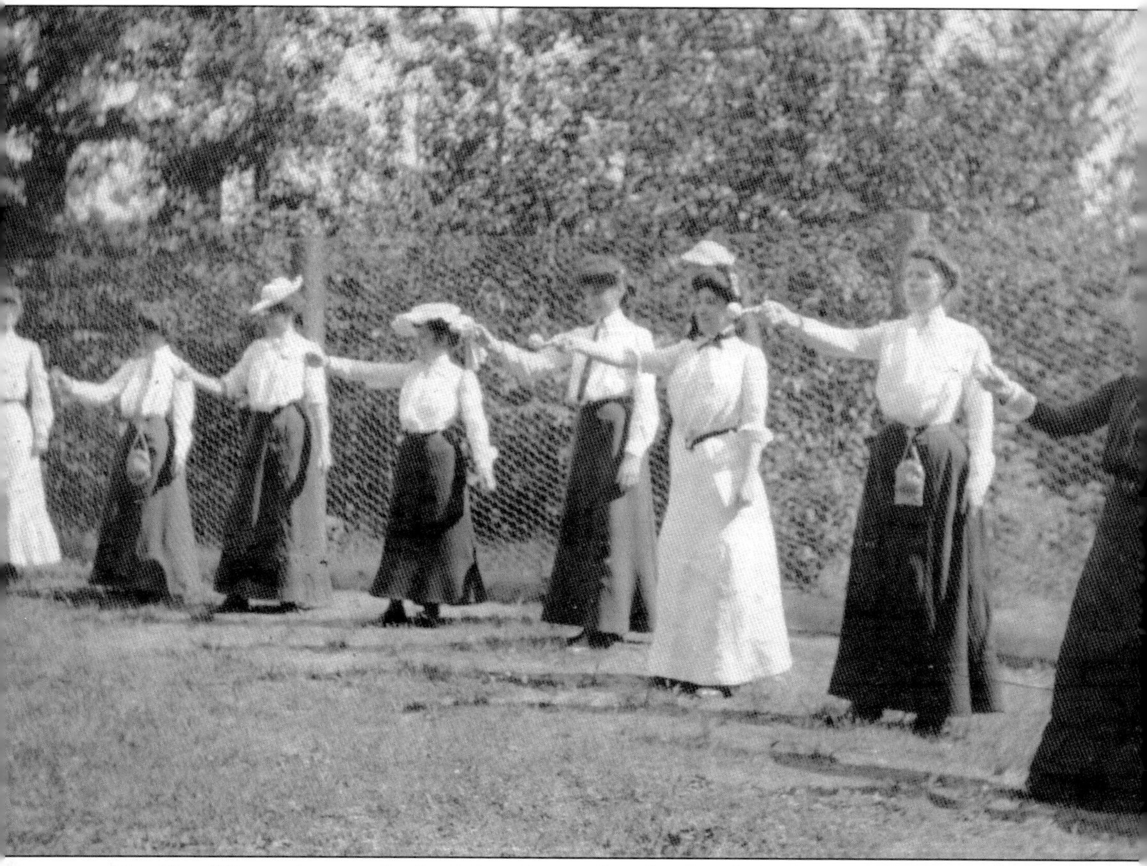

THE EGG WALK. Among the festivities featured at the Star Lake Inn was the egg walk—in full Victorian dress. (SLCHA.)

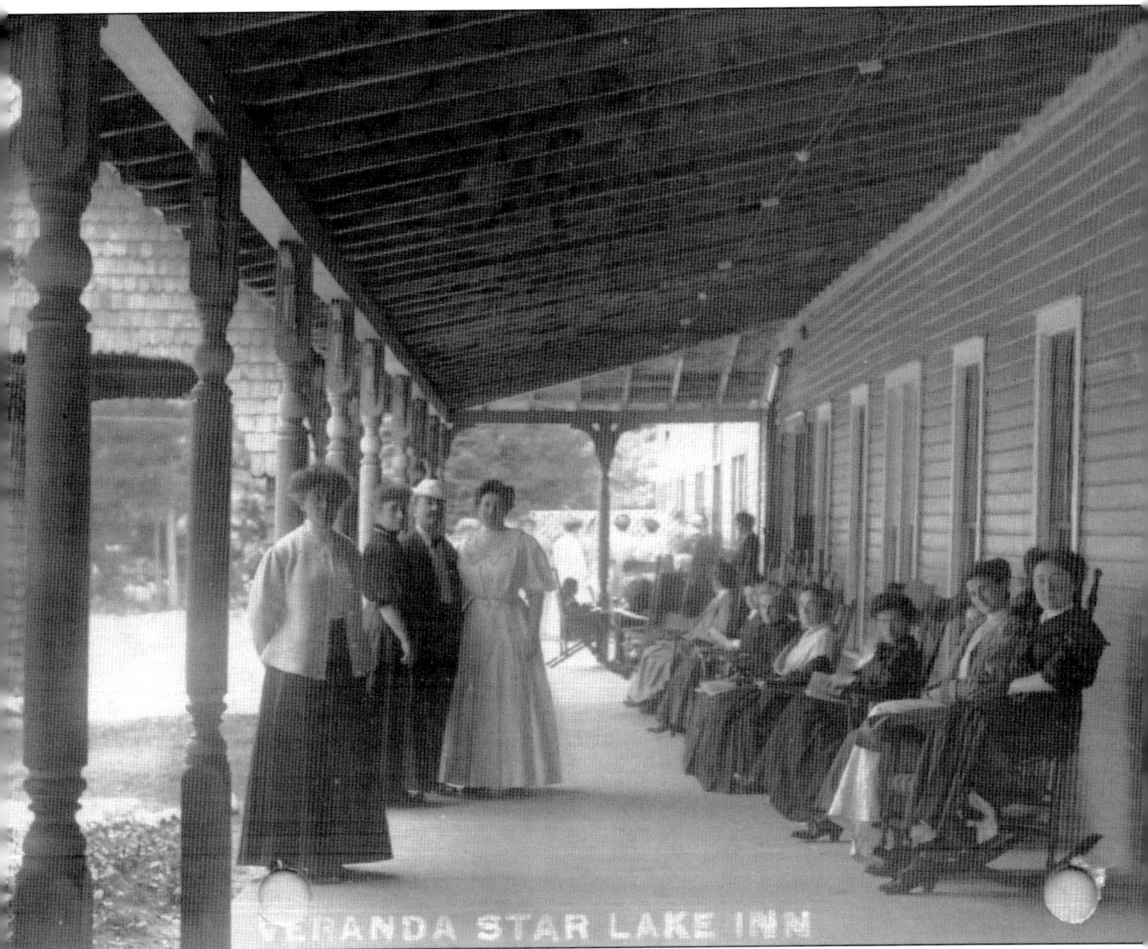

The Star Lake Inn Veranda. After the games, the guests gather on the veranda of the Star Lake Inn. (SLCHA.)

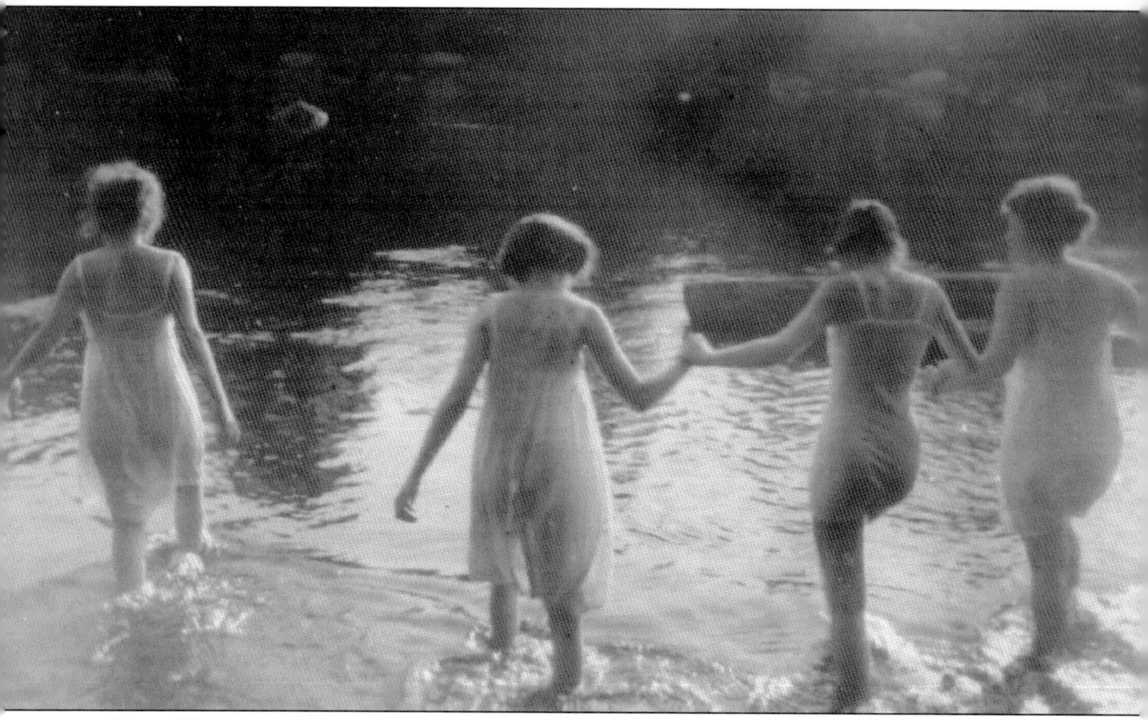

FOUR WOODLAND NYMPHS, EARLY 20TH CENTURY. Dwight Church was an innovative early photographer who experimented with many unusual subjects, including that of this rather risqué image. (Dwight Church photograph, SLCHA.)